Elektra Reference Manual

A catalogue record for this book is available from the Hong Kong Public Libraries.

Published in Hong Kong by Samurai Media Limited.

Email: info@samuraimedia.org

ISBN 9789888407620

Acknowledgements

Physics isn't the most important thing. Love is.

— Richard Feynman

First of all thanks to all people involved in ELEKTRA. Many people contributed over the years. Others helped by participating in user studies. Special thanks to Kai-Uwe Behrmann and Harald Geyer, who are the pioneer users of ELEKTRA. We had many fruitful discussions about many topics concerning configuration.

Thanks to the reviewing committee for finding time.

Thanks to the staff of my institute who proofread many of my papers and helped in all aspects around research. I want to give distinct gratitude to Franz Puntigam for guiding me through the work and for being highly responsive to all my concerns and questions. I thank TU Wien for financial support.

Furthermore, thanks to the people for helping me with reviews and discussions. In particular, reversely sorted by alphabet, I am grateful to Uwe Zdun, Tianyin Xu, Stefan Winter, Patrick Sabin, Nedko Tantilov, Milan Nosál, Maike Löhndorf, Katharina Spiel, Jens Knoop, Helmut Toplitzer, Harald Geyer, Gergö Barany, Geraldine Fitzpatrick, Franz Puntigam, Erik Schnetter, Elisabeth Raab-Steiner, Christian Amsüss, Aotani Tomoyuki, Andreas P. Priesnitz, Andreas Mohrhammer, Andreas Krall, Andreas Falkner, and the anonymous reviewers.

I build upon the work of many people who contributed to free software, science, and society. Without them I would not have been able to even start this work. I do apologize to all the people I cannot mention here!

Last but not least, I am deeply grateful for the backing I got from my family and friends, especially Natalie Kukuczka and Elisabeth Raab.

Abstract

With the help of configuration settings—usually stored in configuration files—applications are highly adaptable. Modern systems give us detailed information about the context the system is situated in. We define context as every information relevant for configuration settings, for example, the location, available hardware, the network settings, settings of other applications, etc.

Today, configuration settings and the context are not connected. Adaptations of configuration settings to better fit the context happen manually—often in complicated interfaces and without proper feedback on errors. Using a questionnaire survey and a source code analysis, we reveal obstacles why applications rarely account for context: Developers do not have context information readily available and dislike dependences to software that would give them the information.

We aim to overcome these problems by introducing a novel system-level configuration specification language, which specifies the relation between context and configuration settings. Including more context into configuration settings improves usability and decreases misconfiguration. Our configuration specification language orchestrates frontends and backends for unified, context-aware access to configuration settings. We introduce a frontend (an API) that maps via code generation the configuration specification language to context-aware variables. We use it to enable context adaptations in dynamic scopes as suggested by context-oriented programming. The configuration specification language modularizes the system into plugins that build up backends. The modularization mitigates the previously mentioned applications' problems of missing context information and unwanted dependences. We implemented different language constructs for the modular configuration specification language to validate our approach.

We evaluate the implications of the novel modular abstractions in the configuration specification language in-depth. We discuss emerging tools, debugging support, introspection, and development time. Furthermore, we measure the overhead caused by the backends and compare solutions, implemented in the frontend and backend, with the result that the overhead in modular backends is small. Despite the context awareness, the frontend enables read access to configuration settings with the run-time efficiency of native variables. Because it is unrealistic that every application gets rewritten to use such type-safe frontends, we demonstrate different ways to connect legacy applications with our backends. With 16 well-known standard applications, such as Firefox, we show the feasibility and practicality of increasing context awareness of configuration settings without modifying any source code.

Kurzfassung

Software ist mit Hilfe von Konfigurationseinstellungen, welche üblicherweise in Konfigurationsdateien gespeichert werden, hochgradig adaptiv. Moderne Systeme beinhalten bereits detaillierte Informationen, in welchem Kontext sich das System gerade befindet. Wir definieren Kontext als jede Information relevant für Konfigurationseinstellungen, zum Beispiel der aktuelle Ort, vorhandene Hardware, Netzwerkkonfigurationen, Konfigurationen anderer Programme, etc.

Heutzutage sind Konfigurationseinstellungen und Kontext nicht verbunden. Adaptionen von Konfigurationseinstellungen, wie besseres Anpassen an den Kontext, werden manuell durchgeführt – oftmals in komplizierten Schnittstellen und ohne hilfreiche Rückmeldungen bei Fehlern. Mit einer in der Arbeit durchgeführten Umfrage und Quelltextanalyse erkannten wir Ursachen dafür, warum Programme derzeit selten Kontext berücksichtigen: Entwickler haben Informationen über den Kontext nicht bequem verfügbar und vermeiden Abhängigkeiten zu Software, welche die Informationen bereitstellen könnte.

Wir zielen darauf ab, diese Probleme durch eine systemnahe Konfigurationsspezifikationssprache, welche die Beziehungen zwischen Konfigurationseinstellungen und Kontext beschreibt, zu lösen. Der Hintergedanke ist, dass die Berücksichtigung von Kontext in den Konfigurationseinstellungen die Benutzerfreundlichkeit erhöht und fehlerhafte Konfigurationseinstellungen reduziert. Unsere Konfigurationsspezifikationssprache orchestriert dabei Frontends und Backends, um den Zugriff auf Konfigurationseinstellungen zu vereinheitlichen. Wir führen ein Frontend (eine Programmierschnittstelle für Entwickler) ein, welches mittels Quelltextgenerierung die Konfigurationsspezifikationssprache in kontextsensitive Variablen abbildet und dabei Kontextsensitivität in dynamischen Sichtbarkeitsbereichen ermöglicht. Die Konfigurationsspezifikationssprache modularisiert Quelltexte in Form von Plugins, mit deren Hilfe die Backends aufgebaut werden. Dadurch werden die zuvor genannten Probleme von fehlenden Kontextinformationen in Applikationen und unerwünschten Abhängigkeiten gemindert. Um unseren Ansatz zu validieren, haben wir mehrere Sprachkonstrukte einer modularen Konfigurationsspezifikationssprache implementiert.

Wir haben die Implikationen unserer neuartigen modularen Abstraktionen der Konfigurationsspezifikationssprache ausführlich evaluiert. Dabei diskutieren wir Funktionalität zur Introspektion, neu entwickelte Werkzeuge, Analysen zur Fehlerbehebung und Entwicklungszeit. Ebenfalls messen wir den durch Backends verursachten Mehraufwand und vergleichen Lösungen, implementiert als Frontends und Backends, mit dem Ergebnis, dass Mehraufwände in modularen Backends gering sind. Trotz Kontextsensitivität ermöglicht das Frontend lesende Zugriffe auf Konfigurationseinstellungen mit der Laufzeit-Effizienz von native Variablen. Da es unrealistisch ist alle existierenden Applikationen auf solche typsicheren Frontends umzuschreiben, demonstrieren wir verschiedene Möglichkeiten, wie bestehende Applikationen ebenfalls an unsere Backends angebunden werden können. Mit 16 bekannten Standardapplikationen, wie etwa Firefox, zeigen wir, dass die Kontextsensitivität der Konfigurationseinstellungen auch ohne Quelltextänderungen verbessert werden kann.

Contents

CHAPTER 0

Introduction

"Begin at the beginning," the King said gravely, "and go on till you come to the end: then stop."

— Lewis Carroll, *Alice in Wonderland*

This book examines context while applications access their configuration settings. **Context** includes all factors that influence an application's configuration settings, for example, information about geographical locations, installed packages, hardware configurations, network connections, and configuration settings of the system. If software better adapts its behavior according to its context, we call it more **context aware** [5]. Applications tend to be adaptable by *configuration settings*. **Context-aware configurations** are configuration settings in accordance with their context.

Many behavioral aspects are not fixed at compile-time but are determined later by reading configuration settings. Applications access configuration settings from configuration files, environment variables, command-line options, etc. at run-time. We subsume these *configuration sources* under the term *execution environments*. Fetching configuration settings from the execution environments is called *configuration access*.

Previously, concerns about context mainly have been addressed with workarounds and ad hoc solutions from both developers and system administrators. Here we address these concerns in a comprehensive and structured way. The book describes a holistic and unified context-aware configuration access. We aim at better abstractions at the system-level to improve user experience.

We write explanations and definitions of terms in *italics*. We bootstrap from minimal explanations in this chapter to definitions later. For example, dissociation of configuration settings to input and sensor data is given in Definition 1.1 on page 28. The index on page 317 contains page numbers for all these terms.

In the rest of this chapter, we discuss the challenges, the goal, the solution, the structure, research questions, and the contributions of the book.

0.1   Challenges in Configuration Access

Configuration access appears to be straightforward: Applications need to read the execution environments and prepare these configuration settings to be accessed in the source code. System administrators, however, experience many surprises around configuration access on a daily basis. Naïve ways to access configuration, which are typically used, are not safe and do not take context into account.

In the systems community, problematic configuration settings are well-known as *misconfigurations* [21, 272, 303, 307]. Misconfigurations are a major cause of system failures [202, 214, 301]. As studies show [179, 202, 238, 307], system administrators need to spend much time to fix misconfigurations. In this section we describe challenges we tackle in this book.

0.1.1   Stakeholder's View

Three different **stakeholders** participate in configuration accesses. Each stakeholder has different interactions and problems with configuration settings and their context [234]:

Developers implement configuration access in their applications and do not foresee every possible context influencing the application. They need to provide interfaces for configuration settings to be used by other stakeholders. For them, context is mainly the system the application is running on.

System administrators prefer direct, precise, and concise ways to change configuration settings. Therefore, their typical interface to configuration settings are low level, such as configuration files [26, 27, 114, 287, 310]. For them, context is mainly the system's settings and other applications' settings. Because constraints on configuration settings concerning context tend to be too complex for manual consideration, system administrators easily miss considering some context. They wish to get concise error messages if configuration settings are invalid, for example, conflicting with context.

End users expect applications to be automatically adapted to their context. Furthermore, they want to customize applications to their special needs, which can be different in different contexts. For end users, context is everything relevant for their interactions with applications.

Although the stakeholder's views are different, the same consequences for configuration access apply: Context puts constraints on the configuration settings, and it is problematic if these constraints are violated.

0.1.2 System's View

Yin et al. [307] discovered that *"a majority of misconfigurations (70.0 %~85.5 %) are due to mistakes in setting configuration"*. The other 14.5 %~30 % of *"misconfigurations are caused by software compatibility and component configuration"*. A main contributor to misconfigurations are configuration settings clearly violating syntactic or semantic rules (38.1 %~53.7 %). Such errors can be avoided with configuration validation. ***Configuration validation***, or ***validation*** in short, rejects invalid configuration settings by checking syntactic and semantic rules. Validation is present in end-user interfaces, but hardly in the interfaces system administrators use. For system administrators, validation only occurs while restarting the application—putting the system at a high risk.

The system administrator's interfaces are confusing, too [26, 27]. System administrators easily confuse syntax because applications have many subtle differences in configuration file formats [27]. Even more traps for system administrators are hidden behind the interfaces. Xu et al. [304] showed that system administrators are not to blame. Instead configuration access code in the applications is leading to unexpected behavior and crashes. Only in 7.2 % to 15.5 % of cases error messages pinpoint the error [233, 307].

Example 0.1. OpenLDAP has the configuration setting `listener-threads`. Its documentation says: *"The default is 1 and this is typically adequate for up to 16 CPU cores. The value should be set to a power of 2."* OpenLDAP's documentation does not mention:

- how to correctly use this setting for more than 16 CPU cores,

- that `slapd` will reduce the value of `listener-threads` to the next number that is *"a power of 2"*, nor

- that `slapd` will crash with values above 16 [304].

Such behavior is a trap for system administrators.   ▲

Now that we have established that applications are vulnerable against misconfiguration, we elaborate on the challenges in providing configuration validation. Problems of the application are located in the configuration access, i.e., along the data flow of configuration settings from the configuration parser to their use in the application. Xu et al. [304] investigated the configuration access in seven applications. The results show that configuration settings are not considered as input to the application and not validated systematically. Even worse, sometimes there are checks and transformations that lead to surprises in behavior. We will subsume all descriptions of the configuration access as **configuration specification**. Their study shows that the available implementations of configuration specifications are woven into the application's source code. As a result, configuration specification cannot easily be separated from the source code nor moved to a separate tool. Applications validate their settings only at startup, or even later [306]. Checking at startup is already too late: Failures at startup can cause outages.

0.1.3 Context and Beyond

Currently applications, which have configuration validation, typically only check consistency within their own settings. They hardly include checks with respect to their context. In particular, system-wide settings or others applications' settings are often prone to mismatch. **Context specifications** describe context relevant for configuration settings. As we will see later, context specifications are an important part of configuration specification. For example, context information about network settings and installed packages are easily available within the network and package managers. Such context information, however, is not readily available within applications. This implies that configuration validation within applications fails to include such context.

A survey from Xu and Zhou [303] gives insights about system approaches to tackle misconfiguration. It shows (by absence of the topic) that most research does not include context of configuration settings, despite empirical research that shows its importance: *"a large portion (46.3 % to 61.9 %) of the parameter misconfigurations have perfectly legal parameters"* (i.e., configuration settings) [307]. If the configuration settings are valid from the view of the application but still invalid in the system, it means that some requirement or context influencing the application was not considered.

Example 0.2. People and their devices often change between different workplaces. Their computers need various network settings where each of them requires different proxy and printer settings. If the user changes workplace, the proxy and printer settings need to be changed according to the network settings. Without changing the proxy, the browser will not be able to connect to the Internet. Configuration settings that are perfectly valid in one situation are invalid in another situation. ▲

Not all misconfigurations with valid settings are due to context unawareness: The second half are violated requirements such as performance, privacy, or security. These factors decide about *suitability* of configuration.

Example 0.3. MySQL has the configuration setting `AutoCommit`: *"But when the user set[s] this parameter to be `True`, she was not aware of the performance impact"* [307]. In this example, the performance is a disregarded requirement. ▲

Applications can avoid misconfigurations if their configuration specification would take context and requirements into account. In some cases, we can avoid any manual interaction and calculate *default values* from context information. We see such software rarely because of the applications' inability to inquire context. System administrators would benefit if the configuration specifications use such context information or at least tell if they are inconsistent.

Usability improvements due to context is not limited to system administrators but applies to all users. Khalil and Connelly [155] conducted a study where all users found context-aware configuration (very) useful. They learned that in 89 % of cases the mapping between activities and settings was consistent for individual users. In the study, context-aware configuration improved satisfaction, even if deduced settings sometimes were not appropriate. For example, a participant stated:

> "I like how it changes state without you having to tell it to. I always forget to turn my cell [off] in class and turn it on after."

Despite these long-known advantages of context-aware configuration, developers hardly implemented them in their applications. Before this work, it was not even known why developers failed to implement these techniques.

0.1.4   Configuration Integration Problem

Developers find it challenging to consider configuration settings and specifications if they belong to other applications. Inter-woven implementations of configuration specifications, missing context information within applications, and different configuration file formats are symptoms of the same problem. Figure 0.1 shows: If n applications read configuration settings and specifications of every other application and the system, we need at least $n * (n + 1)$ ways to extract configuration settings and specifications. The same applies to tools for system administrators. It is unfeasible to take the hurdle to implement access to all configuration settings and specifications. We call the problem *configuration integration problem*[1].

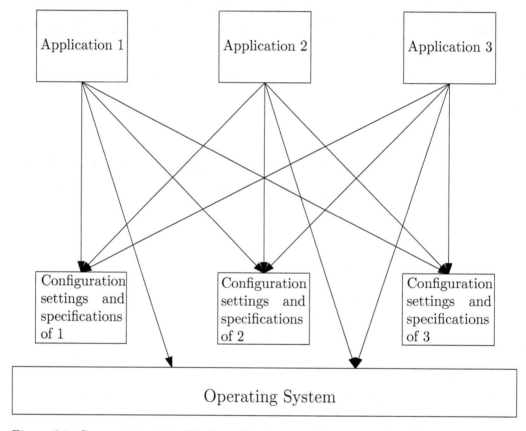

Figure 0.1: Current situation: For 3 applications and 4 sources of configuration settings and specifications, we need $3 * 4 = 12$ configuration accesses.

---

[1]Based on the name given by Keidel et al. [152] *"IDE portability problem"*.

Because of the configuration integration problem, applications do not use configuration settings and specifications from other parts of the system. Even applications, for that other configuration settings are highly relevant, often have no awareness of this context. The configuration integration problem hinders us to create better tools badly needed by system administrators. Furthermore, the configuration integration problem restrains the context awareness of applications, reducing usability.

Example 0.4. OpenLDAP is unable to determine the value for `listener-threads` because it lacks context information about the number of CPUs present in the system.▲

0.2 Methodology, History, and Goals

The aim of the book is to find a system-oriented, computer-language-based solution to the configuration integration problem. In this section we discuss the methodology, history, gaps, goals, and limitations.

0.2.1 Methodology

Before we start designing a formal language, we must understand precisely what we want to express in this formal language. We did an in-depth gap analysis and conducted empirical studies to better understand the configuration integration problem. From these unveiled requirements we started to design a framework and a formal language.

We used the methodological framework *"theory building from cases"* [80, 83] with different methods embedded:

1. an observation report, to learn about fundamental requirements,

2. a questionnaire survey, to learn about goals of potential users, and

3. a source code analysis, to validate statements of potential users.

To countervail weaknesses of individual methods, we mixed them in a way to minimize the threats of validity of our overall results [138]. There is a huge gap between empirical studies of problems and software requirements. We tried to fill it with experience, but it would be unrealistic to claim that there is no room for improvements in the requirements. With the unveiled requirements, we redesigned and reimplemented a framework, called ELEKTRA, and evaluated it.

0.2.2   Elektra

In this book we present the framework ELEKTRA that consists of several parts:

1. The library LIBELEKTRA is a *configuration library*, which means it provides access to configuration settings. It already existed before the book was started.

2. The modular *configuration specification language* SPECELEKTRA is the main contribution of this book.

3. Several tools and frontends are built on top of LIBELEKTRA. In this book we will mostly discuss the code generator GENELEKTRA.

LIBELEKTRA is a library that aims to provide unified access to configuration settings and specifications as found in the execution environment. It works similar to a virtual file system but is based on key-value pairs. LIBELEKTRA enables introspection for both config-

Figure 0.2: Elektra's Logo.

uration settings and specifications. Developers use the configuration specifications to externally specify their configuration access, validations, and default value calculations. *Plugins*, implementing configuration access, enforce these configuration specifications. The idea of the plugins is to provide system-level dependence injection [233].

0.2.3   Elektra's History

The development of LIBELEKTRA started in 2004, sponsored by IBM at that time. The author of this book joined in the same year. A community, called ELEKTRA *initiative*, gathered around the source code repository of LIBELEKTRA. Initially the initiative only aimed at the straightforward idea to unify *application programming interfaces (APIs)* for *configuration access*. From its beginning, ELEKTRA was *free/libre*[2] *and open source software (FLOSS)*. LIBELEKTRA started by introducing an API with many language bindings. The bindings were contributed by different people who felt an API, to unify configuration settings, is important.

---

[2]The word "free" here is interpreted with the meaning of the word "libre". The term FLOSS is designed for the purpose of not taking political position between free software and open source software, see also https://www.gnu.org/philosophy/floss-and-foss.en.html.

The idea of introducing a configuration access API was not new: Most proprietary software systems already had similar APIs for a long time. Nevertheless, it was clear that there was no portable configuration library available to be used for typical FLOSS applications. For example, the configuration libraries X/Q/GSettings, KConfig, dconf, plist, and Windows Registry are tied to their respective platforms.

Grave mistakes in initial versions led to several redesigns of the API. Due to that, ELEKTRA lost many FLOSS users. Despite different efforts to change the situation, rather companies than FLOSS software developers used ELEKTRA. Focus was often at patching applications that led to quality problems in LIBELEKTRA itself. Unfortunately, redesigns had new flaws and unnecessary features were introduced. In particular, developers started implementing a daemon, which did not offer advantages but introduced many complications. Reimplementing security features of the operating system frustrated developers, who then left. The ELEKTRA initiative was in a deep crisis that escalated in 2006 when IBM canceled their sponsoring. On the positive side ELEKTRA was well-known and had supporters [233].

In 2007 the author of the book continued the work on ELEKTRA mostly alone and thus progress was at a slow pace. In 2012 the author did a major cleanup and in 2014 the author restarted the initiative. More than ten students supervised by the author started to work on topics related to ELEKTRA for their Bachelor's and Master's theses. The author of the present book started to lead this revived ELEKTRA initiative. The newly formed initiative is referred as "we" in the following paragraphs about history. Additional contributors, early adopters, and package maintainers also joined the effort. A separation of what was done by the author follows much later in Section 6.4.1 after we had explained all parts of ELEKTRA in detail.

The new lead shifted the goals towards a more technical solution to mitigate the configuration integration problem: We focused on inventing new abstractions other configuration access APIs did not have. We oriented towards the highly competitive market of configuration libraries. As unique selling point our abstractions forced less ideology onto users because ELEKTRA avoids prescribed configuration validation techniques or configuration file formats. In a first step, this was achieved by introducing different backends, chosen by users at run-time. An implementation providing only a single backend for the whole system proved to be too limited: Individual applications cannot customize their backends for their own needs. We implemented a layer similar to a virtual file system, which enables applications and system administrators to mount configuration files [236]. Furthermore, dependences in the core made ELEKTRA unattractive. To solve this problem, we modularized ELEKTRA [225] so that users can select exactly the features they need [233].

Such changes made part of the software more complicated. At first, we provided too little documentation for newcomers to grasp the abstraction mechanisms [225]. Then we started to put efforts into rebuilding the community by overhauling documentation, introducing more regression tests, writing tutorials, and designing a new website. We succeeded by other FLOSS initiatives willing to use ELEKTRA, and ELEKTRA being packaged for many distributions [233].

0.2.4   Scientific Gaps

Now back from the history of ELEKTRA to this book. When the book started in 2013 (shortly before reviving ELEKTRA) the author searched for scientific gaps to be solved to explain the previously mentioned phenomena. The following scientific gaps refer to the situation at that time.

The research topic of *context-aware applications* is well-known [24, 248]. *Context-oriented programming* is a novel programming paradigm that aims at programming-language support to implement context-aware applications [17, 132, 145, 151]. It allows us to describe context, in which the application is situated in, as state of the application. Context-oriented programming languages did not consider the execution environment and did not have desired performance characteristics.

Configuration accesses did not have support for context awareness. Naïve ways to implement context awareness led to the problems mentioned earlier. Accounting context in configuration access differs in some aspects from earlier work on context-oriented programming:

1. We cannot start sensing context within the application before it starts up. Nevertheless, the configuration access at startup must be efficient.

2. We shall not assume developers to know every possible context during development.

3. We shall not assume developers to rewrite large-scale software for context-aware configuration.

4. Improved simplicity for configuration access is essential: For developers the status-quo is a viable option.

Because of these reasons, earlier work of context-oriented programming could not be applied. There was no concept telling us how context-oriented programming can be used without large overhead [235]. Neither did the previous approaches permit multi-threading [226] nor multi-process [231] configuration access. No previous surveys about context awareness for configuration access were done. Therefore, despite developing ELEKTRA since nearly 10 years, we were unaware about some expectations, goals, and challenges.

Configuration specification languages [34, 96, 112, 127, 178] did not have configuration access in their scope. The configuration specification languages did not have capabilities for local configuration validation of configuration files [228]. Furthermore, they were usually not as extensible as needed for the needs of the many different applications. For example, they did not have a practical way to be extended with application-specific run-time checks. We found a scientific gap for a configuration specification language that is easy to use for simple tasks but can be extended to domain-specific, complex tasks.

Configuration libraries did not have an abstraction for programmable configuration access [230, 233]. Research was needed to investigate the solution space. Another scientific gap was the missing way to specify requirements used at configuration access [230]. Previous solutions had specifications that generated configuration files causing problems in a bidirectional work flow.

Behrang et al. [30] found ill-tested applications in which errors caused by co-evolution will not be automatically detected by a test suite. Instead configuration settings, that were in fact not used by the application anymore, were still presented to users. Jin et al. [139] found configuration settings present in the source code but not shown to the users, for example `autoadmin.append_emailaddr` in Firefox. We had to find a configuration specification language that eliminated such inconsistencies.

Holland et al. [134] defined *futzing* to denote *"tinkering or fiddling experimentally with something."* Instead of having a straightforward way to achieve a goal, the user needs to use trial-and-error methods. With ***no-futz computing*** Holland et al. [134] mean *"that futzing should be allowed, but should never be required."* Many situations, however, required system administrators to futz, for example, to reverse engineer configuration access code to know the state of configuration settings [134].

Last but not least, no method existed that allowed applications without any modifications in the source code to have context-aware configuration access [232]. Or more generally, there was no way to apply context-oriented programming in another way than rewriting applications.

0.2.5 Goals

Let us elaborate on our aim to solve a computer-language design problem with the goal to improve on the configuration integration problem. ELEKTRA is a vehicle to study candidate techniques whether they enable developers to build a futz-free configuration system. To validate if ELEKTRA mitigates the configuration integration problem, we define the following goals. As precondition, we must understand the requirements by looking at the developer's challenges:

Goal (Requirement). *A goal of this book is to unveil requirements by empirically analyzing how applications access configuration settings and why developers programmed it that way.*

With these requirements, the next goal can be tackled:

Goal (Abstraction). *We create an abstraction by designing the configuration specification language* SPECELEKTRA. *This abstraction shall enable users to reduce effects of the configuration integration problem by unifying configuration access, simplifying configuration validation, and enabling context awareness.*

Then we want to implement the abstractions defined in SPECELEKTRA within the ELEKTRA framework. With this better abstraction, we grapple the next goal:

Goal (Context). *We aim at a run-time system that automatically chooses the best suitable configuration settings with regard to the context. We want to enable users to consistently manipulate and introspect which configuration settings an application receives. Making changes in configuration settings shall be futz-free.*

If new contexts and requirements arise, we ideally only need to change configuration settings and specifications—without any need to modify the source code of applications. The best run-time system is of little benefit if it is used incorrectly, thus we need to fulfill:

Goal (Frontend). *We aim at a context-aware, type-safe frontend that mitigates problems unveiled before. The effort to let applications participate with this run-time system shall be kept at a minimum.*

0.2.6 Limitations and Assumptions

In *configuration management* [58, 137] taking control over *execution environments* is an essential part. We call such necessary modifications in the execution environments

producing configuration settings. Configuration management tools produce configuration settings and applications ***consume*** configuration settings. While the discipline of producing configuration settings is well researched since a long time [45], we focus on the consumption of configuration settings and specifications in applications from its source to its target:

Source is the execution environment, such as configuration files.

Target is a set of variables used within APIs of the applications.

Nevertheless, configuration access is needed for both consuming and producing configuration settings. Ideally, the same implementation of configuration access is used for both the applications and the configuration management tools.

We will barely discuss the actual management of configuration settings—only as far as we need it to interface with the outside world. Our work is limited to local applications consuming configuration settings, i.e., on single nodes, computers, or devices. Local configuration settings are always necessary, because nodes need at least to know where they can fetch further configuration settings. For most setups the limitation to a single node is irrelevant because configuration management already solves the problem to distribute configuration settings to all nodes in a network.

In the spirit of *infrastructure as code*, we assume that system administrators want to use automation techniques for configuration management. We expect that they want to work systematically, and not by futzing [134].

We will only evaluate applications that have FLOSS licenses. Only FLOSS developers gave us the permission (via the license) for their source code to be analyzed and improved. This implies that other researchers have better possibilities to validate our findings by repeating them [37, 289].

Because previously discussed problems around misconfiguration prevailed in most software intractably since decades, it would be unrealistic to promise that a single piece of software will fix all problems. Instead we can only provide a framework and language that enables developers to improve over the current state. Developers will still be in charge for writing high-quality configuration specifications. We can only offer them a more suitable language to express themselves. With correct specifications, however, we might be able to exclude some kinds of misconfigurations completely.

0.3 Solution

As depicted in Figure 0.3, we use ELEKTRA to improve on the configuration integration problem. Based on the results of Goal Requirement, we will introduce an operating-system-independent and application-independent representation for configuration settings and specifications.

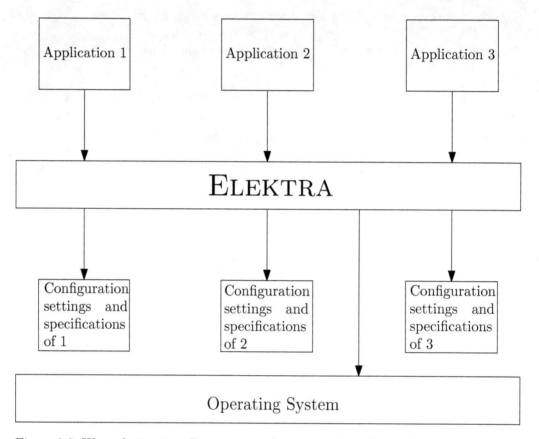

Figure 0.3: Wanted situation: ELEKTRA as abstraction layer for configuration access of applications. We only need $3 + 4 = 7$ configuration accesses.

Applications need to participate in the abstraction layer. Therefore, we have to pursue Goal Frontend to give developers attractive solutions.

As stated in Goal Abstraction, we propose to unify configuration access via LIBELEKTRA. To avoid losing any flexibility or modularity, we introduce the configuration specification language SPECELEKTRA, which enables applications to specify individual needs.

From our studies we found that fixed configuration specification languages are too limited to serve different domains [34, 96, 112, 178]. Instead we propose a *modular configuration specification language* that allows individual domains and applications to define their own extensions for the modular configuration specification language. Only application-specific languages are suitable to specify configuration access for specific needs of individual applications. As shown in Figure 0.4, the modular configuration specification language is implemented by a chain of plugins. Plugins support customized configuration validation and applications-specific functionality.

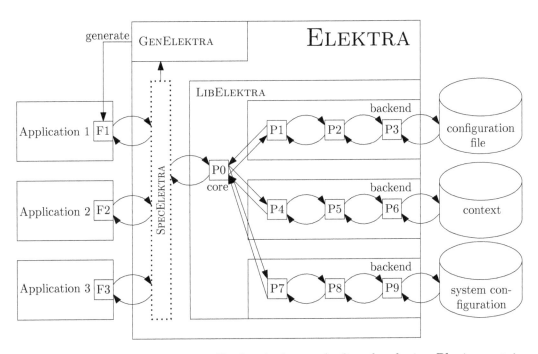

Figure 0.4: LIBELEKTRA consists of backends that are built up by plugins. Plugins contain application-specific or generic source code. F? are frontends, which can be generated by GENELEKTRA as shown for F1. The other arrows indicate data flow of configuration settings and specifications. P? are plugins nested in backends, and in this example, with P0 being part of every backend.

As main use case, extensions to the configuration specification language are used to build customized configuration access. It is up to the designer of the extensions to put focus on context awareness or configuration validation. In our book, our extensions focus towards context awareness, as described by Goal Context. Because of SPECELEKTRA's modularity and extensibility, ELEKTRA supports specific requirements how to validate or derive configuration settings, without adding complexity to applications not needing such language constructs.

Example 0.5. Applications with a complex module system need a new language construct that is implemented using a constraint solver [97] to find optimal instantiations for the application's modules.   ▲

To demonstrate the usefulness of the modular configuration specification language SPEC-ELEKTRA, we designed and built several language extensions with focus on context-aware configuration. Together with ELEKTRA, which enables every application to access configuration settings of the system and any other application, we leverage more context for configuration. SPECELEKTRA can be seen as a glue language that is neutral to both programming languages and execution environments.

SPECELEKTRA shall fully enable developers to specify all relevant parts of configuration access. Relevant parts include validity, transformation, context awareness, etc.

Example 0.6. To solve the problems of Example 0.1 on page 3, we specify:

```
1  [slapd/threads/listener]
2    check/range:=1,2,4,8,16
3    context:=/slapd/threads/%cpu%/listener
4    default:=1
5    description:=One thread is adequate for up to 16 CPU cores.
6    type:=long
```

Instead of calling the configuration setting `listener-threads`, we give it a unique name, written in `[]`. The name makes the configuration setting and specification accessible in the whole system. We use the hierarchy separator / that gives us flexibility when configuration settings are extended. The other lines, which use : =, are *properties* of this configuration specification. All properties together fully specify access to this configuration setting. Line 2 describes that only 5 values are valid, avoiding surprises and crashes. Line 3 specifies that the configuration setting shall be contextually dependent on the number of CPUs available in the system. The string `%cpu%` is a placeholder that is replaced with the current number of CPUs by a plugin. We can create a mapping from the number of CPUs to the respective configuration values. The resulting configuration value of this mapping then utilizes all CPUs. If the calculation fails, for example, because the number of CPUs is unknown on that system or no mapping is available, we use the default value, which is 1 (line 4). The last line specifies the data type for code generation with GENELEKTRA. ▲

Overall, ELEKTRA aims at creating a better abstraction of local configuration access for applications. The abstraction mitigates the configuration integration problem and enables users to program local configuration access for their needs. This novel way of programming empowers developers, system administrators, and end users to:

1. ensure validity of configuration settings in terms of the context,

2. calculate default values honoring the context, and

3. enable introspection of the resulting configuration settings and specifications.

The enriched context awareness and improved configuration validation capabilities will be facilitated to exclude the possibility of some kinds of misconfiguration.

We claim that with such a simple specification language, accessing configuration settings and specifications for any participating application improves the goals Abstraction, Context, Frontend, and the requirements unveiled in Goal Requirement. As a result of the context awareness, we improve usability: Applications will have more context-aware configurations.

0.4   Structure, Research Questions, and Contributions

After stating the main question and the overall contributions we will walk here chapter by chapter through the thesis to clarify research questions, contributions, and structure.

The main question of the book is:

RQ 1. Why is current FLOSS configuration access rarely context aware and how can we improve on the situation?

Raab [226, 227, 228, 229, 230, 231, 232], Raab and Barany [233, 234], Raab and Puntigam [235] contributed answers to the question. **RQ 1** is both a design and research challenge:

1. research the challenges in context-aware configuration access,

2. solve the design problem, i. e., find the best candidate to tackle the challenges, and

3. research the implications of the design we have chosen and evaluate if it improves on the configuration integration problem.

The main contribution of this book are improvements on context awareness for configuration access, resulting in more context-aware configurations:

- We enable software to be more context aware via their configuration settings [227].

- We enable developers and system administrators to improve context awareness without a change of their programming language and, with some limitations, without any change of the applications' source code [232].

- We improve introspection and debugging of configuration access. Our contributions are steps towards a no-futz system [134].

- We analyze the performance situation of configuration accesses and suggest simple but effective optimization techniques [235].

- We improve abstraction and modularization using a modular configuration specification language that supports context-aware configuration [230].

- As contribution to the FLOSS ecosystem, ELEKTRA is available as free software at: https://www.libelektra.org.

0.4.1   Terminology and Background

We establish terminology and background in Chapter 1. We surveyed literature in misconfiguration, configuration specification languages, context-oriented programming, and context-aware configurations, answering the following research questions:

RQ 2. What is configuration, context, and context-aware configuration?

RQ 2.1. What are the viewpoints of context-aware configuration?

Contribution 1. *We consistently establish terminology, viewpoints, and background for context-aware configuration. At least three viewpoints, i. e. sensors, users, and time, constitute the distinction between ordinary and context-aware configurations.*

RQ 2.2. Which configuration specification languages are suitable to improve configuration access of FLOSS applications?

Contribution 2. *Despite conducting a systematic, large-scale literature survey, we did not find any configuration specification language that focused on the configuration integration problem.*

0.4.2 Relevance to the Community

While there is generally no doubt about the presence of many problems surrounding misconfiguration, the analysis of their details proves to be difficult and is still ongoing. We pioneered new aspects, framed as the configuration integration problem, mainly ourselves. In Chapter 2, we describe how we unveiled these challenges. We report on a large-scale source code analysis, a questionnaire survey, and ELEKTRA's community experience, answering the question:

RQ 3. Why do FLOSS applications lack *context awareness* and *configuration validation* for configuration settings and what are the challenges in providing them?

For the empirical source code analysis we classified 2,683 call sites of configuration accesses in 16 real-world applications encompassing 50 million lines of code. Additionally a questionnaire was shown to 672 persons, 286 of these persons started to answer, 162 of these persons completed the questionnaire, and 116 persons handed their email addresses to be contacted by us afterwards [233].

Contribution 3. *We found many different problems causing the described symptoms and collected requirements for potential solutions.*

RQ 3.1. Which problems in configuration access are observed while developing FLOSS with state-of-the-art techniques?

Contribution 4. *We observed different maintenance problems such as duplication and inconsistencies of configuration accesses and settings.*

RQ 3.2. What is the current state of configuration access in FLOSS?

Contribution 5. *We found that different types of execution environments are equally popular and unveiled details about why the decision, which one to use, is often arbitrary.*

RQ 3.3. Which proportion of configuration accesses is already context aware or can be made so without any source code changes?

Contribution 6. *We learned that developers are striving to support context awareness. In other cases, configuration accesses were used as if they were context aware, even though they are not. We found that such configuration accesses provide potential for run-time adaptations without modifying the source code of the applications.*

In the following sub-questions from **RQ 3.3**, we mainly looked at the configuration access API `getenv`. We expected `getenv` to be widely adopted because of its standardization. We present the adoption rate of `getenv` and show that non-context-aware configuration accesses exist in the source code of applications:

RQ 3.3.1. What are the usage patterns of `getenv` invocations in the source code of popular applications?

Contribution 7. *In a source code analysis of 16 FLOSS applications we found that a particular kind of configuration accesses, namely the* `getenv` *API, is used pervasively in 2,683 call sites [234]. It is inevitable that in many of these places the context is forgotten: we found confirmed cases.*

We have to show that these configuration accesses are used in a way exploitable for run-time adaptations:

RQ 3.3.2. How often is `getenv` repeatedly used at run-time?

Contribution 8. *We found* `getenv` *invocations to happen extensively across all studied applications. Many* `getenv` *invocations happen repeatedly and can be exploited for improving context awareness.*

Putting the pieces of Chapter 2 together, we compiled a list of requirements to improve on the configuration integration problem:

RQ 3.4. What are the challenges and requirements in providing configuration access for context-aware configuration?

Contribution 9. *Overall, Chapter 2 contributes towards a better understanding of the problem and unveils the first list of empirically founded requirements for context-aware configuration access.*

0.4.3   Elektra

In Chapter 3, we formalize a model of ELEKTRA's central parts. ELEKTRA introduces a novel form of abstraction yielding context-aware configuration.

Contribution 10. *Chapter 3 contains the first formalization of a framework to access context-aware configuration. It includes a simple proof for eliding an instantiation of misconfiguration, namely missing configuration settings.*

Different from Chapter 3, the next two chapters 4 and 5 will elaborate on why this model fulfills the requirements and how the abstractions work in practice.

0.4.4   Frontends

Frontends are the parts of configuration accesses that are compiled into applications. Every application accessing configuration settings needs some kind of frontend. At minimum the frontend consists of configuration access API invocations, at maximum applications include everything found in configuration libraries. In ELEKTRA, frontends are minimal or generated with GENELEKTRA.

Most developers include source code within their applications that implements configuration access. Configuration transformations and validations within these frontends are an important factor of the configuration integration problem. In Chapter 4, we discuss how we simplify frontend code with context-aware APIs, answering the following research questions:

RQ 5. Which concepts are needed for context-aware frontends to fulfill the requirements as unveiled in Chapter 2?

RQ 5.1. What is the design space for context-aware frontends?

RQ 5.2. Which implementation technique for implementing context-aware frontends has the best trade-off for time versus space?

RQ 5.3. How can we improve on the usability of context-aware frontends if being used concurrently from several threads?

RQ 5.4. How can we share context between applications?

Contribution 11. *We establish a context-aware frontend that:*

1. *fulfills the requirements unveiled in Chapter 2 and integrates context-oriented programming with the execution environment,*

2. *has zero overhead for read access even if used in multi-threaded applications, and*

3. *guarantees some properties of configuration specifications, improving on the configuration integration problem.*

0.4.5 Backends

Backends are all parts of configuration access that are not part of the frontends. Our implementation of the backends is LIBELEKTRA. Different to the frontends, the backends are shared among all applications in a system.

In Chapter 5, we will investigate parts of the configuration integration problem that cannot be solved by frontends. In particular, problems that involve several applications written in different programming languages need a solution within the backends.

RQ 6. Which concepts are needed for context-aware backends to fulfill the requirements as unveiled in Chapter 2?

RQ 6.1. What is the design space for abstractions of context-aware configuration in backends?

RQ 6.2. How can we enable context awareness in backends without support from frontends?

RQ 6.3. Which abstractions retain and improve modularity of configuration access in FLOSS applications?

RQ 6.4. Which techniques enable applications to become more context aware without any changes in the source code?

Contribution 12. *The main results in Chapter 5 are:*

1. *Using simple specifications, ELEKTRA provides programmable backends fulfilling the requirements unveiled in Chapter 2.*

2. *Abstractions enable us to keep the current modularity of FLOSS applications, and even extend it for configuration access.*

3. *ELEKTRA allows legacy applications to become context aware without any source code modifications.*

4. *It is possible to share configuration settings, specifications, and contexts across the whole system.*

0.4.6   Implications and Open Topics

Even though each individual part of our implementation is lightweight because of ELEKTRA's modularity, altogether we propose a rather heavyweight, system-oriented abstraction. One must carefully consider whether the advantages outweigh the risks.

In Chapter 6, we will consider the implications ELEKTRA has on the FLOSS ecosystem. The implications are complex and sometimes, not surprisingly, beyond the problems we initially wanted to tackle. We will reflect on experiences with users and case studies:

RQ 7. What are the risks and implications of introducing ELEKTRA?

RQ 7.1. Which risks and implications does ELEKTRA have for administrating configuration settings?

Contribution 13. *A unified interface for configuration settings brings control to the system administrator. On the downside, system administrators need to learn ELEKTRA's concepts. We demonstrate that our solution is applicable to a variety of use cases. We show* *that* ELEKTRA *is not only feasible, but also practical and seamlessly supports debugging and introspection of configuration settings and specifications.*

RQ 7.2. How does ELEKTRA influence risks of development and time effort if used in a large real-world project?

RQ 7.3. Which features are elegantly realizable in ELEKTRA to configure non-trivial embedded systems?

Contribution 14. *We were able to use* ELEKTRA *within several large real-world and embedded projects successfully. Due to* ELEKTRA*'s extensibility and due to reuse of already existing components, developers saved time. On the downside, some additional complexity needs to be mastered.* SPECELEKTRA *enables us to defer decisions, reducing some risks.*

RQ 7.4. How can we improve debugging support of context-oriented programs?

Contribution 15. *We present debugging techniques that deal with additional flexibility introduced by context awareness.*

RQ 7.5. What are the risks and implications on security, safety, and quality in systems using ELEKTRA?

RQ 7.5.1. What are the source code metrics of ELEKTRA and who develops ELEKTRA?

RQ 7.5.2. What are the implications of ELEKTRA on misconfiguration?

Contribution 16. *In Chapter 6, we demonstrate the practicality and generality of our solution by porting different applications to* ELEKTRA*. We cannot claim the resulting systems to be always more secure and free of misconfiguration. Nevertheless, we argue that some classes of misconfiguration get much more unlikely with* ELEKTRA*. Some classes of misconfigurations would only be possible because of bugs in the implementation and not due to operator mistakes. Furthermore, we argue that a centralized implementation improves on quality, reliability, and security. We are positive that* ELEKTRA *raises the bar for future configuration libraries.*

0.4.7 Evaluation

In Chapter 7, we conduct benchmarks and measure further software characteristics in applications using ELEKTRA, answering the research question:

RQ 8. Which software characteristics change if ELEKTRA is applied?

RQ 8.1. What are the performance characteristics for applications specifically programmed for ELEKTRA?

RQ 8.1.1. How much can we improve the performance of configuration access using context-oriented programming?

Different from non-context-aware applications, context-aware applications need to track all *context changes* occurring in the system. Thus we focused our investigations to measuring overhead of context changes.

RQ 8.1.2. What is the overhead of context changes in an embedded, multi-threaded use case?

RQ 8.1.3. What is the cost of ELEKTRA's individual operations?

RQ 8.1.4. How is ELEKTRA's resource utilization of hard disk storage?

RQ 8.1.5. What are the performance trade-offs towards high-level abstractions for context changes?

RQ 8.1.6. What is the overhead of high-level abstractions for context changes in embedded scenarios?

The contribution of **RQ 8.1** is:

Contribution 17. *All overheads are either constant or increase linearly in execution time. Although some high-level abstractions have considerably more overhead, even context changes every few milliseconds have little impact.*

RQ 8.2. What are the considerations to implement a feature in the frontends versus in the backends?

Contribution 18. *While there is a difference in overhead, we nevertheless recommend implementing virtually all features—except thread-safe, dynamically-scoped, context-aware configuration access APIs—in backends. Only then the features can be interpreted dynamically and can be easily shared between applications in different programming languages.*

RQ 8.3. What is the overhead of ELEKTRA's modular abstractions?

Contribution 19. *The overhead does not give a reason to avoid modularity.*

One of the main contributions is that completely unmodified applications (concerning the source code) can use ELEKTRA. Our assumption is that applications already have configurable behavioral variations. The basic idea is to have a run-time system that computes which behavior variations shall be active to match the context. We strive to answer the research questions:

RQ 8.4. What are the characteristics of a system in which context-unaware software was made more context aware without any modifications in the source code?

RQ 8.4.1. How many `getenv` invocations can be exploited to improve context awareness without any modifications in the source code?

RQ 8.4.2. How can we practically make applications more context aware without any modifications in the source code?

RQ 8.4.3. What overhead occurs in applications intercepted by ELEKTRA?

RQ 8.4.4. What is the performance implication that occurs on context changes?

The main contributions of **RQ 8.4** and its sub-questions are:

Contribution 20. *We collected profound evidence that* ELEKTRA *improves context awareness in FLOSS applications even though we did not change a single line of source code in the respective applications [234]:*

1. *No evaluation of context-aware applications was conducted before using such complex, large, and popular applications [234]. The contributions are steps in the effort of understanding the software-engineering perspective of context-aware configuration.*

2. *In a practical case study, with focus on Web browsers, we improved context awareness for flexible workplaces. We conduct a software-engineering process in which we systematically improve context awareness without any source code modifications.*

0.4.8 Related Work

In Chapter 8 we will discuss related work. As we will see, state-of-the-art techniques assume that applications need to be rewritten in architectures unusual for FLOSS. We avoid this assumption and investigate in methods that can be realized for legacy applications.

RQ 9. Why does related work not solve the configuration integration problem?

0.4.9 Conclusion and Future Work

Our work showed that it is feasible and practical that a high-level configuration specification language unifies configuration access and mitigates the configuration integration problem. In Chapter 9, we will conclude the book with a discussion about the achieved goals. In this light, we will elaborate on perspectives left open as future work.

Finally, we give a summary of the value our line of research has for the *stakeholders*:

Developers get better frontends that enable them to directly work with variables that contain context-aware configuration. With this higher level of abstraction, they do not have to care about configuration validation and context awareness within the application's source code. Another main contribution to developers is SPEC-ELEKTRA that allows them to define valid, context-aware configurations more concisely without bringing further dependences in the application's source code.

System administrators get better tooling that allows them to introspect and change configuration settings without any syntactic hurdles and futzing. SPECELEKTRA empowers them to understand and improve the validations and context awareness on a system level. Our main contribution to system administrators is better user interfaces that make some kinds of misconfiguration much more unlikely. Misconfiguration gets rejected earlier with better error messages.

End users mainly benefit from having more context awareness in applications. Our main contribution to end users is that ELEKTRA enables them to personalize every configuration setting for every context.

CHAPTER 1

Terminology and Background

If you're a baker, making bread, you're a baker. If you make the best bread in the world, you're not an artist, but if you bake the bread in the gallery, you're an artist. So the context makes the difference.

— Marina Abramovic

In this chapter, we introduce terms, elaborate on the already mentioned terms, and discuss the background of our work. We will use the terms in the way as used in the introduction and also as used by the cited papers, unless we say otherwise. We will answer the research question:

RQ 2. What is configuration, context, and context-aware configuration?

1.1 Configuration

The ***execution environment*** is information outside the boundaries of each currently running process [59]. The operating system introduces these boundaries. Controlling the execution environment is essential for configuration management [58, 137], testing [285, 292], and security [105, 170, 213, 260]. For our considerations, the most important parts of the execution environment are configuration files, environment variables, and command-line options [235].

An ***application programming interface (API)*** defines boundaries on source code level. Better APIs make the execution environment easier and more uniformly accessible.

Free/libre and open source software (FLOSS) is software from which the source code can be studied without limitations. In particular, **FLOSS** guarantees that source code can be (0) executed, (1) studied, (2) shared, and (3) published with or without modifications [268]. ***FLOSS initiatives***[1] are communities behind FLOSS.

Modifications in the execution environment change the run-time behavior of ***configurable applications***. We are not aware of any relevant FLOSS application that is not configurable, for example, even `hello`, `cat`, and `echo` can be configured.

While file systems have APIs with specified behavior since decades [192, 256], access to the execution environment is reimplemented differently within every programming language or even application.[2] Some parts of the execution environment cannot be influenced by other applications after the program has started.[3] Other parts of the execution environment can be changed during run-time and as such are subject to ***inter-process*** communication.[4]

Definition 1.1. *A **configuration setting**, or **setting** in short, fulfills these properties:*

1. *It is provided by the execution environment.*

2. *It is* consumed *by an application.*

3. *It consists of a key, a configuration value, and potentially* metadata*. The **configuration value**, or **value** in short, influences the application's behavior.*

4. *It can be* produced *by the maintainer, user, or system administrator of the software.*

A ***configuration file*** is a file containing configuration settings. For example, a Web server configuration file includes many configuration settings such as `port=80` and `address=127.0.0.1`. Their configuration values are `80` and `127.0.0.1`, respectively. Other information in the configuration file is metadata for the configuration settings (such as comments). This book is only concerned about configuration settings but not about other forms of configuration. For example, we configure a computer by assembling its parts, but this is not configuration settings.[5]

---

[1] We avoid the term FLOSS projects because a project has by its definition a fixed end date.

[2] With the notable exception of environment variables, where configuration access is standardized.

[3] For example, environment variables and command-line options.

[4] For example, the file system and shared memory.

[5] Unless we talk about an application that assembles computers.

There are different viewpoints of configuration, for example, configuration as activity [254], decision process [244], or task [265]. In this book, we will interface with such activities. But for us only the result of such activities is of importance, i. e., the configuration settings.

In the literature many synonyms for configuration settings exist. ***User preferences*** [139] and ***customization*** [8] stress that users make the change although that might not always be the case. ***Variability points*** [112, 186, 194, 286, 288, 291] aim at describing the capability of software to adapt its behavior. ***Derivation decision*** [60, 64] puts the decisions to make and not the result in focus. ***Configuration parameter*** [10, 307] is easily confused with other kinds of parameters. ***Configuration item*** [13] or ***configuration option*** [238, 309, 310] are sometimes not applicable, for example, "proxy option", or "language item". ***Configuration data*** [137] is often used in the context of programmable gate arrays and has a different meaning in that domain. We will avoid all these synonyms in the rest of this book, except if we need the term for the distinguished meaning as described here.

From the application's point of view configuration settings are indistinguishable from other input/output data. What are input/output data for one application, are configuration settings for another application.

Example 1.2. Let us consider a Web server. The following discussion is only valid from the Web server's perspective, for a browser it would be different. The Web server's address and port clearly are configuration settings. Web server requests clearly are not settings. The contents of the pages delivered are potentially influenced by settings. Users have server-side settings stored, for example, languages-specific settings. If the data is stored in cookies, however, it is not a configuration setting because cookies are sent within every request. In our terminology, Apache's configuration file `.htaccess`[6] contains configuration settings even though it is located next to data files. ▲

Configuration Access

Configuration access is the part of every software system concerned with fetching and storing configuration settings from and to the execution environment. There are many ways to access configuration [139, 157, 304]. ***Configuration access APIs*** are APIs that enable configuration access. Within the source code the ***configuration access points*** are configuration access API invocations that return configuration values.

---

[6]It provides configuration files on a per-directory basis.

Example 1.3.

```
1 char * getenv (const char * key);
2 int main ()
3 {
4     getenv ("PATH");
5 }
```

The forward declaration on line 1 specifies the configuration access API getenv. In line 4 we have a configuration access point.   ▲

Configuration access happens at various points in time throughout deployment and runtime [13]. Kang et al. [147] distinguish between compile-time, load-time, and run-time configuration access. We will use more elaborate distinctions:

Implementation-time configuration accesses are hard-coded settings in the source code repository. For example, architectural decisions [120] lead to implementation-time settings. Often developers decide that configuration access shall be postponed, leading to the other points in time below.

Compile-time configuration accesses are configuration accesses resolved by the build system while compiling the code. Similar to implementation-time configuration accesses, run-time lookups are not necessary and compilers can optimize away not-executed paths. Different from implementation-time, the build process also considers the execution environment outside the source code repository. This technique is often discussed along with software product lines [188, 286]. The implementation techniques range from special-purpose programming languages, generated code, and definitions substituted by preprocessors. Because avoiding complexity in the build system is rarely a pursued goal, the number of such configuration settings can be extremely large in FLOSS [211]. Nevertheless, these settings are hardly used by non-maintainers because changes require recompilation. Systems providing compile-time settings usually provide alternatives. For example, although Linux has many preprocessor directives, loadable kernel modules with parameters[7] (next to other techniques) enable us to set nearly all configuration settings at later points in time.

---

[7]They were added to Linux in 1995, and around 2000 modules were used everywhere in Linux.

Deployment-time configuration accesses are configuration accesses while the software is installed. Techniques that do configuration access solely during deployment are used rarely in FLOSS. For example, in Debian GNU/Linux the installation procedure of alternative tools changes symbolic links so that the favorite tool is preferred.

Load-time configuration accesses are configuration accesses during the start of applications. The application accesses the execution environment only while initializing but does not synchronize its in-memory configuration settings with the execution environment later. For example, accesses to environment variables and command-line options are load-time configuration accesses.

Run-time configuration accesses are configuration accesses during execution not limited to the startup procedure. To trigger configuration access at run-time we usually have to notify the application. Then the application rereads its execution environment and updates its in-memory configuration settings.

We focus on run-time configuration accesses because it is straightforward to avoid configuration accesses to reoccur at a later point of time.[8] Considering run-time configuration accesses in applications that do not support them already, however, usually implies rewriting code. Furthermore, the user's decision about a configuration value can always be earlier than the point in time the configuration access happens but not vice versa.

1.1.1 Libraries

Configuration libraries provide implementations for a configuration access API.

Abstractions

It is an old idea to use an API to abstract from irrelevant details when accessing configuration settings. The first interface, that is still commonly in use, is `char *getenv(const char *name)`. It was first standardized in 1986 with 4.3BSD and is included in the C89 standard.

The essential operations for configuration libraries are those to get and to set configuration settings in two different ways: *transient* and *persistent*. The APIs for environment variables only provide transient access, i. e., changed configuration settings are lost after restart. For persistence, *serializers* transform the transient data structures to a byte

---

[8]By ignoring notifications that the configuration settings have been changed.

stream to be written into configuration files. They have other drawbacks in their abstraction, for example, the environment is easily corrupted by directly accessing `environ`.

Other examples of standard APIs are:

- `long pathconf(const char *path, int name)`,

- `long sysconf(int name)`, and

- `size_t confstr(int name, char *buf, size_t len)`.

These APIs are less generic because they only allow us to request values from a predefined list. But such APIs are safer: Typos in the constants to be used for the name are caught by the compiler.

Based on these first steps, the next generation of APIs provided persistence, too. These libraries usually originated from applications and are often dedicated to special-purpose configuration settings. This often lead to some specialties, such as function names, that indicate the original application. For example, `xf86HandleConfigFile` parses the `XF86Config` configuration file (now called `xorg.conf`).

Later, FLOSS developers introduced dedicated, general-purpose configuration libraries. They filled the main gap that was often left by libraries written for specific applications: They were able to persist configuration files and not only to parse them. For example, Java Properties and the Universal configuration library parser (`libucl`) are such libraries.

A *configuration source* is an entity containing configuration settings. For example, configuration files, command-line options and environment variables are configuration sources.

Another fundamental abstraction introduced by configuration libraries is cascading lookup. *Cascading lookup* allows users to merge different sources of configuration settings in the following way: If a specific configuration setting is missing in one configuration source, we continue the search in other configuration sources. For example, cascading lookup was used to *"abstract annotation and XML-based configuration sources"* [199].

Yet another abstraction handles several configuration sources of different configuration file formats in a unified way. Both the Apache Commons Configuration [95] and Zend Config framework [277] convert to a common data structure. The solution of Nosál and Porubän [199], Porubän and Nosál [218] extends this idea by using a meta-model and a declarative translation specification.

Configuration File Formats

At any point during the invention of the abstractions mentioned above, in parallel, developers invented many configuration file formats. Passwd might be the first configuration file format that has documentation still available[9]. After 10 more years, the number of configuration files suddenly began to explode. Both UNIX (for example, hosts) and DOS (for example, CONFIG.SYS in DOS 2.0) invented one configuration file format after the other. In the early history, UNIX preferred comma-separated value (CSV) file formats (for example, next to passwd: fstab, inetd, and crontab) but DOS started with key-value formats. Then INI got a popular configuration file format across all operating systems. Evard [87] evaluated UNIX systems and found 58 important configuration files with up to 45 revisions each (4.6 mean, 2 median). He says: *"These configuration files are a good area of study because they are relatively simple but can lead to complex issues."* Later popular configuration file formats include XML [264], JSON [62], and YAML [32].

Semi-structured data is a representation of irregular, implicitly-structured data [3]. In particular, it allows data to be missing, which is not possible in structured data. It became clear that some forms of semi-structured data are better suitable than others if configuration files are serialized. Siméon and Wadler [264] describe two properties:

> ***Self-describing*** means that from the configuration file alone we are able to derive the correct internal representation.
>
> ***Round-tripping*** means that if a file is serialized and then parsed again, we end up with an identical internal representation.

Older formats, such as S-expressions [184] fulfill these properties. Many popular formats, such as XML, do *not* possess these properties [264].

A property of configuration libraries is the conservation of all metadata found in the configuration files. Most configuration libraries have limitations in this property. For example, they do not preserve comments and white spaces.

The configuration library Augeas [177] systematically avoids loss of metadata and ambiguities in round-tripping using lenses. Lenses are designed in a way that losing information causes extra effort [41]. Furthermore, instead of separating the parser and the serializer, a lens as sole specification is sufficient. Because lenses are interpreted from up and from

---

[9]It was already part of the original UNIX Programmer's Manual `http://man.cat-v.org/unix-1st/5/passwd` from 3rd November, 1971.

down, they are called bidirectional programs. The current implementation, however, does
not provide:

- the level of abstraction as often needed because some (structural) properties of
  configuration files leak through [36],

- configuration access APIs for applications since it is only intended to be used by
  system administrators,

- useful error messages on parse errors, and

- support for some popular formats such as YAML (type-safe lenses are limited to
  regular expressions).

Despite these limitations lenses are an important puzzle piece to provide support for
non-standard legacy configuration files. Augeas' ability to completely preserve all white
spaces is not achieved by other configuration libraries.

Many configuration libraries are already included within the core libraries of programming languages. For example, Java provides `java.util.Properties`, and Python
has `ConfigParser`. Because of the availability, such already included libraries are the
most popular ones. If not included, successful configuration libraries are often specialized
to some niche. For example, `fontconfig` allows system administrators to configure
available fonts on the system and performs specialized convenience functionality such as
font name substitution.

Most likely more configuration file formats than programming languages exist.[10] Some
of them were hyped and then were already forgotten before tools around them matured.
Most of them are unintentional fragmentations, with minor differences such as case
sensitivity, key-value separation character, comments[11], and encoding[12]. While these
differences are confusing in practice, we will only discuss fundamental differences here.
We will distinguish between document-oriented formats, object-oriented formats, and
configuration file formats designed as such. The distinction must be taken with a grain
of salt [79], the concepts behind these different formats are nevertheless useful.

---

[10] Nearly every programming language can be used as configuration file format.

[11] For example, subversion uses INI with # instead of ; to start comments.

[12] For example, Java properties use ISO 8859-1 and Flex properties files use UTF-8 as described in http://help.adobe.com/en_US/FlashPlatform/reference/actionscript/3/mx/
resources/IResourceBundle.html.

Document-oriented file formats are intended to describe complete documents. These formats provide many structural elements and have a rather heavyweight syntax. Nevertheless, they are popular for configuration settings. Strangely, they are hardly used to produce documents even though a literal style is often preferred by system administrators. One of the rare examples is that in Lynx the configuration file is converted to an HTML page for online documentation. A typical document-oriented file format is XML [264].

Object-oriented file formats are intended to serialize objects from programming languages. Typical formats include JavaScript Object Notation (JSON) and Object Exchange Model (OEM). As another example, AIX introduced the Object Data Manager (ODM) [150] for most of its configuration. ODM allows us to create classes, and their instances are serialized. S-expressions [184] and JSON are subsets of programming languages. XML can also be used to serialize configuration settings in an object-oriented fashion [149]. Object-oriented file formats seem handy at first but one has to continuously resist to not leak internals, such as names and state, into the configuration files.

Other ***configuration file formats*** are formats exclusively designed to contain configuration settings and to be edited by humans. Earlier representatives are the already mentioned INI, `XF86Config`, and CSV formats. For the CSV formats it was soon clear that they are too limited: The number of keys they can represent is defined by the number of columns. Thus in newer software like Xinetd, the CSV format was replaced. In other cases like fstab and crontab, extensions were invented to circumvent limitations. One trend is to revitalize INI avoiding some of its limitations, for example, as done by systemd or TOML [207].

Some configuration file formats contain code, for example `sendmail.cf`. They are harder to comprehend and cannot be edited by programs. Nevertheless, they are still popular, for example, to configure some window managers. While all these formats above have many differences, all of them represent configuration settings as ***key-value pairs*** [139, 165, 238, 304]. For scripts key-value pairs are the result after execution. Thus we will, without loss of generality, assume that configuration file formats can be mapped to key-value pairs.

1.1.2 Configuration Specification

Misconfigurations are configuration settings that cause misbehavior in software [179, 307]. In some situations, misconfiguration becomes manifest because of problematic configuration access, such as wrong transformations [304].

Configuration specification, or ***specification*** in short, describes the behavior and result of configuration access. Configuration specifications assign ***configuration properties***, shortened as ***properties***, to individual configuration settings. Properties can be informal, for example, containing documentation, or formal, for example, describing a data type and a transformation rule. Configuration specification can be internal and external, i.e., embedded within the application and in external files, respectively. External configuration specifications can be written in the same file format as the configuration settings. Configuration specifications are on a different meta-level than configuration settings. As shown in Figure 1.1 we separate the universe of all possible configuration specifications into five subsets.

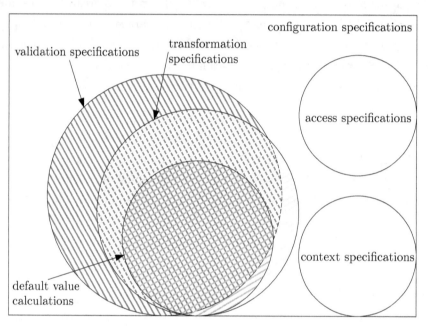

Figure 1.1: Types of configuration specifications. The sizes of the circles suggest the number of language constructs for the different specifications but such numbers vary widely for different configuration specification languages.

Validation specification describes all possible valid configuration settings to enable
  configuration validation. Murata et al. [193] says that validation specifications *"are
  more precise than those in prose and that we can rely on validators rather than
  carrying out human inspections"*. Complete validation specifications reject all misconfigurations, and accept all other configuration settings. Validation specifications
  are usually incomplete, i.e., there exist invalid configuration settings, which do

not get rejected [137]. We call source code implementing validation specifications ***validation code***. In other work, validation specification is called ***schema*** [56, 79]. While it is clear that validation specifications shall be checked as early as possible, this is currently rarely achieved. Xu et al. [306] wrote a tool to find validation specifications executed too late and aims at pushing configuration validation to the startup of applications. Ideally, the configuration validation would already happen before the configuration settings are persisted and thus misconfigurations are never present in configuration files.

Transformation specification describes how configuration settings shall be transformed. Because not every transformation accepts arbitrary strings as input most of these specifications are implicitly validation specifications.

Default value calculation complements other forms of configuration validation [44, 81]. While technically a subset of transformation specifications, it has tremendous importance for configuration settings. Instead of creating a need to synchronously change configuration settings, ***default values*** are calculated from other configuration settings.

Access specification describe which configuration file and format shall be used for retrieving configuration settings.

Context specifications are discussed thoroughly in chapters 3 to 5; and for the definition see Section 3.2.4.

1.1.3 Configuration Management

Configuration Management is a discipline in which configuration (in the broader sense) is administered. Configuration management makes sure computers are assembled from desired parts and the correct applications are installed. Furthermore, configuration management ensures that the execution environment of installed applications is as required.

Configuration management tools help people involved in configuration management. Usually, source code describes the desired configuration of the whole managed system. Then the configuration management tool tries to converge the actual configuration to the desired one [45]

A currently challenging task within configuration management tools is ***configuration file manipulation***. The use of configuration libraries eases this task. It makes configuration file manipulation more precise and safe. Because default value calculations influence the configuration settings the applications receive, additionally local introspection of configuration settings is important for configuration management tools.

System Administrators

The *system administrator* is the most important stakeholder within configuration management. System administrators need to configure every component in a way so that the overall system has desired properties. This usually implies solving a constraint satisfaction problem [254]. Higher-level configuration management tools help us find solutions to such constraint satisfaction problems [58, 137].

System administration research tries to better understand system administrators [310]. The interest of understanding system administrators emerged rather recently [8, 27]. System administration research uses surveys, diary studies, interviews and observations. Barrett et al. [26] tried to initiate a workshop at CHI 2003 to draw the attention of the HCI community towards system administration. The workshop was already dropped in the next year. Later Haber and Bailey [114] repeated an ethnographic field study similar to the one by Barrett et al. [27]. In the study of Velasquez et al. [287] interviews and a survey were combined. In interviews, they found that tools used by system administrators varied widely. One main result of these studies is that system administrators lack tools that have awareness of the context.

Configuration settings are often centered towards the need of developers. Thus system administrators and end users struggle to understand the consequence of configuration settings. State-of-the art is that system administrators and developers need to work together tightly, also known as DevOps [249].

History

One of the first ideas for configuration management was to clone complete machines— often in combination with file synchronization tools like `rdist`—and then do necessary modifications with scripts or profiles. *Profiles* are groups of configuration settings between which the user can easily switch. This allows us to copy all needed configuration settings onto every machine and afterwards decide which machine is used for which purpose. While the approach is powerful if all machines are nearly identical, it shows severe limitations once the machines start to differ significantly. This was state of the art for a long time, until in 1994 when *"the community nearly exploded with four new configuration systems"* [87]:

lcfg from Anderson [10]. The development of lcfg started first in 1991 [9, 10]. Nevertheless, its development still continues [11, 131].

GeNUAdmin from Harlander [119].

omniconf from Hideyo [129].

config from Rouillard and Martin [251].

According to Hintsch et al. [131], in 2016 the number of papers published with a configuration management tool in focus is: 15 papers about CFEngine, 11 papers about Puppet, 9 papers about Chef, 7 papers about lcfg, and 3 papers about BCFG2.

1.1.4 Context-aware Configuration

As adapted from Chalmers [53]:

> **Context** is the circumstances relevant to the configuration settings of the application.

We extend the definition with:

> **Context-aware configurations** are configuration settings that are consistent with its context. **Context-aware configuration access** is configuration access providing context-aware configuration.

Next we investigate the research question:

RQ 2.1. What are the viewpoints of context-aware configuration?

Types of Configuration

According to Wielinga and Schreiber [297] we have three different types of configurations (valid, suitable, and optimal). We will extend it with a fourth type, orthogonal to all others that we will call context-aware configuration:

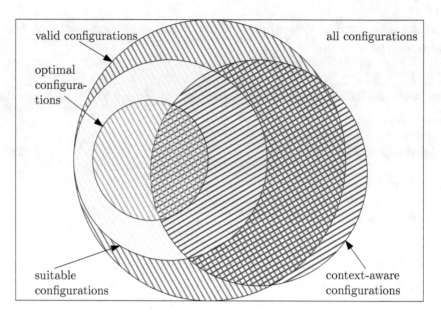

Figure 1.2: Types of configurations. The size of circles does not have a meaning here.

Valid configuration does not contradict the present validation specifications. With a valid configuration, applications can start but they may not do what the user wanted or may be inconsistent with context.

Suitable configuration is valid with respect to additional specifications from the user that describe the system the user requires [159].

Optimal configuration is optimal with respect to given optimization criteria. Optimization criteria are important if managing configuration of many computers but are rarely needed for configuration access discussed in this book.

Context-aware configuration is in accordance with its context. Unlike configuration settings, the context changes in ways outside of our control. Context-aware configuration can also be valid, suitable, and optimal.

Viewpoints

Three *viewpoints* are important for context-aware configuration:

Sensors: *Context sensors* derive context from information sources of the system. Adding new context sensors increases the context available in a system. Configuration that was context aware before, can be context unaware with respect to the context acquired from the new context sensors.

Users: Context awareness can be subjective with respect to the needs of a user. For different users, we may need different context specifications. Configuration that is context aware for one user, can be context unaware regarding the wishes of another user. According to Khalil and Connelly [155, 156] personalization is essential.

Time: Because context varies in time, on changes, we need to renew the context awareness of configuration settings. In such situations we speak of ***context changes*** [103, 145]. Without renewing configuration settings, configuration settings context aware in one moment of time, can be context unaware in the next moment.

These viewpoints imply that fully context-aware configuration is only possible with a closed-world assumption. With an open-world assumption, we can always construct differences in the viewpoints that make previously context-aware configurations inappropriate. Thus it is essential that users have possibilities to personalize and extend context specifications to cope with differences in the viewpoints.

Time and users are not only a viewpoint but can be a context, too. For example, context sensors can look into the working schedule to change the context according to currently ongoing meetings.

We answer the research question:

RQ 2.1. What are the viewpoints of context-aware configuration?

Finding. *At least three viewpoints, i. e. sensors, users, and time, decide about how to interpret the current context. There may be further viewpoints, too.*

1.2 Configuration Specification Languages

Configuration specification language is a relatively vaguely defined term—it is a language where some kind of configuration is specified. In this section, we will investigate different kinds of configuration specification languages.

We aim at configuration specification languages that provide background for SPEC-ELEKTRA. We investigated who already created configuration specification languages to improve configuration access, answering the following research question:

RQ 2.2. Which configuration specification languages are suitable to improve configuration access of FLOSS applications?

Hypothesis (RQ 2.2). *We expect to find a large variety of configuration specification languages that already solve some parts of the configuration integration problem.*

1.2.1   Method

We did a survey of all configuration specification languages as revealed by Google Scholar with the search term:

```
language
"configuration specification" OR
"configuration description" OR
"configuration definition" OR
"configuration declaration"
```

This search yielded several thousand articles. We grouped them by dates because of download limits:

```
1950–1998      946 articles
1999–2004      919 articles
2005–2007      786 articles
2008–2010      872 articles
2011–2012      723 articles
2013–2016      810+ articles
```

The + sign means that we subscribed to the search term to keep track of new incoming articles. We scanned through the titles of all papers—or if this was not enough, we read the abstract—to filter off-topic papers. In particular, we removed all articles that describe general purpose languages, behavioral descriptions, or that are domain-specific. After this process, we grouped papers that described the same configuration specification language. As result, we found 92 configuration specification languages. Due to lack of time, we only further processed the ones that are at least remotely related to SpecElektra and are of interest for this book. In this step, we excluded about ¾ of the configuration specification languages.

In the rest of the section, we will describe four selected properties, i. e. expressiveness, reasoning, modularity, and reusability, for some configuration specification languages. Others are mentioned in "Others".

1.2.2 UML

Felfernig et al. [88, 89, 90] describe an approach where the unified modeling language (UML) is used as notation to simplify the construction of a logic-based description. The papers formally describe the semantics. Tools are available and experimental results show feasibility.

Expressiveness: All UML features, including cardinality, domain-specific stereotypes and OCL-constraints are available. The basic structure of the system is specified using classes, generalization and aggregation. Resources impose additional constraints on the possible system structure. Finally, the require-relation and incompatible-relation allow us to limit valid configurations.

Reasoning: Customers provide additional input data and requirements for the actual variant of the product. The logical sentences are range-restricted first-order-logic with a set extension and interpreted function symbols. For decidability, the term-depth is limited to a fixed number. It is possible to show that the configuration is consistent or that no solution exists.

Modularity: Generalization is present without multiple inheritance with disjunctive semantics, i. e., only one of the given subtypes will be instantiated.

Reusability: For shared aggregation additional ports are defined for a part.

1.2.3 CFEngine

CFEngine [45, 206] is a language-based system administration tool that pioneered idempotent behavior. It uses declarative class-based decision structures. Burgess [46] introduces theory behind it.

Expressiveness: CFEngine allows us to declare dependences and facilitates some high-level configuration specification constructs. In its initial variants it neither had validation specifications, cardinalities, nor higher-level relationships.

Reasoning: NOT SUPPORTED

Modularity: NOT SUPPORTED

Reusability: Existing system administrator scripts can be profitably run from CFEngine.

1.2.4 NIX

The NIX language [77] claims to be purely functional as a novel feature. The main concept is the referential transparency both for the configuration specification language and for the system itself. A large-scale deployment shows that the approach is feasible and practical.

Expressiveness: NIX expressions, for example functions, describe how to build software packages. The unit of variability is a package. Additionally, a hierarchical set of properties describes the configuration specification. Otherwise, the expressiveness is low, NIX describes neither cardinalities nor relationships.

Reasoning: Because of the referential transparency of the system itself, every solution derived from the NIX expressions should be valid, so no reasoning or conflict handling is necessary. Some operations, however, might lead to a completely new system.

Modularity: The NIX expressions are modular because they ensure absence of side effects and thus can be easily composed.

Reusability: Derivations that describe atomic build actions are reused in other derivations. Import and inherit features are used to create packages, improving reusability.

1.2.5 Pan

Cons and Poznanski [58] invented and used PAN for many machines within CERN. Furthermore, the language is still used by Quattor. The configuration database in Pan comprises high-level and low-level descriptions. The low-level descriptions are in XML syntax. Here we focus on the declarative, high-level description.

Expressiveness: The Pan language allows users to specify data types, validation with code snippets and constraints. It only supports lists but no configurable cardinality nor is-a/part-of relationships. The compiler uses a 5 step process: compilation, execution, insertions-of-defaults, validation, and serialization.

Reasoning: Pan focuses on validating configurations, it is not able to generate new configurations. Pan provides type enforcement with embedded validation code.

Modularity: The language has user-defined data types (called templates) but otherwise has only minimal support for modularity. In particular, side effects and assignments hinder modularity of validation code.

Reusability: Reusability and collaboration is only possible via simple include statements and a simple inheritance mechanism of templates.

1.2.6 ConfValley

Huang et al. [137] introduce systematic validation for cloud services. ConfValley uses a unified configuration settings representation for tens of different configuration file formats. Its configuration specification language, called CPL, does not aim to be a type-safe configuration specification language. It enables, however, system administrators of cloud services to write declarative specifications of properties with correctness constraints.

Expressiveness: CPL introduces many concepts and has non-trivial language features. Its most expressive elements are first-order quantifiers. CPL is not able to specify dynamic and complex requirements.

Reasoning: Constraints can be inferred by running an inference engine on configuration settings that are considered good (black-box approach). Within the validation engine, however, no constraint solver is available.

Modularity: CPL aims at easy grouping of constraints. Its extensibility has limitations, for example, adding language primitives need modifications in the compiler. The authors claim, however, that these changes can be done in a straightforward way—at least for predicates.

Reusability: Using transformations and compositions, predicates can be reused in different contexts. Also with language constructs like `let`, specifications can be reused.

1.2.7 Others

Lock [173] invented Strider that supports modeling and analysis of complex systems.

PROTEUS [282] shows the tight relation between software configuration management, like Git or Svn, and configuration specification languages. PROTEUS combines both worlds in a powerful build system.

ConfSolve [127, 128] is a configuration specification language that is translated to a standard constraint programming language called MiniZinc. Their focus is in finding configurations for machines and not to compute configuration settings. ConfSolve generates Puppet code for deployment.

Many other configuration specification languages have been found during the survey [11, 34, 69, 96, 104, 112, 130, 136, 176, 178, 201, 206, 250, 266], but they do not provide configuration access specifications for FLOSS applications.

1.2.8 Result

The result of the survey was that we could not find a configuration specification language to be used as basis. Instead all configuration specification languages we investigated had a different focus, which leads us to our answer of:

RQ 2.2. Which configuration specification languages are suitable to improve configuration access of FLOSS applications?

Finding. *We have to reject our hypothesis for **RQ 2.2**: We did not find any configuration specification language that supports our goal of solving the configuration integration problem. Instead earlier work had at least one of the following two assumptions:*

- *Configuration access in applications needs to be used as given. Configuration management tools have this assumption.*

- *Applications need to be reimplemented using new development methods. Architecture description languages, software product lines, and similar approaches have this assumption.*

Both assumptions hinder progress in fixing the configuration integration problem.

1.3 Programming Paradigms

In this book we will extend from several existing programming paradigms. This section explains the necessary foundations.

1.3.1 Data-driven Programming

Data-driven programming is a very popular programming paradigm available in most programming languages. Raymond [242] says that *"in data-driven programming, the data [...] defines the control flow of the program. Where the primary concern in OO [object-oriented programming] is encapsulation, the primary concern in data-driven programming is writing as little fixed code as possible. Unix has a stronger tradition of data-driven programming".* Raymond [242] further elaborates *"Lisp and Java programmers call this introspection; in some other object-oriented languages it's called metaclass hacking."* We will use the terminology from Lisp and Java and will call the facilities for applications to look up configuration settings and specifications ***introspection***.

1.3.2 Object-oriented Programming

Simula is believed to be the immediate ancestor of object-oriented programming [246]. Smalltalk further evolved the paradigm [197]. In homogeneous designs the premise of "everything is an object" goes quite far, next to primitive types and classes, even expressions are objects. But the premise needs to be broken at some level, for example messages normally cannot be objects we can send messages to [197]. But particularly the sending of messages is central to the object-oriented programming mechanism.

There are different reasons why object-oriented programming got popular. While first the immediate code-reuse, for example via inheritance, rose to prominence, it soon became clear that subtyping is even more powerful on large-scale systems. A long-standing problem was nominal versus structural subtyping. Malayeri and Aldrich [180] found a solution to combine both ways of subtyping. Object-oriented programming has all building blocks for design patterns [98]. Sometimes, subtyping even presents elegant solutions for problems that were thought to be intractable [293].

For details on how to implement an object-oriented system, we refer to Schwartzbach and Palsberg [261]. For configuration libraries, object-oriented programming had little impact for two reasons:

- Encapsulation has little use in a scenario without behavioral specifications. Classes exclusively consisting of trivial getter and setter methods have no advantage to directly accessing data.

- Subtyping is hardly used in configuration settings. The reasons are similar: The benefit of subtyping on simple data types is limited compared to subtyping on objects with behavior.

1.3.3 Persistence in Object-oriented Programming

The main limitations of persistence in object-oriented programming is figuratively described as *"Fitting Round Objects Into Square Databases"* [283]. Databases and configuration libraries emphasize data independence, which is different from the focus of object-oriented programming [283]. **Data independence** aims at separation of the persistent data and their applications using it.

Objects in Smalltalk are persistent, which can be used as replacement for configuration settings from the developer's point of view. Later systems provided dedicated object serialization [126]. While it is a good idea to have the persistence format decoupled from objects, efforts usually do not go far enough to have a serialization that fulfills all desired properties for configuration settings. The fundamental problem is that objects are coherent with the implementation design, which usually has nothing to do with the system administrator's needs.

1.3.4 Aspect-oriented Programming

While **core concerns** are the functionality software was designed and modularized for, **cross-cutting concerns** are usually scattered throughout the code base. Typical examples for cross-cutting concerns are persistence and logging, both relevant for configuration access.

Kiczales et al. [158] suggested to weave separately implemented modules (the cross-cutting concerns) into the main module (the core concern). After the first implementations for Lisp and Java, other implementations, for example, for C++ [15], followed. While it is straightforward to show that aspect-oriented programming improves modularity, there is doubt if aspect-oriented programming increases development speed [117] or has advantages during maintenance [85].

Chiba et al. [54] proposed a radically different approach: Instead of extending syntax, they suggested a synchronous copy and paste. To do so, they remember all concerns in a tree. This approach allows us to handle cross-cutting concerns over documentation and other non-code artifacts.

Immensely successful (and without alternative) got aspect-oriented programming in system-level tracing frameworks. For example, DTrace and SystemTap allow system administrators to collect data about the running system.

1.3.5 Feature-oriented Programming

Feature-oriented Domain Analysis (FODA) pioneered methods to reuse requirements [147]. It distinguishes between compile-time, load-time, and run-time features.

Mostly unrelated but with the same goals, *feature-oriented programming* emerged. Feature-oriented programming or software product lines is an appropriate technique to implement program families [167, 190, 286]. Prehofer [220] described them to be similar to (abstract) subclasses or mixins. Instead of rigid class structure, features are composed when creating objects. The central problem of *feature interaction* is resolved by *lifting* function of one feature to the context of another. The basic idea is that only *"a quadratic number of* $\binom{n}{2} = \frac{n^2-n}{2}$ *of lifters, but an exponential number* $\binom{n}{k}$, $k = 1,...,n$ *of different feature combinations can be created."* [220]

Apel et al. [15] extended the approach with multiple inheritance and templates. Furthermore, they integrated aspect-oriented features. Thüm et al. [279] created a framework based on Eclipse used for educational purposes. Different from previously mentioned solutions it embeds the feature-oriented domain analysis.

Batory [29] gives a short introduction on product lines, which is a design methodology and tool for program synthesis. The idea is to specify products via features, as done in non-software products such as assembled personal computers. Such a specification contains programs as constants, and feature refinements as functions with a feature-augmented program as return value. These constants and functions define a relational algebra. It is possible to synthesize non-code artifacts or product lines of product families.

1.3.6 Subject-oriented Programming

Harrison and Ossher [121] coined the term *subject-oriented programming* in order to bring awareness that real-world objects cannot be objectively described. This would assume that all attributes are intrinsic and not depending on their relation to other objects. The authors introduced a new paradigm that allows us to describe subjectivity. For example, a tree has some intrinsic properties, such as its mass and height. But for most applications, we are interested in subjective, extrinsic properties. The extrinsic properties are viewpoints about different perceptions of the object. For example, a woodman wants to compute a sale price and a squirrel wants to compute the food value of a tree. For subjects only object identity is shared.

Ossher and Tarr [203] added lifetime features for subjects, including traceability. They mainly see benefits of subject-oriented programming for programs in the large. They claim that within subject-oriented programming design patterns can be implemented as subjects, thus separating code to which they apply.

1.4   Context

Context is a natural thing, at least for humans. It creates more conversational bandwidth and contributes more bits of information to communication. As downside, we miserably fail in understanding the message if we do not put enough attention on the context. In this section, we look at challenges and discuss techniques that tackle the challenges.

1.4.1   Context-aware Applications

In the last years the shape of computers changed radically. They often fit into our pocket or even glasses and are fully packed with sensors. This gives many opportunities to take more context into account.

Context awareness aims to give users the impression of applications and devices to be smart [226]. We want applications to react according to properties of their physical environments. For example, when an application notices that the device is on battery, energy savings should be given priority. In the same way, if a tool tells the system administrator that the Web server's and the firewall's configuration settings are inconsistent, the tool is more context aware. The increased context awareness implies that the relationship between the Web server and the firewall is known to the tool.

Most software has at least some context awareness but often without any explicit consideration in the program design. Thus it is implemented in the same way as other features are, interwoven in the core concerns. For others applications, context was an important design goal [24]. Riva et al. [248] searched for design patterns in code that support context awareness in software.

Context-oriented Programming

One of the many systematic ways to write context-aware applications is called ***context-oriented programming*** [5, 14, 16, 17, 24, 61, 74, 106, 133, 141, 145, 151, 216, 255, 259, 267, 275, 290, 294]. Contrary to other techniques to improve context awareness, it focuses on the language level. Its run-time system is rather small, it does not need sophisticated frameworks, databases, or middleware. Context-oriented programming supports implementation of context-aware applications.

Gassanenko [100, 101] provided the first implementation using the name context-oriented programming in Forth. In response to this first work, Costanza et al. [61] criticized that Forth did not have object-oriented programming concepts. According to Costanza et al. it is *"not clear whether Gassanenko's contexts must be fully defined or can be partial and combinable"*. Later context-oriented programming languages extended from object-oriented and often aspect-oriented programming. For example, Tanter et al. [276] combined context awareness and aspects.

Context-oriented programming is a modularization technique on programming language level [16]. So instead of having `if` conditions spread within the core concerns of the application, context-oriented programming allows us to separate code for different contexts [74, 255, 259]. Improving on previous paradigms, context is multi-dimensional and dynamically changed as needed.

The ***layer*** is the main concept of context-oriented programming. Each layer represents a part of the context, and together they compose the context awareness of the application. ***Activation*** and ***deactivation*** of layers dynamically adapt the application to a new context. The ***layer switch*** is the response for context changes: They imply activations or deactivations of the layer as needed by the context. Information about currently active layers is usually stored in a data structure. Layers naturally cut across the whole system and provide a natural modularization concept [17]. Context-oriented programming has no restrictions on when layer switches occur. This dynamic behavior poses challenges related to efficiency [17, 226]:

1. Activation and deactivation of layers can be inefficient.

2. Execution time, even without any layer switches, can be problematic.

For both problems, improvements were suggested: For layer activation Costanza et al. [61] build upon heavily optimized language features. Bockisch et al. [40] employed control flow pointcuts in a virtual machine. Despite these optimizations, Appeltauer et al. [17] revealed that performance penalties of 75 % to 99 % are common [226].

Context-oriented software engineering facilitates a *"methodology that guides us to a specification of context-dependent requirements"* and a *"methodology to systematically organize context-dependent requirements."* [145]. One of the hypotheses underlying context-oriented software engineering is: *"The factors dynamically changing the system behavior are candidates for contexts."* Context engineers derive a design model on the basis of a requirements model. It provides a systematic mapping from context-dependent use cases to layers [145].

1.4.2   Contextual Values

Tanter [275] introduced a lightweight extension to context-oriented programming: **Contextual values** are variables whose values depend on the context in which they are read and modified. They *"boil down to a trivial generalization of the idea of thread-local values"*. The key idea is to use layers as *"discriminate amongst possible values, not only the current thread"* [275]. Side effects are limited to the respective context [232]. Furthermore, contextual values naturally work along with layers as introduced in context-oriented programming.

The semantics of contextual values are like variables, but their observed values change according to the context. When reading a contextual value within a different context, the value can be different even though no assignment occurred. When writing to a contextual value, the written value is only visible within the current context that allows us to limit the contextual value's scope.

CHAPTER 2

Relevance to the Community

All of humanity's problems stem from man's inability to sit quietly in a room alone.

— Blaise Pascal

In this chapter we present reasons why the community should find our challenges relevant and unveil requirements to avoid some of the problems. We answer the research question:

RQ 3. Why do FLOSS applications lack *context awareness* and *configuration validation* for configuration settings and what are the challenges in providing them?

The chapter is structured as follows:

In Section 2.1 we discuss what we observed in FLOSS initiatives and companies.

In Section 2.2 we conduct a study investigating the current state of configuration access.

In Section 2.3 we discuss the current state of context awareness in FLOSS applications.

In Section 2.4 we derive requirements from community feedback.

2.1 General Observations

Because of the omnipresence of the configuration integration problem, developers invented many ad hoc solutions and workarounds. The ad hoc solutions and workarounds are important puzzle pieces to understand the situation of the configuration integration problem. The author of this book made many general observations during the years. In this section we walk through important problems repeatedly found in many FLOSS initiatives and companies, answering the research question:

RQ 3.1. Which problems in configuration access are observed while developing FLOSS with state-of-the-art techniques?

2.1.1 Method

We were involved in various FLOSS initiatives ourselves, for example, Performous (a karaoke application). In this first section, we mainly rely on our own experience but we discussed the problems with experts, and other persons involved in FLOSS initiatives.

Personal observations and experience reports involve high subjectivity. In particular, it is well-known that bias spreads across several cases. If something is believed to be true because of multiple observations, it can be due to bias such as the illusory truth effect [123]. Because no findings here are inconsistent with other findings in the book, we likely forgot our wrong observations because of recall bias. Unfortunately, knowing about a bias does not avoid having it. Thus this material must always be considered critically and supplementary.

2.1.2 Configuration Libraries

From our experience FLOSS initiatives and companies tend to develop their own configuration libraries. To make developers consider using existing configuration libraries, from the authors experience, it is essential that:

Requirement 1. *A configuration library must be simple to use, easily available, lightweight, efficient, and have an excellent out-of-the-box experience.*

Often there are some constraints because of legacies, such as:

1. Customers already use legacy configuration file formats, and

2. it shall be possible to configure legacy software with the same configuration interfaces.

Requirement 2. *A configuration library must be able to integrate (legacy) systems and must fully support (legacy) configuration files.*

2.1.3 Duplication

In larger applications duplicates related to configuration settings arise and have to be kept in sync. Even in mature FLOSS initiatives, for example PostgreSQL—where the problem is already known and effort has been put into it—similar information needs to be synchronized in at least four places [73]. Typically redundant, but with current approaches often unavoidable duplicates, are:

1. command-line interfaces (CLIs), graphical user interfaces (GUIs), and Web interfaces showing configuration settings,

2. command-line options and environment variables for overwriting a configuration setting,

3. validation code scattered and duplicated at several places,

4. several configuration files for different purposes[1],

5. test cases that run the application with different configuration settings,

6. documentation of the configuration settings, and

7. places where configuration settings are used within the application.

The duplication makes it time-consuming to change, remove, or add existing configuration settings because always various places need to be considered. Furthermore, the duplication makes it hard to get reliable information about configuration settings.

Requirement 3. *A single configuration specification must be able to include all information to generate all artifacts needed for configuration settings.*

We saw several teams introducing their own identical configuration settings instead of sharing the configuration value of already given configuration settings. This approach works nicely for the developers, who can avoid any collaboration and communication. It creates, however, problems for system administrators who need to keep the duplicated configuration settings in sync.

Requirement 4. *A configuration library must allow us to share configuration settings.*

---

[1]Such as configuration examples and default configuration files.

2.1.4   Inconsistencies

Developers, maintainers, documentation writers, and system administrators easily create mismatches related to configuration settings. In many cases this problem results from the duplication mentioned before. We saw that:

- a configuration setting is misspelled at one of the duplicated places,

- developers convert a configuration setting to a wrong type,

- developers invent non-documented default value calculations and transformations,

- the used configuration settings are not synchronized with the configuration settings of the configuration file,

- data types or semantics of configuration settings differ between code and documentation, and

- settings are hidden, i. e., used in the source but invisible otherwise. System administrators do not know about such settings.

Of course, mismatches easily happen anywhere and anytime related to software. The problem with configuration settings is that they cannot be tested exhaustively. Testing is limited because all configuration settings can interact and create an exponential number of combinations. In FLOSS software, often only the configuration settings as used by the (package) maintainer, developers, and testers are tested. Thus system administrators have a good chance to find misbehavior if they facilitate rarely-used configuration settings.

Requirement 5. *The specification must enable code generation and inconsistencies must be ruled out during compilation.*

For users and system administrators it is confusing if the configuration file has the correct content but applications do not use it. For example, in a commercial application configuration settings only take effect after the next startup [139]. We should avoid situations in which applications do not behave as their configuration files suggest:

Requirement 6. *Configuration libraries must provide ways to keep transient and persistent views consistent.*

Users must be able to know which configuration settings exist, and which values are valid for them. In case of doubt, it must be possible for system administrators to query which configuration settings and specifications are actually used:

Requirement 7. *Configuration settings and specifications must be introspectable.*

2.1.5 Maintenance

As long as many similar and duplicated configuration settings exist, co-evolution is unavoidable. It happens that:

- abundant code is accumulated around configuration accesses,

- unused configuration settings are not visible and therefore cannot be cleaned up,

- validation and transformation specifications need to be updated according to reported problems, and

- outdated documentation for configuration settings needs to be corrected.

Such activities are time-consuming and error-prone, mainly because of the duplication. Because these situations happen frequently, the source code likely gets inconsistent with the documentation. Intensive testing would be needed but problems are often left for system administrators to find.

We found many workarounds because of bad API design. In particular, in some applications we often found code that bypasses configuration access APIs.

Requirement 8. *The configuration access API must be minimal and crafted carefully.*

A large technical debt is validation code spread over the whole source code. We found that most of the code around configuration accesses tries to validate and transform configuration values. This code was often executed much too late, causing hard-to-find misconfigurations.

Requirement 9. *Validation of configuration settings must happen systematically before the application is even started.*

We found complicated constructs that assign the return values of configuration accesses to variables. Here people wanted to optimize the program and avoid calling configuration accesses within loops.

Requirement 10. *Developers must have guarantees that read-only configuration access is fast and updates only happen if wanted.*

2.1.6 Result

Here we answer the research question:

RQ 3.1. Which problems in configuration access are observed while developing FLOSS with state-of-the-art techniques?

Finding. *Due to observations we found that many small duplications of configuration settings and specifications lead to inconsistencies and increase maintenance costs.*

We have listed requirements that intend to reduce these problems.

2.2   Current State of Configuration Access

For the book we want to focus on configuration access that is indeed relevant and popular. In this section we investigate which kind of configuration access FLOSS developers prefer and how configuration access is currently done, answering the research question:

RQ 3.2. What is the current state of configuration access in FLOSS?

2.2.1   Method

In the main part of this section, we use labels to indicate which method we used. The label "*Q:*" (without quotes) indicates that data was collected from the questionnaire survey and the label "*S:*" (without quotes) represents that data was gathered from the source code analysis.

Questionnaire (Label *Q:*)

The author of the book formulated questions with FLOSS developers as main target. Three students added some questions for their bachelor book. They created two questionnaires using LimeSurvey and Google Forms. Then we organized several pilot surveys with colleagues, FLOSS developers, and experts for surveys. Based on the feedback, we decided to use LimeSurvey and improved the questions, answers, and visual appearance [233].

To be sure that we reach our main target group, we posted requests for participation in many relevant FLOSS communication channels. We rewarded non-anonymous answers by donations to initiatives related to FLOSS. For quality assurance, we cross-checked these non-anonymous answers with the complete pool of participants [233]. The survey was reachable from 20th June, 2016 to 18th July, 2016. After the survey was completed, we sent an email to all non-anonymous participants.

LimeSurvey version 2.50+ aided us for conducting the survey. The questionnaire started with an introduction and personal questions to have characteristics of our group. The personal questions included education, occupation, age, and FLOSS participation [233]. We did not ask any gender-related questions because we did not expect enough participation for significant conclusions. The main part consisted of questions about why and how developers use configuration. We added open questions at the end of the questionnaire for a qualitative touch.

In this book original questions are written down using the format *O: "Original question"*. We report the percentages relative to the number of participants (n) answering the particular question. We note standard deviations (s) and means for samples of $n \geq 95$. We utilized the Kolmogorov-Smirnov test [171] for samples of smaller size [233].

Source Code Analysis (Label *S:*)

Different from earlier work [139, 154, 304, 310], we do not want to limit ourselves to configuration files. Instead we extend our studies to `getenv`, which is a configuration access API to query *environment variables*. We chose it because it is unique in its availability[2] and standardization[3] [233].

Application	Version	Application	Version
0ad	0.0.17	Gimp	2.8.14
Akonadi	1.13.0	Inkscape	0.48.5
Chromium	45.0.2454	Ipe	7.1.4
Curl	7.38.0	LibreOffice	4.3.3
Eclipse	3.8.1	Lynx	2.8.9dev1
Evolution	3.12.9	Man	2.7.0.2
Firefox	38.3.0esr	Smplayer	14.9.0~ds0
GCC	4.9.2	Wget	1.16

Table 2.1: Versions of applications studied.

We analyze the usage of the function `getenv` in the source code. We carefully elected 16 FLOSS applications across different domains such as desktop, development, mobile, games, and system utilities. Our selection criteria were popularity, code size, and a thriving community. We included individual other applications for diversity. As shown in Table 2.1, we consistently used the versions as part of Debian GNU/Linux 8 (Jessie) [233].

---

[2]It is readily available in nearly all programming languages, for example, it is included in the standard libraries of Java, C, C++, Python, Lua, and many more.

[3]It is standardized by SVr4, POSIX.1-2001, 4.3BSD, C89, and C99 [1].

We downloaded packages with `apt-get source` from `http://snapshot.debian.org` [233]. To determine the code size we facilitated Cloc 1.60 [66].

We wanted to know how many of the textual `getenv` occurrences are real `getenv` invocations, i. e. configuration access points, as opposed to occurrences in comments etc. Thus we counted them manually for the versions as specified in Table 2.1 [233]. Obvious wrapper functions that include `getenv` within their name are evaluated identically to `getenv` itself [234]. We excluded some `getenv` occurrences:

- We did so if the `getenv` invocation is obviously related to debugging, logging and testing. Such situations were determined by looking at the `getenv` parameter.

- We did so if the `getenv` invocation is obviously related to the build system, and not used in the application.

The rationale behind these exclusions is that our study should be generalizable to run-time configuration access, and not be specific to `getenv`.

History Analysis

For the analyses of the histories we looked at the same applications as specified in Table 2.1. We used Git repositories, even if the official repository used a different version control. Because of the immense number of commits in the application's repositories, we could not use Cloc for the histories[4]. Manually counting `getenv` in every commit was also out of question. Therefore, we used the line-counting tool `wc -l` and `grep -rio getenv` (with binary and project files filtered out).

2.2.2   Threats to Validity

As proposed by mixed methods, the combination of different analyses returns a more complete picture [138]. Nevertheless, each of the individual methods needs to be conducted with great care. Threats to validity concern the questionnaire, the source code analysis, and the history analysis. Here we describe our mitigation strategies categorized by these methods.

---

[4]It took weeks to run through all commits even without Cloc.

Questionnaire (Label *Q:*)

Surveys reflect beliefs and wishful thinking of participants. Hence, we cross-checked with other methods for facts in the source code of the applications. Nevertheless, opinions assist in understanding reasons and goals, thus the survey is an essential part of the overall work. We consider it as important supplement to source code analysis [233].

For the questionnaire survey's validity we had to make sure that only FLOSS contributors participate. To mitigate this threat [233]:

- We made clear in the introduction that the study is related to FLOSS, by starting with *O: "This survey targets developers of free and open source software (FLOSS) applications"*.

- We prompted the participants about involvement in FLOSS initiatives.

- We invited persons via communication channels that are most likely read by FLOSS contributors.

- We advertised with donations to FLOSS initiatives.

Anonymized raw data for better reproducibility and the questions in full for better repeatability are found at [37, 233, 289]:

`https://rawdata.libelektra.org.`

Source Code Analysis (Label *S:*)

Manual analysis has the danger of oversight and subjective classification. To minimize such errors we incorporated second opinions and only report large differences [234].

An important matter is whether the applications and their developers are representative. We address it by studying 16 mostly diverse applications. We added both large and small applications. We took care that various development teams, domains, and programming languages are represented. The browsers are also used in mobile contexts [234].

We have to acknowledge that the majority of evaluated software is implemented in C/C++. Nevertheless, Java, JavaScript and Python are represented with 4.3, 3.3, and 1.1 million lines of code, respectively. Furthermore, we included Eclipse to have a huge FLOSS initiative mainly implemented in Java [234].

An equally important threat to validity is whether `getenv`, our prime subject of study, represents configuration access points in general. According to previous studies [139, 238, 304], configuration access points are in their essence simple key-value accesses. Higher-level configuration accesses, for example with complex data types, would only complicate the implementation of the configuration access APIs [30, 234].

Some FLOSS initiatives contain `getenv` invocations in scripts used to configure their compilation. These invocations are not part of the final executable and are irrelevant for our goal of making software context aware at run-time. We did not include such invocations to `getenv` in our classification. It is not always easy to tell which parts of the source code actually end up in a given binary. We might have included some `getenv` invocations in the analysis that are actually not included in the executable of the application. Thus we might slightly overestimate the number of `getenv` occurrences.

Because we conducted a source code analysis, we were not able to pick closed-source applications. A portion of the evaluated software, however, has its roots as closed-source applications. Also based on our experience within companies, we are confident that our conclusions hold for closed-source applications, too [234].

History Analysis

Some applications did not have a linear history. In some cases, different repositories without common ancestors were merged. Even though we worked with great care, it is possible that we did not always pick the right commits. If this often happened, we might have missed trends that are there.

2.2.3   Configuration Access in FLOSS

What was the population of the survey?

Q: From 672 persons visiting the survey 286 started to answer. From them, 162 persons completed the questionnaire and 116 persons left their email address.

The age of the population ($n = 220$) has a mean of 32 years ($s = 9$, *O: "How old are you?"*). As occupation, 56 % of the persons selected software developer, 21 % system administrator, and 16 % researcher (multiple choice question, $n = 287$, *O: "What is your occupation?"*). The participants ($n = 242$, *O: "Which country are you from?"*) said they are from Germany (50), Austria (41), United States (32), France (25), Australia (9), and 31 other countries (85). The reported degrees of the persons ($n = 244$, *O: "Which is the highest degree that you have?"*) are: master (38 %), bachelor (25 %), student (18 %), no degree (13 %), and PhD (6 %).

In the questionnaire we asked to fill out information for up to five different FLOSS initiatives (*O: "In which free and open source software (FLOSS) projects have you been or are you involved?"*). For the first FLOSS initiatives, persons estimated their participation time with a mean of 5.3 years ($s = 5$, $n = 180$, *O: "Length of Participation [years]"*). Of these persons, 60 % reported a second FLOSS initiative, 36 % a third, 17 % a fourth, and 9 % a fifth. All persons together reported that they participated in 400 FLOSS initiatives, from which 282 were unique[5]. Debian was the most often mentioned initiative (28), then GNOME and KDE (9), and then Linux (7).

Which methods for configuration access are popular?

Finding. *Command-line arguments, environment variables, and configuration files are equally popular. Developers are very satisfied with them. Other configuration accesses are less popular—both in reported use and satisfaction [233].*

The finding leads to the requirement:

Requirement 11. *A configuration library must support all three popular ways for configuration access: configuration files, command-line options, and environment variables.*

Q: Command-line arguments (92 %, $n = 222$), environment variables, for example, via `getenv` (79 %, $n = 218$), and configuration files (74 %, $n = 218$) are the most popular ways to work with configuration settings (*O: "Which configuration systems/libraries/APIs have you already used or would like to use in one of your FLOSS project(s)?"*).

Others—namely X/Q/GSettings (4 %, 11 %, 9 %), KConfig (5 %), dconf (7 %), plist (7 %), and Windows Registry (13 %)—were used less (≤ 13 %, $n \geq 185$). Freedesktop standards' usage, for example shared-mime-info, is in between (20 %, $n = 205$).

Persons seldom found it (very) frustrating to work with the popular systems (*O: "What is your experience with the following configuration systems/libraries/APIs?"*): `getenv` (10 %, $n = 198$), configuration files (6 %, $n = 190$), and command-line options (4 %, $n = 210$). Less-used systems frustrated more (≥ 14 %, $n \geq 27$): X/Q/GSettings (41 %, 14 %,

---

[5]With normalized names and collapsed "various" and "personal" FLOSS initiatives.

35 %), KConfig (21 %), dconf (42 %), plist (32 %), or Windows Registry (69 %). QSettings is the most popular API from the lesser-used ones with 51 % of (very) satisfied users.

Finding. *The API* getenv *is used omnipresently with 2,683 occurrences.*

S: Table 2.2 shows the number of occurrences of getenv per application as we counted them manually.

Application	1k lines of code	counted getenv	lines per getenv
0ad	474	55	8,617
Akonadi	37	13	2,863
Chromium	18,032	770	23,418
Curl	249	53	4,705
Eclipse	3,312	40	82,793
Evolution	673	23	29,252
GCC	6,851	377	18,172
Firefox	12,395	788	15,730
Gimp	902	56	16,102
Inkscape	480	19	25,255
Ipe	116	21	5,529
LibreOffice	5,482	284	19,304
Lynx	192	89	2,157
Man	142	62	2,293
Smplayer	76	1	76,170
Wget	143	32	4,456
Total	49,556	2,683	18,470
Median	477	54	

Table 2.2: Manually counted getenv [234]: The column *1k lines of code* are the lines of codes of the applications divided with a factor of 1,000. The column *counted* getenv contains our manual count of getenv invocations. The column *lines per* getenv is the ratio of the lines of code and manually counted getenv.

Why are currently so many configuration file formats present?

Finding. *New configuration file formats were introduced by 19 % of the persons.*

Q: The 19 % persons (*n* = 251, *O:* *"In which way have you used or contributed to the configuration system/library/API in your previously mentioned FLOSS project(s)?"*), who claim to have introduced a configuration file format, confirm that regularly many new configuration file formats get invented. Furthermore, 29 % implemented a configuration file parser. Fewer persons (15 %) introduced a configuration system/library/API. Using internal (35 %) and external configuration access APIs (34 %) is more popular than reinventing new formats or APIs.

Discussion: More configuration file formats are invented (19 %) than configuration system/library/API(s) introduced (15 %). This suggests that many configuration file formats do not have a proper library/API for them.

2.2.4 Purpose and Trend of `getenv`

What is the purpose of `getenv`?

Finding. *In most aspects* `getenv` *has the same purpose as other configuration access APIs. Specific to* `getenv` *is its utilization for:*

1. *bypassing other configuration accesses (Q: 45 %),*

2. *locating configuration files,*

3. *debugging and testing (Q: 55 %, S: 1,152, i. e. 43 %), and*

4. *sharing configuration settings across applications (Q: 53 %, S: 716, i. e. 47 %).*

Item 4 of this finding is an indication that there is a need for our Requirement **4**:

Requirement 4. *A configuration library must allow us to share configuration settings.*

Q: In a multiple choice question we found that the reasons to use `getenv` vary ($n = 177$, *O: "At which places in the code would you use a* `getenv`*?"*):

55 % say they would use it for debugging and testing,

53 % say they would use it for configuration integration, i. e., sharing configuration settings (answer "environment variables" from question *O: "Which effort do you think is worthwhile for providing better configuration experience?"*),

45 % would use `getenv` to bypass the application's main configuration access,

20 % would use `getenv` if they consider configuration settings unlikely to be changed
    by a user, and

2 % say they would use `getenv` in a loop (*O: "even when it is used inside a loop, for
    example:* **for** *(int i = 0; i < K; ++i) getenv("HOME");"*).

S: Out of the 2,683 `getenv` invocations, we classified 1,531 `getenv` invocations, i. e. 57 %,
not to be used for logging, debugging, testing, or similar. By analyzing which parameters
are passed to non-testing `getenv` invocations we found 716 invocations (47 %) using
shareable parameters, such as `PATH`.

As mentioned in the method section, we separated the `getenv` invocations for debugging
and testing because we wanted to avoid that our results are specific to `getenv`. Configuration settings in configuration files usually do not have so many settings dedicated to
debugging and testing. Thus further investigations in this book elaborate exclusively on
these 1,531 `getenv` invocations.

Application	conf	uniq	Application	conf	uniq
0ad	45	25	Gimp	27	22
Akonadi	8	5	Inkscape	16	11
Chromium	387	234	Ipe	19	12
Curl	26	20	LibreOffice	207	120
Eclipse	33	24	Lynx	79	53
Evolution	13	11	Man	52	35
GCC	218	127	Smplayer	1	1
Firefox	376	245	Wget	24	17

Table 2.3: Counted number of `getenv` invocations without debugging and testing.

S: Table 2.3 presents the results of the classification. The column *conf* shows the number of
`getenv` invocations broken down from the before-mentioned 1,531 `getenv` invocations.
The column *uniq* displays how many of them had different parameters.

Most `getenv` invocations pass a string parameter defined nearby in the source code
(95 %). Only in 71 cases it was unclear which string is passed to the `getenv` invocation.

Analysis of `getenv` parameters: 357 configuration access points (105 unique) manage
configurable file system locations, for example, download directories or paths to configuration files. Some configuration access points configure the user interface, such as
whether native widgets shall be used, for example, `AQUA_NATIVE_MENUS`. Furthermore,

97 configuration access points (15 unique) configure the language, for example, LANG. Some applications have a large amount of application-specific parameters to getenv, for example, Firefox has 117 configuration access points (89 unique) with MOZ_* or GECKO_* as parameters. Some parameters ensure compatibility with previous or standard behavior, for example POSIXLY_CORRECT. Other parameters probe hardware, for example, 58 parameters (42 unique) probe OpenGL support. For common parameters, we found different spellings or capitalizations, for example, TMP, TEMP, or TMPDIR.

We found configuration accesses that were outdated and not used anymore. We wrote 4 bug reports, 2 of them were acknowledged and 1 was fixed.[6]

Discussion: Overall we found the characteristics of getenv parameters to be very similar to other configuration accesses like configuration settings in configuration files. One special property of getenv is that parameters are commonly shared between applications (such as PATH) but with some fragmentation. The analysis of the getenv invocations surprised us by very different uses: In some cases, environment variables are misused as global variables. Some getenv invocations obviously bypass the application's main configuration access. We found different reasons for bypasses:

- To locate the configuration files avoiding otherwise necessary *bootstrap* code.

- Because getenv was more readily available, for example, a pointer to the data structure of main configuration access was missing at that place.

- It was added temporarily but never removed.

What is the trend of getenv occurrences?

Finding. *In an analysis of the development histories of the 16 applications we observed that getenv occurrences rarely decrease.*

Figure 2.1 shows the historical development of textual getenv occurrences and the textual lines in the repositories for Firefox and Chromium.

Implication. *This inflation indicates research on getenv is future-proof and system administrators may get even more complex interfaces in the future.*

---

[6]Reported by us in https://savannah.gnu.org/bugs/index.php?47989.

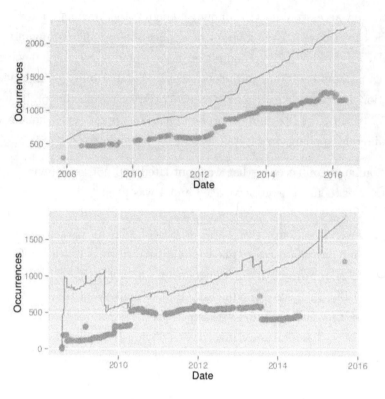

Figure 2.1: The red points show occurrences of the text `getenv` in the repository of Firefox (above) and Chromium (below). We suppress points where the number has not changed between commits. The continuous, thin line indicates total lines of the application's source code. They are counted with `wc` and expressed as multiples of *10,000*. The repository contains files not present in the Debian source package we analyzed. The *date* dimension goes beyond the release date of the manually evaluated Firefox version (22nd September, 2015). In Chromium, we added the manually evaluated version. The graphs are representative for about half of the evaluated software, others are highly irregular.

How are `getenv` parameters documented?

Finding. *The documentation of* `getenv` *parameters is not satisfactory.*

Method: Using `startpage.com` we searched for every parameter passed to `getenv` invocations. If there were too many results, we added the name of the application. We did not look at the second page, i. e., we only investigated the first ten links.

Result: S: For only 283 non-shared `getenv` parameters we found documentation. We could not find explanations of the behavior of the 387 other `getenv` parameters [233].

Discussion: We found different ways how FLOSS initiatives deal with lacking documentation of `getenv` parameters. Many FLOSS initiatives declare `getenv` use as internal: They officially do not recommend using them, even if no other workaround exists. Such statements contradict our finding that only 20 % of FLOSS developers consider environment variables unlikely to be changed. In some FLOSS initiatives the contributors compile lists of available parameters. For example, LibreOffice contributors find `getenv` invocations with `grep`[7] [233].

2.2.5 Result

Here we summarize our results for the research question:

RQ 3.2. What is the current state of configuration access in FLOSS?

Finding. *We found that three types of execution environments are especially popular: configuration files, environment variables, and command-line options.*

We unveiled details about why it is often arbitrary which of the execution environments is chosen:

- *Often the most convenient method is used.*

- *In the survey, people often could not agree what* `getenv` *shall be used for (Most results are around 50 %.)*

The `getenv` API supports all characteristics for configuration access and can be used to investigate challenges in configuration validation.

Environment variables cannot replace configuration files because they do not support to be persisted or to be changed from outside during execution.

---

[7]Which has limitations regarding `getenv` aliases and is also not intended for users, see `https://bugs.documentfoundation.org/show_bug.cgi?id=37338`.

2.3   Current State of Context Awareness

In this section we answer the research question:

RQ 3.3. Which proportion of configuration accesses is already context aware or can be made so without any source code changes?

Hypothesis (RQ 3.3). *We expect at least some configuration accesses to be context unaware as candidates for improvements.*

2.3.1   RQ 3.3.1: What are the usage patterns of `getenv`?

In this part we investigate if configuration access points already consider context. We focus on the configuration access points using the API `getenv`.

Method

We refined our classification by determining whether `getenv` invocations for configuration *provide* or *require* configuration context. We say that some configuration access code *requires context* if it is executed conditionally depending on some configuration value. The configuration access code controlling such conditional branches is said to *provide context* for the conditionally executed code.

Example 2.1. Consider the following code snippet adapted from Lynx:

```
1 if (lynx_cfg_file == NULL) {
2     if ((cp = getenv ("LYNX_CFG")) != NULL)
3         lynx_cfg_file = strdup (cp);
4 }
```

Here the `getenv` invocation *requires* configuration context: It is conditionally executed depending on the existence of a configuration file in a place that may have been configured by a command-line option. This `getenv` invocation *provides* context for further configuration access code because it controls where configuration settings will be searched.   ▲

We only looked at code snippets with 20 surrounding code lines. In some cases this made it difficult to judge whether a `getenv` invocation needed or provided context. In such cases we were conservative and did not count the invocation as needing or providing context, except for invocations which are presumably used to locate configuration files. Our results may be skewed by the fact that some FLOSS initiatives include source code from others. For example, Chromium and Firefox both include source code of the SQLite library that contains `getenv` invocations. Chromium even contain two slightly different versions of at least some of this code.

Then we tagged contexts of configuration access points into categories. The categories classify the purpose of the context, for example, **if** `(running_os_X) getenv(..);` is in the `os_X` category.

Result

As shown in Figure 2.2 we identified 837 configuration access points where context is needed. We found 750 places where the return value of `getenv` provides context for configuration related code.

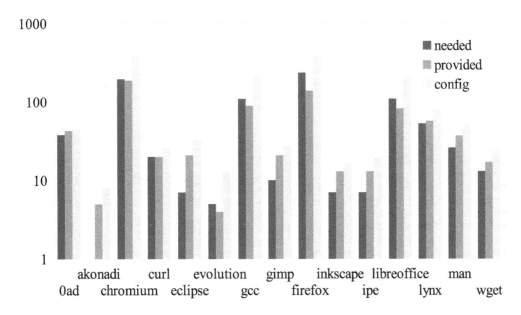

Figure 2.2: Classification of *needed* and *provided* contexts per application with a logarithmic scale; *config* is the number of configuration-related configuration access points (in total 1,531).

We introduced 152 categories of contexts. The categories include operating systems `os_*`, `getenv` invocations `getenv_*`, locales, network, cmdline, build system, debug, hardware specifics `hw_*`, system specifics `sys_*`, file system paths `path_*`, and others. Developers put by far the greatest effort into correctly handling the context the operating system provides. They considered 36 different operating systems, with most occurrences for different versions of Windows (155), various UNIX clones (127), Android (59), and VMS (23).

We found 102 invocations to `getenv` depend on other invocations to `getenv`, often because of fallback chains that support similarly named settings (for example, `TMP`, `TEMP`, or `TMPDIR`). Hardware-based features were not often used as context but they were diverse, for example, configuration access points checking for AES or SSE instruction set features. In 38 places the name or presence of files formed a context. Many contexts occurred only for a single configuration access point, for example, a specific software dependence.

Discussion

We searched for places where more context would be useful. Here, by nature, subjectivity is involved. We only report the numbers we found but avoid building any finding or implications on the number. We found 129 such places, with complaints on the Internet in 23 cases.

We answer the research question:

RQ 3.3.1. What are the usage patterns of `getenv` invocations in the source code of popular applications?

Finding. *Source code to consider context often occurs around configuration access points. We found 837 configuration access points where context is manually considered, and 750 configuration access points that provide context for others. Developers focus on support for various operating systems. It is inevitable that in many places the context is forgotten: we found cases with complaints in the Internet.*

Implication. *Based on the 837 needed and 750 provided contexts around configuration access points, we assume developers tried hard to support context awareness.*

2.3.2   RQ 3.3.2: How often is **getenv** repeatedly used at run-time?

As we learned from the questionnaire survey, nearly no developer thought `getenv` should be used in a loop. Therefore, if `getenv` is nevertheless repeatedly invoked with the same parameters, it is possible that developers assumed different semantics than `getenv` actually has: All `getenv` calls within the process return a value initialized at application's start. Thus `getenv` return possibly-outdated, non-context-aware values repeatedly, which is a lost opportunity for better context awareness.

Method

To improve reproducibility we freshly installed Debian GNU/Linux Jessie with KDE and GNOME desktop, respectively. Only one measurement (of the boot up) was done with the GNOME variant. We applied only small modifications after the fresh installation: We installed the mentioned applications[8] and ELEKTRA [232]. Furthermore, we configured Akonadi to use an IMAP account.

For more accurate interpretation of the numbers it is important to know that usage patterns vary widely between different hardware, operating systems, and installed packages. For example, Firefox executed within GNOME[9] triggered 11 GNOME-specific and 8 GTK-specific `getenv` invocations [232]. In the KDE desktop, these `getenv` invocations would not occur. The differences caused by the environment are drastic. For example, on the author's laptop EliteByte (running KDE with many additionally installed applications), we counted 210.276 `getenv` invocations during startup. This number is 21 times more than the number counted on a freshly installed KDE.

We examine how applications use `getenv` repeatedly. Only APIs that are repeatedly used at run-time flawlessly support context awareness. To learn about usage patterns of `getenv`, we count executions of `getenv` by logging all invocations [232].

Result

In Table 2.4 we use the following columns [232]:

lines of code: Counted lines of code.

getenv all: Counted `getenv` invocations while using the applications.

getenv init: Counted `getenv` invocation while starting up the applications.

all unique: From *getenv all*: How many different parameters were used?

later unique: From `getenv` invocations after initialization, how many different parameters were used? (For Wget and Curl we count the first download as initialization.)

---

[8]If not already part of the default installation.

[9]Which was not used in the main experiment.

Application	lines of code	getenv all	getenv init	all unique	later unique	same
Akonadi	37,214	10,357	8655	110	12	5126
Chromium	18,032,183	6006	1803	1118	192	165
Curl	249,380	19	8	12	8	4
Eclipse	3,311,712	2790	2696	389	42	1495
Evolution	672,789	4407	1488	1060	24	163
Firefox	12,394,938	3371	2049	276	70	895
Gimp	901,703	2551	1115	217	137	364
Inkscape	479,849	722	457	160	51	166
LibreOffice	5,482,215	3354	2891	258	59	1493
Lynx	192,012	1931	961	27	27	923
Man	142,183	2862	13	86	76	2
Smplayer	76,170	212	164	71	8	53
Wget	142,603	11	10	8	1	3
Median	479,849	2790	1115	160	42	166
Total	41,821,956	38,593	22,310	3792	707	10,852
KDE	*	*	9606	265	*	2634
GNOME	*	*	144	47	*	4
Debian	*	*	5317	430	*	286

Table 2.4: Count of `getenv` during run-time. The star (*) means that any of the above applications can be started in the session [232].

same: From the `getenv` invocations during startup (*getenv init*), what is the highest number of `getenv` invocations with the same parameter?

The 13 applications of Table 2.4 requested a median of 2790 environment variables. Akonadi had the largest number of `getenv` invocations. The environment variable `LANGUAGE` alone was requested 5126 times. We observed a similar effect during the KDE startup: 27 % of all `getenv` invocations used the parameter `LANGUAGE`. Other applications had a more uniform use of different parameters. Thus the ratios of overall requested and unique parameters differs greatly: Its median is 14 % but for Akonadi it is only $\sim 1\%$ [232].

Discussion

We answer the research question:

RQ 3.3.2. How often is `getenv` repeatedly used at run-time?

Finding. *From Table 2.4, we conclude that* `getenv` *invocations happen extensively across all studied applications at run-time. Applications do not stop querying environment variables after startup: For example, user interactions cause further* `getenv` *to be invoked [232].*

We assume that developers spend little effort in counting or optimizing `getenv` invocations. Quality assurance also unlikely finds such unnecessary occurrences. We conclude that excessive use of `getenv` can be undeliberate [232].

Because developers expect configuration access points to be cheap, which is the case for `getenv`, there is further support of Requirement **10**:

Requirement 10. *Developers must have guarantees that read-only configuration access is fast and updates only happen if wanted.*

2.3.3 Discussion

After investigating in the sub-questions, we answer the main question:

RQ 3.3. Which proportion of configuration accesses is already context aware or can be made so without any source code changes?

Finding. *We accept the hypothesis for* **RQ 3.3***:*

   1. In the quantitative study we validate that `getenv` *invocations are pervasive [232].*

   2. We found `getenv` *invocations to happen frequently at run-time after startup [232].*

   3. Many manual considerations for context exist throughout all applications. We found 837 such places. We also found 750 places that provide context. Nevertheless, in many places context is forgotten or not available.

Implication. *The high number of* `getenv` *invocations is a prerequisite for run-time adaptations of applications towards better context awareness without source code modifications [232].*

2.4 Configuration Challenges

Now that we have established that configuration accesses are widely used and popular, we investigate challenges of providing configuration validation. We use the same methods as described in Section 2.2.1, again with the labels *"S:"* and *"Q:"*. We investigate the research question:

RQ 3.4. What are the challenges and requirements in providing configuration access for context-aware configuration?

2.4.1 Reduction & Effort

Here we give empirical foundations to our observations in Section 2.1.

Why should configuration be reduced?

> **Finding.** *Many developers do not want to reduce configuration (30 %) while others say reduction would prevent errors (43 %).*

Q: Many participants (30 %, $n = 215$, multiple choice, *O: "Why do you think configuration should be reduced?"*) think that the number of configuration settings should *not* be reduced (*O: "I do not think it should be reduced"*). Other participants, however, argue that configuration settings should be reduced to simplify code maintenance (50 %), to prevent errors and misconfiguration (43 %), to provide better user experience (40 %), because they prefer auto-detection (29 %) (with a possibility to override configuration settings: 32 %), *O: "because use-cases which are rarely used should not be supported"* (13 %), and *O: "because only standard use-cases should be supported"* (1 %). Of the positive answers, 9 % admitted they *O: "never find time for this task"*.

Discussion: We found the high number of negative answers (30 %) surprising:

- Xu et al. [305] proposed to reduce the number of configuration settings to avoid misconfigurations. They found that many configuration settings can be completely removed without any replacement needed.

- It is the multiple choice question in which most persons rejected all positive answers. As shown in the results above, we gave many reasons why reduction is a good idea in the answers. Saying no to the question disallowed picking one of the positive answers. People who are not sure would most likely pick one of the arguments.

- We even considered more sophisticated arguments for reduction and added the answer "auto-detection should always be overridable" (29 %). People who gave this answer, were not counted to the 30 %. Popular FLOSS applications already successfully used auto detection, for example X-server, and are well-known.

Which effort provides better configuration experience?

Finding. *Most developers have concerns adding dependences for more validation (84 %) but consider good defaults important (80 %).*

From the finding we derive the requirement:

Requirement 12. *Dependences exclusively needed to validate configuration settings must be avoided.*

Q: We got mixed answers ($n = 177$, multiple choice, *O: "Which effort do you think is worthwhile for providing better configuration experience?"*): Developers agree that good default values are important (80 %). Most techniques to provide better configuration experience, however, exceed the effort considered acceptable by the majority of participants. The only majority was found in using `getenv` for a better configuration experience (53 %). Many persons (44 %) would use other configuration access APIs next to `getenv`. Fewer persons (30 %) would use OS-specific sources. Only 21 % of the participants would use dedicated libraries, 19 % would read other application's configuration settings, and 16 % would use external configuration access APIs that add new dependences.

Discussion: Because of dependences, FLOSS developers currently expect users to manually configure their applications to be consistent with other configuration settings.

2.4.2   Validation & Specification

Which challenges prevent us from supporting validation?

Finding.

- *Currently, validation specifications are manually implemented by hard coding them into applications.*

- *The validation code is scattered around as it is the case for other cross-cutting concerns.*

- *Essential information needed for configuration validation (most often system configuration settings) is often not available in applications.*

Because sharing system configuration settings would make the information needed for configuration validation more easily available, the finding supports Requirement **4**:

Requirement 4. *A configuration library must allow us to share configuration settings.*

S: We did not find a single application that kept validation code separated. Instead we found validation code to be scattered around similar to other cross-cutting concerns [233].

Furthermore, we found that information necessary for configuration validation is often missing. In 204 places we assumed that a dependence to additional configuration access points was missing. In 58 places we even found several hints, for example, missing cases in fallback chains and complaints in the Internet. A real-life example of incomplete context awareness—despite immense effort to fully detect the context—is given by Raab and Barany [233].

Discussion: Configuration validations are easily forgotten if not done in systematic ways. This leads to important configuration settings not being available from the expected configuration source. In some situations the effort to get necessary information for validation is too high. For example, information about installed packages, network connections, firewall settings, hardware configurations, etc. are nearly impossible to get in a portable way [233].

Why would you specify configuration?

Finding. *Many developers (79 %) would like to use configuration specifications for different reasons.*

Q: We found that 21 % of the persons would not specify their configuration because they are too complicated (14 %), might introduce inconsistencies (3 %) and other reasons[10] (4 %; $n = 215$, multiple choice, *O: "Configuration specification (e.g. XSD/JSON schemas)*

---

[10]Such as problems with manual editing or problems with JSON/XML technologies.

allows you to describe possible values and their meaning. Why do/would you specify configuration?").

Those who would introduce specifications said:

58 % for *O: "looking up what the value does"*,

51 % it helps users to avoid common errors (*O: "so that users avoid common errors"*),

46 % to simplify maintenance,

40 % for rigorous validation,

39 % for documentation generation (for example, man pages, user guide),

30 % for external tools accessing configuration,

28 % for generating user interfaces,

25 % for code generation, and

24 % for specification of links between configuration settings.

Discussion: Even though many developers would like to specify their configuration, most do not.

How important is it to mitigate the configuration integration problem?

Finding. *Mitigating the configuration integration problem is considered to be important to improve user experience (96 %).*

The finding demands:

Requirement 13. *A configuration library must mitigate the configuration integration problem.*

Q: From the multiple choice question (*O: "Configuration integration is an effort to adapt applications better to the system. How important are the following reasons to introduce configuration integration? (e.g. reading /etc/papersize)"*), we got the following answers (at least "moderately important", excluding "slightly important" and "not important"):

96 % *O: "to improve user experience"* (43 % very important, $n = 173$).

90 % *O: "because common/default settings are already available (e.g. in /etc/papersize)"* (24 % very important, $n = 161$).

84 % *O: "because guidelines recommended it (e.g. $HOME in POSIX)"* (21 % very important, $n = 165$).

70 % *O: "because I am convinced it should be done"* (18 % very important, $n = 152$).

2.4.3 Documentation

How should configuration be exposed?

Finding. *The most important interface for configuration is configuration files (49 %).*

The finding supports Requirement **2**:

Requirement 2. *A configuration library must be able to integrate (legacy) systems and must fully support (legacy) configuration files.*

Q: In detail, the persons answered (multiple choice, $n \geq 121$, *O: "How important is it to expose configuration options in the following ways?"*) that it is very important that configuration settings shall be exposed:

49 % as configuration file,

36 % as command-line utility,

17 % via native GUI,

17 % via library API,

9 % via inter-process communication,

6 % via REST API[11], and

4 % as Web UI.

How do you backup your configuration settings?

Q: Already 72 % of the persons have configuration files in version control system repositories, and 42 % use `rsync` ($n = 159$), again supporting the requirement:

Requirement 2. *A configuration library must be able to integrate (legacy) systems and must fully support (legacy) configuration files.*

---

[11]Representational state transfer uses URLs and HTTP to provide an API.

How do you inform yourself about configuration options?

Q: In detail, persons found it very important that (multiple choice, $n \geq 150$, *O: "You want to configure a FLOSS application. How important are the following ways for you?"*):

48 % documentation is shipped with the application

36 % configuration examples are shipped with the applications

17 % *O: "google, stackoverflow... (looking for my problem)"*

14 % looking at the website of the application

14 % use UIs that help them

14 % look into the source code

11 % *O: "wiki, tutorials... (looking for complete solutions)"*

5 % look into the configuration specification

2 % ask colleagues and friends

Discussion: The results suggest that configuration specification shall be used to generate documentation and examples: On the one hand, developers think that the main reason for specifying configuration is documentation (58 %, for *O: "looking up what the value does"*). On the other hand, developers hardly use configuration specification to directly look up documentation about configuration settings (5 %). This is supported by 40 % of the persons, who would specify configuration to generate documentation.

Requirement 14. *There must be a support for shipping correct documentation and examples generated from the configuration specifications.*

2.4.4 Community Feedback

Q: We found helpful community feedback in the questionnaire. As last question we asked *O: "Finally, which benefits do you think are essential in order to add a dependency to a configuration system/library/API? (e.g. Elektra)"*.

Persons acknowledged that a configuration library must be *"lightweight and efficient"* (80 %, $n = 153$). Developers had consensus about that a configuration library *"must be available anywhere and anytime"* (84 %, $n = 153$) [233]. A majority agreed that it *"must be a trivial API (e.g. like getenv)"* (53 %), which supports our Requirement **1**:

Requirement 1. *A configuration library must be simple to use, easily available, lightweight, efficient, and have an excellent out-of-the-box experience.*

Most participants (70 %, $n = 150$) recognize it as important to have a supportive community. Even more persons find it important that bugs are fixed promptly (88 %, $n = 150$) [233].

Many persons found support for readable configuration files important (65 %, $n = 152$), which again confirms our Requirement **2**:

Requirement 2. *A configuration library must be able to integrate (legacy) systems and must fully support (legacy) configuration files.*

Other Selected Feedback

- *"Must be extensible/adaptable. If it is, users can take care of many of the above aspects themselves".*

- *"It must offer a compelling reason to switch from e.g gsettings. [sic!]*[12] *For example a killer feature that others don't have, etc. Otherwise, the status quo wins."*

- *"env vars are great for trying out settings before baking them into config files."*

- *"All generic configuration should come with a library, not be read directly; that allows the library to migrate to new mechanisms without breaking applications that use it."*

- *"envs are difficult to track, you cannot assume them in every environment, it's still a bit tricky to work with them platform-indepentent [sic!]".*

- *"In 0 A.D., we found it hard to use a cross-platform configuration system, which is why our source code has its own simple configuration system."*

---

[12]We indicate typos with [sic!]. In this case the author most likely wanted to say "e.g. GSettings", which is a configuration system used in the GNOME desktop environment.

CHAPTER 3

Elektra

You never change things by fighting the existing reality. To change something,
build a new model that makes the existing model obsolete.

— Buckminster Fuller

In this chapter we formalize a model of ELEKTRA's central parts. They capture the whole framework of ELEKTRA. We do not provide any rationale but explain internal dependences of the model. We concisely describe all parts relevant for further development of this book, including the modular configuration specification language SPECELEKTRA. In later chapters, we will present the rationale and the connection to the requirements.

In Section 3.1 we discuss a common data structure all other parts of the framework ELEKTRA relies on. We use it to represent configuration settings and specifications for both in-memory access, code generation, and persistent configuration files. We introduce a syntax suitable for this book to denote configuration settings and specifications.

In Section 3.2 we explore the user's view of ELEKTRA. We elaborate on the fundamentals of the modular configuration specification language SPECELEKTRA and how SPECELEKTRA provides guarantees for users concerning configuration access. We discuss how to facilitate the contextual classes that implement type-safe contextual values.

In Section 3.3 we take the system's perspective. We describe the essence of backends and the algorithms used by LIBELEKTRA. We introduce how LIBELEKTRA keeps the in-memory data structure in sync with the execution environment. We discuss the default behavior of the key database and how the behavior is redefined via SPECELEKTRA.

In Section 3.4 we accustom us with the details of frontends. We introduce another abstraction to transform configuration settings and specifications to source code. Based on this abstraction, we show how GenElektra generates contextual classes and prove the absence of a run-time error concerning unavailable configuration settings.

3.1 Data Structure

A key-value pair is the simplest generic data structure [271]. While syntactically plenty of different configuration files are available, they all can be represented as key-value pairs as discussed in Section 1.1.1. In this section we define a key-value data structure suitable to contain configuration settings and specifications thereof.

3.1.1 Preliminaries

We start by defining the characters and strings needed to create key-value pairs:

Definition 3.1. *The **character set** C includes all needed characters. There is a total order on C with the character slash ('/') being the smallest character:*

$$\forall x, y \in C : \text{'/'} \leq x \land (x \leq y \lor y \leq x) \land ((x \leq y \land y \leq x) \implies x = y)$$

*A **string** $\vec{C}$ is a (possibly empty) sequence of characters in C. A **non-empty string** $\vec{C_{\geq 1}}$ has a length of at least one. A **value** $\vec{C_\epsilon}$ is a string, that additionally can be ϵ (which is different from an empty string). We call the set of all possible strings $\mathbb{C}$, the set of all possible non-empty strings $\mathbb{C}_{\geq 1}$, and the set of all possible values $\mathbb{C}_\epsilon = \mathbb{C} \cup \{\epsilon\}$.*

We employ values $\in \mathbb{C}_\epsilon$ as configuration values. The value ϵ represents an available configuration value that intentionally was set to be not available.

We use the extended Backus–Naur form notation to specify syntax [262, 269, 300]. We have two forms to denote nonterminals:

- We write nonterminals in ⟨*angles and italics*⟩. They are case-sensitive and either defined within grammars or in the surrounding text.

- We write nonterminals as symbols representing sets, such as C and $\mathbb{C}_{\geq 1}$. Here each element of the set is supposed to be in the specified syntax.

To avoid name collisions, some nonterminals defined within the grammar start with capitals. We write terminals in 'quotes and in typewriter'. The quotes contain strings $\in \mathbb{C}$ (or characters $\in C$, only in the next definition). Furthermore, we write productions with ::=, union with |, options with [], groups for preferences with (), and any number of repetitions (including zero repetitions) in {}.

Definition 3.2. *A **white space** (in grammars denoted as '␣') is a character in C to represent vertical space. The set of **special characters** $P \subset C$ is:*

$$P \quad\quad ::= \text{'/' | '\%' | '=' | ',' | ':' | ';' | '␣' | '[' | ']'}$$

We denote a **line break** in grammars as '↩', but assume for the discussion here that they are not considered as characters $\in C$ and thus cannot be part of strings or values.[1]

Definition 3.3. *A **clean string** $\overrightarrow{C'}$ is a sequence of non-special characters in $C \setminus P$, and $\overrightarrow{C'_{\geq 1}}$ is a non-empty sequence thereof. We call the set of all possible clean strings $\mathbb{C}'$ and the set of all possible **non-empty, clean strings** $\mathbb{C}'_{\geq 1}$. We denote literal strings with 'string' and string concatenation with $x +\!\!+ y$ $(x, y \in \mathbb{C})$.*

Example 3.4. The literal 'example' is a string $\in \mathbb{C}$, a clean string $\in \mathbb{C}'$, and a non-empty, clean string $\in \mathbb{C}'_{\geq 1}$. It is identical to the string 'ex' $+\!\!+$ 'ample'. The string 'hello, world' is a string $\in \mathbb{C}$ but not a clean string, i. e., $\notin \mathbb{C}'$. It contains two special characters: a comma and a white space ('␣'). ▲

3.1.2 Key Names

Definition 3.5. *The set of **relative key names** $\mathbb{R}$ is a subset of non-empty strings $\mathbb{C}_{\geq 1}$ according to the following grammar:*

$$\langle \textit{hierarchy level} \rangle \quad\quad ::= \mathbb{C}'_{\geq 1} \text{ | '\%'}$$

$$\langle \textit{basename} \rangle \quad\quad ::= \langle \textit{hierarchy level} \rangle$$

$$\mathbb{R} \quad\quad ::= \{ \langle \textit{hierarchy level} \rangle \text{'/' } \} \langle \textit{basename} \rangle$$

As shown in the grammar, a basename is a special case of a **hierarchy level**: We call the right-most hierarchy level **basename**. The meaning of the special characters in the relative key names are:

'/' is the hierarchy separator, splitting up the relative key name into hierarchy levels.

---

[1] In the implementation special characters such as line breaks are escaped with complicated rules not relevant to the model. We assume escaped line breaks to be characters different from '↩'.

'%' denotes an empty hierarchy level.

Example 3.6. The string 'slapd/%/bar' is a relative key name. Its hierarchy levels are 'slapd', '%', and 'bar', where 'bar' is additionally called basename.   ▲

Definition 3.7. *The set of **key names** $\mathbb{N}$ is defined by the following grammar, where each element in N is a **namespace**:*

$$\mathbb{N} \qquad ::= [\, N \text{ `:'} \,] \text{ `/'} \, \mathbb{R}$$

$$N \qquad ::= \text{`spec'} \,|\, \text{`proc'} \,|\, \text{`dir'} \,|\, \text{`user'} \,|\, \text{`system'}$$

If a key name does not have the optional namespace and starts with '/', we say the key name has namespace ϵ (which is not included in N).

The elements of N represent the namespaces SPEC, PROC, DIR, USER, and SYSTEM. They have fixed semantics described in Section 5.2.1.

To avoid name collisions of key names we have two options:

- If we speak of the same configuration setting from different *configuration sources*, we use namespaces. The namespaces N resolve conflicts between otherwise identical key names.

- Otherwise, we introduce further hierarchy levels.

Example 3.8. The string 'user:/slapd/%/bar' is a key name. Its hierarchy levels are the strings 'slapd', '%', and 'bar', where the string 'bar' is the basename. The string 'user' acts as its namespace USER.   ▲

For simplicity and easier distinction with other strings, we leave out the 'quotes' for (relative) key names.

Example 3.9. The string /slapd is a key name. Its namespace is ϵ. The only hierarchy level is also the basename, which is slapd.   ▲

We define the following operators on key names.

Definition 3.10. *Using $x, y \in \mathbb{N}$ and $n \in N$:*

$$x \leq y \quad \text{is defined by lexicographical comparison of the characters.}$$

$$removeNamespace(x) = \begin{cases} x \text{ if the namespace of } x \text{ is } \epsilon \\ y \text{ otherwise, where } x = n \mathbin{+\!\!+} \text{`:'} \mathbin{+\!\!+} y \end{cases}$$

Example 3.11. For every $x \in C$, `user:/a/a` $\leq$ `user:/axa` is true. A further example of lexicographical comparison is given in Example 3.34 on page 96. ▲

Example 3.12. *removeNamespace*(`user:/slapd/%/bar`) gives `/slapd/%/bar`. ▲

3.1.3 Keys and Key Sets

Definition 3.13. *The set of **metakey names** M is a subset of the set of relative key names $\mathbb{R}$. G is a set of grammars. The metafunction Ψ is a global mapping from every defined metakey name $m \in M \subset \mathbb{R}$ to a grammar $g \in G$, i. e., $\Psi \colon M \mapsto G$. $X_g \subseteq \mathbb{C}$ is the set of strings that forms the language described by $g \in G$. **Metakey values** are elements of the set $\bigcup\limits_{g \in G} X_g$.*

In the extensible meta-specification describing SPECELEKTRA, we define all grammars $g \in G$ for the metakey names M. We give some of these grammars in the course of this chapter. Users can extend M but cannot redefine Ψ for existing elements in M. With every new element in $m \in M$, the user also needs to add a grammar $g \in G$ and add $(m, g) \in \Psi$. Every extension automatically adds to the set $\bigcup\limits_{g \in G} X_g$ because it is the set that includes all strings according to the languages described by all grammars in G.

Example 3.14. Given $\langle number \rangle$ as decimal number, let us define $\langle property\ check/range \rangle$ $\in G$ for 'check/range' $\in M$ assigned by Ψ(`check/range`):

$$\langle property\ check/range \rangle ::= \langle range \rangle\ \{\ `,'\ \langle range \rangle\ \}$$

$$\langle range \rangle \qquad\qquad ::= \langle number \rangle\ `-'\ \langle number \rangle$$
$$\mid\ \langle number \rangle$$

Thus `1,2,4,8,16` as given in Example 0.6 on page 16 is a valid metakey value for `check/range`. ▲

Example 3.15. Let us define $\langle property\ type \rangle \in G$ for 'type' $\in M$ assigned by Ψ(`type`):

$$\langle property\ type \rangle \quad ::= `boolean' \mid `string' \mid `short' \mid `unsigned\_short'$$
$$\mid\ `long' \mid `unsigned\_long' \mid `long\_long'$$
$$\mid\ `unsigned\_long\_long' \mid `float'$$
$$\mid\ `double' \mid `char' \mid `any' \mid `octet'$$

Thus `long` as given in Example 0.6 is a valid metakey value for `type`. ▲

Definition 3.16. *A key is a record $\langle k, v, \mu \rangle$ with the following fields:*

k *is a key name from* $\mathbb{N}$.

v *is a value from* $\mathbb{C}_\epsilon$.

μ *is a function, defined as* $\mu \colon M \mapsto \bigcup_{g \in G} X_g$, *which maps from metakey names to metakey values. The grammar of each metakey value is defined by:* $\forall r \in M \colon \mu(r) \in X_{\Psi(r)}$.

We call the set of all keys $\mathbb{K}$.

A key x holds the configuration value $x.v$ for a configuration setting with the name $x.k$. The function $x.\mu$ assigns **metadata** to this configuration setting. We write Key if we refer to the class implementing keys.

Example 3.17. The key $x = \langle$user:/slapd/threads/listener, 4, {check/ range $\mapsto$ 1, 2, 4, 8, 16}$\rangle$ has the key name $x.k$ user:/slapd/threads/listener, the value $x.v$ which is 4, and the metadata $x.\mu$ that maps the metakey name check/ range to the metakey value 1,2,4,8,16. ▲

Example 3.18. The key $x = \langle$user:/slapd/threads/enabled, 1, {type $\mapsto$ boolean}$\rangle$ has the configuration value $x.v = 1$, which represents true. ▲

We define the following operators on keys:

Definition 3.19. *We use* $x, y \in \mathbb{K}$, *and* $n \in N$:

$$x = y \iff x.k = y.k$$
$$x \le y \iff x.k \le y.k$$
$$n \mathbin{:\!/} x = y \quad \text{where } y.k = n \mathbin{+\!\!+} \text{`:'} \mathbin{+\!\!+} removeNamespace(x.k)$$

Example 3.20. With x from Example 3.17, applying system :/ x yields the key y with the key name $y.k = $ system:/slapd/threads/listener. ▲

Definition 3.21. *We say a key* x **is of** *the namespace* n *iff* $x.k$ *has the namespace* n. *A* **cascading key** *is of the namespace* ϵ.

Example 3.22. The key $x = \langle$/slapd, ϵ, {}$\rangle$ is of the namespace ϵ and thus is a cascading key. ▲

If a configuration value represents a boolean, by convention, we use the string 0 to represent false, and 1 to represent true.

Definition 3.23. *Iff the key x is of the namespace* SPEC, *we call a metakey name also a **property name**, a metakey value also a **property value**, and the mapping $x.\mu$ also a **property**.*

Property names define the syntax of property values via Ψ.

Example 3.24. The key $x = \langle$`spec:/slapd/threads/listener`, ϵ, $\{$`check/range` $\mapsto 1, 2, 4, 8, 16\}\rangle$ has the (only) property name `check/range` with its property value $1, 2, 4, 8, 16$. Thus the (only) property of x is `check/range` $\mapsto 1, 2, 4, 8, 16$. ▲

Definition 3.25. *A key set $K \subseteq \mathbb{K}$ is a totally ordered set of keys where ordering is defined by $\leq$ on keys. We call the set of all key sets $\mathcal{K}$. The key set without any key is called the **empty key set** κ. The nullary operator $\varnothing$ returns a special key that indicates the absence of a key. The key $\varnothing$ cannot be part of a key set. The set with all keys including this special key is $\mathbb{K}_\varnothing = \mathbb{K} \cup \{\varnothing\}$.*

We write `KeySet` if we refer to the class implementing key sets.

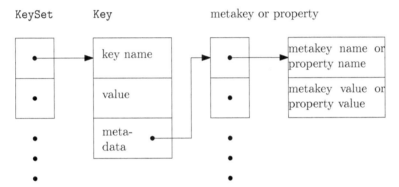

Figure 3.1: `KeySet`: ELEKTRA's data structure.

A key set represents configuration settings and specifications. Figure 3.1 gives us a visual representation of a key set.

In the next two sub-sections, we define the two most important operations on a key set.

3.1.4 Appending

Let us start with the definition of the `ksAppend` operation for K.

Definition 3.26. *We use $x, y \in \mathbb{K}$ and $s \in \mathcal{K}$:*

$$ksAppend(s, x) = \begin{cases} s \cup \{x\} & if\ \forall y \in s : y.k \neq x.k \\ (s \setminus \{y\}) \cup \{x\} & if\ y \in s,\ y.k = x.k \end{cases}$$

The result of the function `ksAppend` is a key set that has the key x appended to the key set s. If a key with the key name $x.k$ is already present, it will be replaced by the key x. Key sets are exclusively constructed as follows: We start with the empty key set κ and repeatedly append keys to it using `ksAppend`.

Example 3.27. After applying `ksAppend(ksAppend(`κ`, `⟨`user:/x, foo, {}`⟩`), `⟨`user: /x, bar, {}`⟩`)`, we have constructed the key set $\{$⟨`user:/x, bar, {}`⟩$\}$.   ▲

Lemma 1. If a key set is constructed by repeatedly applying `ksAppend` to the initially empty key set, then keys within the constructed key set are unique with respect to their key name k. Given the natural numbers n, m, b (including 0), the keys $x_1, \ldots x_n \in \mathbb{K}$, and the key set $s \in \mathcal{K}$, where s was constructed using `ksAppend(`$\ldots$ `ksAppend(`κ, x_1`)`$\ldots, x_n$`)` the following statement $A(n)$ is always true:

$$\forall x_m, x_b \in s : x_m \neq x_b \implies x_m.k \neq x_b.k \tag{3.1}$$

Proof. ***Base case:*** The only possible way to construct a key set is by subsequent use of `ksAppend`. Given the key $x_1 \in \mathbb{K}$ the induction start must be `ksAppend(`κ, x_1`)`. Trivially, $x_1.k$ is unique in a key set only containing x_1, i.e., $A(1)$ always holds.

Induction step: Suppose the hypothesis—that $A(n)$ is true—holds for the appended keys $x_1, \ldots x_n \in \mathbb{K}$, we have to show that $A(n) \implies A(n+1)$ holds for all n. The proof—that adding a key x to s cannot change the uniqueness of $x.k$—directly follows from the definition of `ksAppend`:

- If $x.k$ is already present as key name in s, then appending x causes the removal of the key that has the key name $x.k$. Therefore, no key with the same key name is present.

- If $x.k$ is not present in s, x is added to s and is the unique entry with the key name $x.k$.   □

3.1.5 Lookup

Let us define the `ksLookup` operation on K.

Definition 3.28. *We use $l \in \mathbb{K}$, $z \in \mathbb{K}_\varnothing$, and $c \in \mathcal{K}$. ksLookup$(c, l) = z$ searches the key l in the key set c and returns $z \in (c \cup \{\varnothing\})$. The key l is the key to be looked up. ksLookup has the signature $\mathcal{K} \times \mathbb{K} \to \mathbb{K}_\varnothing$. The nullary operator $\varnothing$ represents the not-found key. Iff the key was found, ksLookup returns a key from c.*

The algorithm `ksLookup` provides two different views on a key set:

1. If l is of namespace ϵ, a ***cascading lookup*** is used. A cascading lookup consists of the following steps:

   a) The function `ksLookup` can be extended. Such extensions allow us to consider more keys to improve context awareness and to visualize the lookup process. If an extension is available, the cascading lookup tries to look up the key l with the lookup logic as provided by the extension. We present an extension `lookupByExtension` later in Section 3.3.1.

   b) The namespace SPEC is considered. If the key `spec`$:/l$ is found, we evaluate its properties. We show the algorithm `lookupBySpec` in Section 3.3.2.

   c) Otherwise, as shown in Figure 3.2, we return a key with one of the following key names: `proc`$:/l$, `dir`$:/l$, `user`$:/l$, and `system`$:/l$ (in this preference).

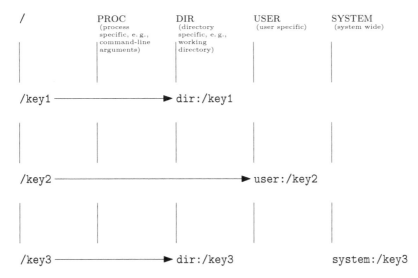

Figure 3.2: Cascading lookup in ELEKTRA. Arrows indicate the lookup procedure if calling `ksLookup` with `/key1` to `/key3`. The arrow ends at the key which is returned. The key `system:/key3` is not found. Explanations about namespaces follow later.

2. If the lookup key l is not of namespace ϵ, `ksLookup` guarantees for every return value x that $x.k = l.k \iff x \neq \emptyset$. I.e. `ksLookup` either returns a key with exactly the same key name or $\emptyset$. This form of `ksLookup` is the non-cascading lookup.

Lemma 2. Given any key set $s \in \mathcal{K}$ and the key $k \in \mathbb{K}$, where k is not of namespace ϵ, the following statement is always true:

$$\forall s, k : \texttt{ksLookup}(\texttt{ksAppend}(s, k), k) = k \qquad (3.2)$$

The proof of Lemma 2 directly follows from the above definition of `ksLookup` and `ksAppend`: we know that k gets appended to s, and because $k.k$ has a namespace it is found by *ksLookup*.

We influence the behavior of `ksLookup` by adding keys of the form `spec` $:/l$ to the key set. This way, we enable the system administrator to specify guarantees for a cascading lookup by modification of persistent keys' properties in the namespace SPEC.

For cascading lookups, it is possible that `ksLookup` finds the same key x for different arguments of `ksLookup`. The function `ksLookup` with cascading lookups is no longer bijective, we only have the properties of a surjective function. Because the key name of the parameter l and the result z can be different, it is important that the key name is part of the key: From the returned key, we know the key name of the found key.

The cascading lookup is an important abstraction and applications exclusively rely on cascading lookups to look up their configuration settings. Thus for applications, ***configuration settings*** are represented by a key set only considering the key names and configuration values returned from cascading lookups. Only tools intended for system administrators use the non-cascading lookup, so that all keys can be administered. ***Configuration specifications*** are written in SPECELEKTRA and are represented by a key set only considering the key names of the namespace SPEC and the key's properties.

3.1.6 Syntax

As we see in Figure 3.3, three meta-levels of ELEKTRA are important. For the three meta-levels, we describe two syntaxes to denote a key set to be used in this book:

1. Meta-specifications consist of a grammar $g \in G$ assigned by Ψ. We explain the semantics mostly informally. We do not need a special syntax for these specifications.

2. For configuration specifications we need a way to denote key names and properties, but we do not need to include configuration values. The grammar for this syntax will be given below.

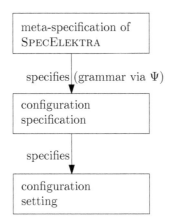

Figure 3.3: Metalevels in ELEKTRA.

3. For configuration settings we only need to denote key names and configuration values without any support for metadata. The grammar for this syntax will be given further below.

The separation of syntax between configuration settings and specifications is purely for practical purposes so that different meta-levels are clearly distinguishable. The distinction between configuration settings and specifications happens via namespaces and not via syntax:

- If a key is in the namespace SPEC, the metadata is used as properties and the key represents a configuration specification.

- If a key is in another namespace, the metadata only describes the key itself, but does not specify the configuration setting. Here the configuration value is the essential information. Such keys are configuration settings.

For this book, we could have used every configuration file format that has a correspondence to a key set, for example, in XML syntax with metadata written as attributes. We use, however, a simple INI-like syntax to illustrate key sets. We exclusively rely on relative key names.

Configuration Specifications

Here we describe a syntax for configuration specifications. They are used to specify configuration settings and configuration access in SPECELEKTRA. A syntax usable for

SPECELEKTRA needs to include relative key names (called $\mathbb{R}$, see Definition 3.5 on page 85) with properties (see Definition 3.23 on page 89):

$\langle configuration\ specifications \rangle ::= \{ \langle configuration\ specification \rangle \{ `\hookleftarrow' \} \}$

$\langle configuration\ specification \rangle ::= `[' \mathbb{R} `]' `\hookleftarrow' \langle properties \rangle$

$\langle properties \rangle \qquad ::= \{ \langle property \rangle `\hookleftarrow' \}$

$\langle property \rangle \qquad ::= \{ `\sqcup' \} \langle property\ name \rangle `:=' [\langle property\ value \rangle]$

The absence of the $\langle property\ value \rangle$ means that the property value is empty. The grammar of the $\langle property\ value \rangle$ is depending on its associated property name x. The meta-specification specifies its grammar to be $\Psi(x)$.

Example 3.29. This is a configuration specification:

```
1 [slapd/threads/listener]
2   property1:=propvalue1
3   property2:=propvalue2
```

In the first line, we write a relative key name within `[]`. *Property values* are assigned with `:=` to *property names*. Every key can be specified with several properties. The key with the key name ending with `slapd/threads/listener` has two properties as shown in lines 2 and 3. The property name is `propertyN` and property value is `propvalueN`. The string `propvalueN` has a syntax according to $\Psi(\text{property}N)$.   ▲

Configuration Settings

For configuration settings we do not necessarily need metadata nor properties. We use the following grammar for configuration settings:

$\langle configuration\ settings \rangle ::= \{ \langle configuration\ setting \rangle \{ `\hookleftarrow' \} \} \langle configuration\ setting \rangle$

$\langle configuration\ setting \rangle ::= \langle relative\ key\ name \rangle \left[`=' [\langle value \rangle] \right] [\langle comment \rangle]$

$\langle comment \rangle \qquad ::= \{ `\sqcup' \} `;' \mathbb{C}$

Absence of ⟨*value*⟩ means that the value is an empty string and the absence of both '=' and ⟨*value*⟩ means that the value is ϵ. Assignment with =, as opposed to :=, is reserved for key-value pairs denoting configuration settings in configuration files. This way, it is apparent for the reader that we are in a different meta-level and talking about concrete settings for applications. For this book, we assume that the values do not have trailing spaces nor red semicolons ';'.

Example 3.30. By the use of the grammar above, we can specify configuration settings:

```
1 slapd/threads/listener=1
2 slapd/key=1 ; comment
3 slapd
```

In the first line, we define that the key, identified with the relative key name `slapd/threads/listener`, has the configuration value `1`. The second line does the same with the key name ending with `slapd/key` but with a comment ' comment'. In the third line, we define the key name ending with `slapd` to have the value ϵ. ▲

3.1.7 Sort Order and Hierarchy

Definition 3.31. *We say a key x is **below** a key y iff the key name of x has the key name of y as prefix separated with a slash:*

$$below(x, y) = \begin{cases} \top & \text{if } \exists s \in \mathbb{R} \colon x.k = y.k \mathbin{+\!\!+} \text{'/'} \mathbin{+\!\!+} s \\ \bot & \text{otherwise} \end{cases}$$

Example 3.32. The function below(⟨'`user:/slapd/threads/listener`', ϵ, {}⟩, ⟨'`user:/slapd/threads`', ϵ, {}⟩) returns $\top$. The function below(⟨'`user:/slapd/threads/listener`', ϵ, {}⟩, ⟨'`user:/slapd/key`', ϵ, {}⟩) returns $\bot$. ▲

Definition 3.33. *A **subtree** of a key x and a key set t is the key set s, which contains all keys in t below x, as well as x. We call x the **root** of the subtree.*

$$s = \{y \in t \mid below(x, y) \vee x = y\} \tag{3.3}$$

According to Definition 3.1 on page 84, we treat the special character / for the lexicographical comparison of keys with $\leq$ differently: It is ranked first in the order of the character's precedence.[2] Because of the special handling of /, keys not within a subtree occur after keys within the same subtree.

---

[2]The implementation is efficient by separately storing key names modified in a way so that they are correctly compared with `memcmp`.

Example 3.34. Given the following key names:

```
1 a
2 a/a
3 a/b
4 a!a
```

Here a/a and a/b are below a. These three keys form a subtree with a as root. The pure ASCIIbetical sort order[3] would put a!a in the middle after a. Our chosen sort order allows us to efficiently operate on a hierarchy, for example, to cut out a subtree. We look up the key a, and keys below it (with respect to the hierarchy), are guaranteed to be subsequent, if there are any keys below a.   ▲

For iterating configuration settings, in most cases, the sort order of keys—within the same hierarchy level—is irrelevant. If the order is important, we do not merely rely on how the key was inserted in the key set. Instead the sort order is clearly visible within the key name. We use a so-called **_array index_** to indicate the order between otherwise identical key names or metakey names. Such array indexes are also used if we have several key names for the same configuration setting. We use the following convention for array indexes:

1. The first array index is '#0'.

2. For the next array index, we increase the numerical part by incrementing it. If the number of digits is increased by one, we add an underscore ('_') between '#' and the digits.

While the algorithm keeps the key set ordered by the array index with any radix, for example, hexadecimal with the characters [A-F], we chose the decimal system. It is trivial to know the quantity of '_' for any number by counting the digits and decrement the result. With this convention we generate array indexes in a compact syntax, readable and writable by humans, while still using the sort order of decimals representing the array index. Given ⟨*number*⟩ as decimal natural number ≥ 0, the grammar is:

⟨*array index*⟩   ::= '#' { '_' } ⟨*number*⟩

---

[3]Sort by string comparison, i.e., the ASCII value of the characters.

Example 3.35. The array index 1 is written down as '#1', 10 is written down as '#_10', 100 is written down as '#__100'. The sort order of these key names is:

```
1 #1
2 #_10
3 #__100
```
▲

Example 3.36. To sort the key names ending with a, b and c in reverse order, we would use the following key names with array index from 0 to 2:

```
1 #0/c
2 #1/b
3 #2/a
```
▲

3.2 User's View

Both system administrators and developers are users of ELEKTRA. In this section we consider these users together and frame ELEKTRA with a focus of context-aware configuration from their point of view. As shown in Figure 3.4, their main interactions with ELEKTRA is by using frontends and SPECELEKTRA. In this section we describe:

- How users get and set configuration settings and specifications (i. e., including specifications written in SPECELEKTRA).

- How users map configuration files into a unified view for all applications.

- How users share configuration settings.

- How users enable context-aware configuration.

Figure 3.4 shows what is required from users to facilitate ELEKTRA: The blue parts need to be supplied by users. ELEKTRA does not help in implementing the application logic. It does, however, disentangle the application from source code specific for configuration access. Applications use LIBELEKTRA via so-called frontends. SPECELEKTRA specifies both the frontends and LIBELEKTRA. We will use a key set to represent SPECELEKTRA.

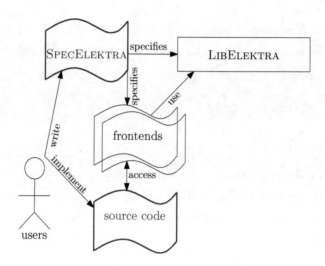

Figure 3.4: The ELEKTRA framework from the users' perspective.

Furthermore, key sets are used for communication between any parts of ELEKTRA, such as between frontends and LIBELEKTRA.

3.2.1   SpecElektra

SPECELEKTRA is a modular **configuration specification language** for configuration settings. In SPECELEKTRA we use properties to specify configuration settings and configuration access. SPECELEKTRA enables us to specify different parts of ELEKTRA.

Plugins are filters, sinks, and sources processing a key set. We aim at SPECELEKTRA to be as modular as possible and make extensive use of plugins:

1. SPECELEKTRA does not have any built-in feature, all features are (or can be) implemented as plugins.

2. ELEKTRA works completely without SPECELEKTRA's specifications.

3. Configuration specifications are present within the execution environment. Thus any tool and plugin can introspect and use the specifications.

Semantics

Several tools and plugins read and implement SPECELEKTRA's specifications. A meta-specification within ELEKTRA defines which property is used by which tool and plugin.

Here we characterize how semantics are defined. We elaborate on SPECELEKTRA's semantics in the rest of this chapter.

In this book, we focus on the central properties and tools. Users can extend SPEC-ELEKTRA by additional properties, but cannot redefine existing ones. We mainly discuss possibilities SPECELEKTRA offers and only elaborate on non-obvious features. Because every property has a grammar assigned by Ψ, the syntax of property values is formally specified. Semantics of the properties are described—usually informally—in the meta-specification of SPECELEKTRA and in this book. Plugins implement the semantics of the properties. The semantics of the configuration values are described—then again mostly informally—by the properties. Applications implement the semantics of the configuration values.

Example 3.37. We give an example of a trivial feature to clarify how the specification is used:

```
1 [slapd/threads/listener]
2   description:=Text to be displayed in application.
```

The specification uses the INI-like syntax introduced in Section 3.1.6. The syntax of the text to the right of $:=$ is given by Ψ(`description`), which is $\mathbb{C}$ (any text). The property puts no constraints on the key `slapd/threads/listener`. If applications present the configuration setting to the user, however, the property `description` shall be part of this presentation. Applications have access to the properties in the same way as the tools and plugins have, therefore they are candidates to give properties meaning. Furthermore, the application behavior must be in accordance with the semantics described in the description.

Different from Example 3.37, other properties than description usually affect the configuration access behavior. The semantics of the individual properties are combined by sequential enforcement of each property. Before introducing more properties, we give an overview how the configuration access works.

3.2.2 Key Database

LIBELEKTRA implements a **key database**. It provides a unified, system-wide, key-value-based view of the execution environment. The view contains all previously defined namespaces, including namespace SPEC, which holds SPECELEKTRA's specifications. The key database is the part shared between all applications in a system and consists of several **backends**. Each backend maps a key set from a configuration file into the key database with the help of plugins. The minimal goal of a backend is to parse and serialize configuration files.

To realize several backends LIBELEKTRA splits and merges the key set in such a way that each backend receives only the part of the key set it is responsible for. At least every namespace is separated in a different backend. The key database can be seen as a tiny middleware between plugins and applications [227].

LIBELEKTRA's main purpose is to present configuration settings and specifications uniformly. To do so, LIBELEKTRA abstracts over all configuration sources (i. e., key set's namespaces) of the execution environment. All applications and tools with the same context see the same configuration settings and specifications.

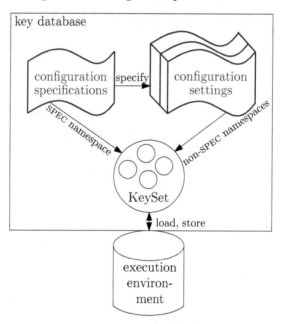

Figure 3.5: The execution environment stores key sets of all namespaces. The namespace SPEC specifies the other namespaces (PROC, DIR, USER, and SYSTEM). Arrows indicate data flow of key sets.

As shown in Figure 3.5 the key database contains configuration specifications in the namespace SPEC. All other namespaces are specified by this single specification written in SPECELEKTRA. Keys with the same key name refer to the same configuration setting. If key names only differ in the namespace, the key in the namespace SPEC specifies the other keys. We enable system administrators to change configuration specifications with the same tooling as used to modify configuration settings.

Example 3.38. Let us assume that the following configuration setting is stored in a configuration file on a system:

```
1  slapd/threads/listener=4
```

If this configuration file is read from a system's configuration source (and assuming that the configuration setting is not found in any of the other namespaces) it is part of the namespace SYSTEM. As result, we get the key with the name `system:/slapd/threads/listener`. For configuration specifications, we assume the namespace SPEC:

```
1  [slapd/threads/listener]
2    description:=Example from the introduction
```

The configuration specification has the key name `spec:/slapd/threads/listener` and refers to the configuration setting above.   ▲

API

LIBELEKTRA provides access to the key database by synchronizing the execution environment and an in-memory key set. The API to access the key database is minimalist and consists of only four functions. We abbreviate the key database with `kdb` and use `KDB` as its type in the implementation.

kdb.open(): The first step is to open a connection to the key database.

> Because LIBELEKTRA is a library, it needs to **bootstrap** itself during the launch of every application. First LIBELEKTRA reads from an initial configuration file from a hard-coded path. Given the content of this initial configuration file, LIBELEKTRA knows about the rest of the execution environment. The initial configuration file contains information about which plugins must be used [227].

kdb.get(KeySet): The application (initially) fetches and (later) updates its configuration settings as a key set of type `KeySet` from the execution environment by one or many calls to `kdb.get`. If all relevant configuration files are unmodified since the last invocation, `kdb.get` will do nothing.

kdb.set(KeySet): When a user finishes editing configuration settings, `kdb.set` is in charge of writing all changes back to the key database. This function atomically persists a whole key set in involved parts of the execution environment. In the case of an error no action takes place.

kdb.close(): The last step is to close the connection to the key database.

ELEKTRA does not provide extra functions for other features with the consequence that every feature related to the key database must be either part of `kdb.get`, `kdb.set`, or `ksLookup`. Configuration settings not conforming to the configuration specification are rejected by plugins in `kdb.set`. Applications that want to validate configuration settings, must serialize configuration settings to configuration files. This principle encourages us to serialize configuration settings early. Applications learn about problems via errors from `kdb.set`. As long as only ELEKTRA is used, the key database is always coherent with its configuration specifications.

Within `kdb.set`, plugins notify other applications that the configuration settings have been updated. Other applications listening to these notifications use `kdb.get` to update their configuration settings. This simple mechanism keeps the in-memory key set in sync with the external representation of a key set in the execution environment.

Example 3.39. A user synchronizes the application's `KeySet` with the execution environment using the following source code:

```
1 KDB kdb;
2 KeySet conf;
3 void onNotification () // triggered by other processes
4 {
5     kdb.get (conf);
6 } // <continues on the next page>
```

```
 7 int main ()
 8 {
 9     kdb.get (conf);
10     // work with conf...
11     kdb.set (conf);
12 }
```

Line 11 notifies other processes and triggers onNotification there.   ▲

3.2.3   Mounting

For better modularity, the key database consists of many backends. In most cases a backend is responsible to parse and serialize a single configuration file. Each of the backends—in turn—is built up by several plugins. Here we introduce how users decide about backends and plugins using SPECELEKTRA.

Mounting integrates a backend into the key database [236]. Hence, ELEKTRA allows several backends to deal with configuration files at the same time. Each backend is responsible for its own subtree of the key database. To integrate a backend into the key database, we mount it by using the property mountpoint in the configuration specification. Its property value is the relative file name to mount. The key that has the property mountpoint is the root of this subtree. Subsequent use of kdb.get and kdb.set assume configuration settings below the mountpoint in the respective configuration files.

Example 3.40. To specify mountpoints, we use the following configuration specification:

```
1 [sw]
2     mountpoint:=configfile.txt
3 [sw/libreoffice]
4     mountpoint:=libreoffice.conf
```

These properties are read by ELEKTRA's tools. The configuration specification achieves that two new backends are instantiated in the key database. These backends are used for all namespaces, except the namespace SPEC. If an application accesses keys in the key database below /sw/libreoffice, the application receives the configuration settings of libreoffice.conf. Otherwise, if an application accesses other keys below /sw, the application receives the configuration settings of configfile.txt. For the key /, ELEKTRA always assumes the property mountpoint to be present, the property does not need to be specified by the system administrator.

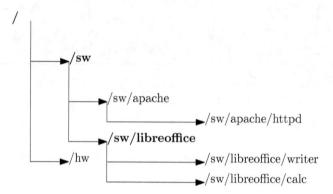

Figure 3.6: Mountpoints in ELEKTRA. Arrows indicate that keys are below another key. Bold keys are mountpoints.

In Figure 3.6 three subtrees are written in bold: /, /sw, and /sw/libreoffice. Backends take care of the configuration settings in their respective subtree. The subtrees are nested, for example, /sw/libreoffice/writer belongs to the mountpoint /sw/libreoffice, while /sw/apache/httpd belongs to /sw.   ▲

The property mountpoint abstracts over configuration settings. Applications do not need to take care about how and where their configuration settings are stored. It is the task of the backends to implement these details.

Relative key names are relative to their mountpoint. If we mount the configuration specification to a different root, also the configuration settings get different key names.

Example 3.41. If we mount the configuration specification from Example 3.40 to spec:/test[4] then, instead of /sw/libreoffice/writer, the resulting configuration setting is /test/sw/libreoffice/writer. The key /hw, however, is not concerned about this change. It still belongs to a ***default mountpoint*** always present at the namespaces' root.   ▲

The property mountpoint is usually specified by:

---

[4]It must be of namespace SPEC because it is a configuration specification.

- The system administrator who prefers separated configuration files.

- Developers that need or want their applications to continue using their previous configuration file. Setting the property is done during the installation process.

Despite the different namespaces in which a configuration setting can be, users need access to properties of any key they currently work with. Here we describe a metadata abstraction. At run-time the properties specified in the namespace SPEC are copied[5] as metadata into the configuration setting of all namespaces. Applications and users facilitate this metadata to learn about configuration specification.

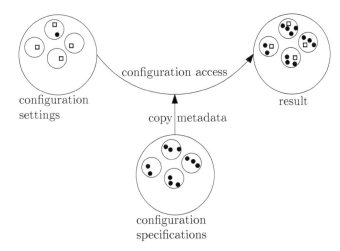

Figure 3.7: Abstraction of Metadata. The large circles are key sets, the smaller ones keys. Configuration values are boxes and metadata are black dots.

As we see in Figure 3.7 in the result the abstraction makes it irrelevant whether metadata:

- has been copied from the properties (i.e., metadata in the configuration specifications), or

- is directly part of configuration settings.

Example 3.42. Let us assume we have the configuration specification from Example 3.37:

---

[5]Copying metadata is efficient by referring to already existing metakeys.

```
1 [slapd/threads/listener]
2   description:=Text to be displayed in application.
```

When an application accesses the key with the key name `/slapd/threads/listener` in any namespace, the property `description` is part of its metadata.   ▲

In the rest of this book, we assume for the configuration settings and specifications given in listings that

- configuration specifications are mounted at the root of the namespace SPEC,

- configuration settings are mounted at the root of any other namespace, and

- properties are available as metadata in every key related to a configuration setting.

3.2.4   Context Specifications

Context specifications are properties of SPECELEKTRA, which make configuration settings more context aware. They are implemented in frontends (generated by GEN-ELEKTRA) and in backends (implemented in LIBELEKTRA).

Namespaces and cascading lookup provide a form of context awareness. For example, they allow the configuration settings to be aware of the current user (namespace USER). Their context awareness is restricted by fixed rules and the fixed number of namespaces. Here we generalize the concept.

For system administrators a central mechanism to work with ELEKTRA is changing properties, i. e., modifying metadata in the namespace SPEC. We show how system administrators—by writing context specifications in SPECELEKTRA—share configuration settings between applications. Sharing configuration settings is a kind of context awareness: We enable applications to be aware of configuration settings of other applications. We only assume that applications, receiving configuration settings, use the key database.

The properties below achieve this goal. They are implemented by `ksLookup` and are thus part of the key database (implemented in LIBELEKTRA). The priority of properties is always fixed and cannot be changed by changing the order of properties in the configuration specifications. Thus we sometimes need properties with identical semantics but different priority. Some properties permit us to use array indexes that enable users to choose order within the functionality of that property. Lower array indexes have higher priority. We indicate support for array indexes by adding a /# suffix. In the order of priority (higher priority first), the properties for context awareness are [227]:

context specifies configuration settings to be preferred to the key itself to better fit the context. With this property we aim at having semantics of contextual values for configuration settings. We discuss its syntax and semantics in Section 3.2.6. It is implemented using the extension interface `lookupByExtension` of `ksLookup` as explained in Section 3.3.1.

override/# specifies configuration settings to be unconditionally preferred to the key itself. This property enables users to create links between configuration settings. The grammar assigned to this property value by $\Psi(\texttt{override})$ is the grammar of key names, as shown in Section 3.1.2.

namespace/# defines alternative namespace priorities using array indexes for the specified key. The grammar of the property value is N.

fallback/# specifies configuration settings to be used if the key itself is only present in the namespace SPEC, and not in any other specified namespace. As in property `override`, we create a link between keys and use the grammar of key names.

default represents a value to be used if no key was found (including consideration of the properties above). The property value is a string $\in \mathbb{C}$, i.e., $\Psi(\texttt{default}) \mapsto \mathbb{C}$, and is used as *default value*. Because property values cannot be ϵ, default values cannot be ϵ.

Example 3.43. If system administrators want a configuration setting that:

- prefers the key /sw/pools/threads/listener if available,

- only considers the namespace SYSTEM (and not PROC, DIR, and USER), and

- has the configuration value 2 if the configuration setting is not found otherwise.

Then system administrators specify:

```
1  [slapd/threads/listener]
2      default:=2
3      namespace/#0:=system
4      override/#0:=/sw/pools/threads/listener
```

The order of the properties in the configuration specification does not matter. The property `override` has a higher priority than properties `namespace` and `default` (as given in the list of properties before the example). We increase context awareness using the property `override`. Without this specification, `slapd` would not be aware of the configuration setting `/sw/pools/threads/listener`. We decrease the context awareness of the namespaces: We do not consider the namespaces PROC, DIR, and USER for the key `/slapd/threads/listener`. Because the key `/sw/pools/threads/listener` has no configuration specification, we will consider all namespaces there. ▲

3.2.5 Frontend

We already introduced features that are part of LIBELEKTRA (the backends). Features in the frontend are part of the application and thus not part of the key database. When adding features in the frontend we have to be careful: Applications do not always use the same frontends. We could easily break the desired globally unified view that the key database promises. Reasons to put functionality in the frontend nevertheless are:

- Performance.

- Ensure presence of configuration settings and specifications even when retrieving configuration settings and specifications from the key database fails.

- Ensure type safety and improving the usability for developers, for example, directly returning correct types.

- Supporting features where configuration settings need to differ in different parts of an application.

Here we focus on the user's view of type-safe access code for contextual values. We prefer type-safe access code as frontends and avoid direct access to the low-level key-value operations (`ksLookup`) of LIBELEKTRA. We call applications that use ELEKTRA's key database via one of its frontends ***elektrified***. Figure 3.8 shows the architecture with code generation used in elektrified applications. When using LibElektra in this architecture, users need to:

- Write a specification in SpecElektra that defines the configuration access of their application.

- Provide an elektrified source code for their applications that directly makes use of the generated, type-safe frontends.

This architecture is the preferred way for newly written applications. In Section 5.4, we will present an alternative architecture for applications without changing their frontend.

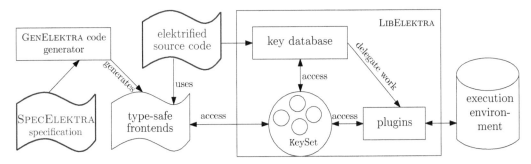

Figure 3.8: Architecture of Elektra with code generation. Bold, blue boxes need to be provided by users of Elektra.

Code Generation

The code generator GenElektra reads SpecElektra specifications and emits high-level APIs to be used in applications. GenElektra facilitates the key names to generate unique API names. We use nested objects (accessed by . via a root object `env`) according to the hierarchy levels of the key name. These objects are used like variables. GenElektra employs the following properties from SpecElektra:

type represents the type to be used in the emitted source code. The emitted variables implicitly cast to the type given here. For property `type`, we use the common object request broker architecture (CORBA) interface description language (IDL) data types, which already have well-defined mappings for many programming languages.

opt is used for short command-line options to be copied to the namespace PROC. Here we can choose between implementations in the frontend and backend with the trade-off performance versus flexibility for system administrators.

> **Example 3.44.** With the property `opt:=p`, the configuration setting with this property can be changed by adding the command-line option `-p`.   ▲

opt/long is used for long command-line options, which differ from short command-line options by supporting strings and not only characters.

readonly yields compilation errors when developers assign a value to a contextual value within the program.

default enables us to start the application even if the backend does not work. GEN-ELEKTRA uses it to hard-code default values into the application. If the backend is available, the property `default` is interpreted by the backend. Without the property `default`, the configuration value can be missing (`ksLookup` can return ∅). In the high-level APIs the user would get a run-time error when trying to access such a configuration value. Thus if the property `default` is not available, GENELEKTRA will not generate a contextual class for the given configuration specification to protect the user from run-time errors.

Example 3.45. The specification `[foo/bar]` alone (without properties) does not generate any code because property `default` is not given. Calling `ksLookup` on such a configuration setting is not safe and can return ∅ (indicating the not-found key).   ▲

Example 3.46. With the specification:

```
1 [foo/bar]
2   default:=Hello
3   type:=string
4   opt:=b
5   readonly:=1
```

GENELEKTRA gives the user read-only access to the object `env.foo.bar`:

```
1 std::cout << env.foo.bar;
2 env.foo.bar = "Other world"; // compilation error
```

Line 1 prints the configuration value of `/foo/bar` or `"Hello"` (without quotes) by default. When invoking the application with `application -b "This world"`, the application would print `"This world"` (without quotes). Line 2 leads to a compilation error because of the property `readonly`. ▲

3.2.6 Contextual Values

The most expressive part of the **context-aware lookup** algorithm is the *layer-based lookup*. It enables configuration access points to have semantics of *contextual values*. **Context-aware configurations** are configuration settings in which context-aware lookups are used. We provide two types of context-aware configurations, implemented in frontend and backend, respectively. Both types share the following syntax:

Definition 3.47. *Layer values are relative key names $\in \mathbb{R}$. **Layer names** are non-empty, clean strings $\in \mathbb{C}'_{\geq 1}$ embedded in a context specification as given in the following grammar (we use $\langle basename \rangle$ and $\langle hierarchy\ level \rangle$ from Definition 3.5 on page 85 and N from Definition 3.7 on page 86):*

$\langle contextual\ key\ name \rangle \qquad ::= [\ N\ \text{'}:\text{'}\ ]\ \text{'}/\text{'}\ \{\ \langle contextual\ hierarchy\ level \rangle\ \text{'}/\text{'}\ \}$
$\qquad\qquad\qquad\qquad\qquad\qquad \langle basename \rangle$

$\langle contextual\ hierarchy\ level \rangle ::= \langle context\ placeholder \rangle\ |\ \langle hierarchy\ level \rangle$

$\langle context\ placeholder \rangle \qquad ::= \text{'}\%\text{'}\ \langle layer\ name \rangle\ \text{'}\%\text{'}$

Every hierarchy level is a contextual hierarchy level and every key name is a contextual key name, thus Definition 3.47 generalizes Definition 3.7 on page 86.

Both forms of contextual values (frontend and backend) share the following semantics:

Definition 3.48. *Layer is a mapping from layer names to layer values and represents the current context. The function `context.evaluate` replaces all context placeholders with layer values given by the layers. If no layer name is found, or the layer value is empty, the layer value `%` will be used. We call a layer **active** if the layer does not have the layer value `%`.*

Example 3.49. Given the contextual key name `/foo/%bar%/hey`, depending on the layer value of the layer name `bar`, the following incomplete list of key names are valid contextual interpretations:

```
1 foo/%/hey=       ; no such layer, or no layer value
2 foo/bar/hey=     ; layer value bar
3 foo/foo/hey=     ; layer value foo
4 foo/some/more/hierarchy/hey=
```

The layer value in line 4 is 'some/more/hierarchy'.   ▲

Backend

In the first type of contextual values the meta-function Ψ assigns the grammar of contextual key names as given in Definition 3.47 on page 111 to the property value of the property `context`. When looking up such a key, LIBELEKTRA substitutes the context placeholder and tries to search the resulting key name. Similar to the property `override`, the key is preferred to the configuration value of the original key.

For the property `context`, layers are specified within the key database. The layer names are wildcards to discriminate between different possible keys.

Example 3.50. We define a context-aware link using the property `context`:

```
1 [foo]
2    context:=/foo/%bar%/hey
3    override/#0:=/foo/hey
```

When looking up `foo`, depending on the layers, key names in the form as given in Example 3.49 are looked up. On failure, the lookup continues with the property `override` because of the priorities as specified in the list of properties in Section 3.2.4.   ▲

Frontend

In the second type of contextual values we do not use properties. Instead we directly use contextual key names as key names in the configuration specification. In the configuration settings' syntax, we denote the contextual key names without their namespace SPEC. It is the task of the frontend to call `context.evaluate` so that context placeholders are resolved before calling `ksLookup`. LIBELEKTRA provides a predefined class `Context`, which is the interface for users to dynamically activate and deactivate layers [235]:

```
 1 class Context : public Subject
 2 {        // for the frontend:
 3     string evaluate(string const & spec) const;
 4 public: // for the user:
 5     template <typename Layer> void activate(...);
 6     template <typename Layer> void deactivate(...);
 7     template <typename Layer> Context & with(...);
 8     template <typename Layer> Context & without(...);
 9     ...
10 };
```

The purpose of the class `Context` is to govern the layers in a data structure (i. e., not in the key database). To change the context, the class `Context` provides four methods for the user:

activate: Activates a layer without scope.

deactivate: Deactivates a layer without scope.

with: Activates a layer in a dynamic scope.

without: Deactivates a layer in a dynamic scope.

While the methods `activate` and `deactivate` affect the rest of the execution (until another context change is done), the methods `with` and `without` are bound to their dynamic scope.

In Chapter 4 we describe the semantics of these methods and different ways how the user specifies the `typename Layer` required in the interface of `Context`.

Contextual classes emitted by GENELEKTRA implement contextual values and can directly be used by the developer. In generated classes, we use the naming conventions for nested objects as described in Section 3.2.5 but with the context placeholders removed. Contextual classes implement contextual values.

Example 3.51. If we change Example 3.46 to have the contextual key name `[foo/%language%/bar]`, we get a contextual value `env.foo.bar`. Then the output differs depending on the layer value of `language`. Assume the configuration settings:

```
1 foo/english/bar=Hello
2 foo/german/bar=Hallo
```

With the layers {language ↦ german}, the application will output `"Hallo"` (without quotes).   ▲

Frontends versus Backends

Here we discuss differences between contextual interpretations in the backend and in the frontend. Contextual key names—used as key names in configuration specifications—are only useful if used along with frontends. Such key names cannot be resolved within backends: They are not valid key names and thus cannot be looked up. The advantage of frontends' contextual values is that layers can be restricted within dynamic scopes.

For the lookup within the backend, the frontend is completely unaware that a context-aware lookup takes place. Thus the property `context` provides a stronger abstraction.

3.3   Backend

In this section we reflect upon the system's view of ELEKTRA, with a focus on the key database. We go into the details of the lookup algorithm with its two main helper functions `lookupBySpec` and `lookupByExtension` implementing the already explained properties. In previous work we discussed an earlier version of the lookup algorithm [227]. After explaining the details of the metadata abstraction, we discuss how plugins are assembled to backends.

ELEKTRA already has many predefined plugins as shown in the figure on page 183. Users add further plugins to extend ELEKTRA's functionality. The plugins we use in the examples are implemented. For brevity, we sometimes shorten information about plugins in the examples. For the full contracts please refer to the source code repository at `https://git.libelektra.org`.

3.3.1   Layer-based Lookup Algorithm

The ***layer-based lookup*** facilitates layers using `context.evaluate`. Layer-based lookup is a special form of the context-aware lookup.

We use $l \in \mathbb{K}$, $z \in \mathbb{K}_\varnothing$, $c \in \mathcal{K}$, $p \in \langle property\ name \rangle$, and $i \in \langle array\ index \rangle$. Let us start with defining small helper functions:

lookupProperty $(l, p) \to z$ returns a new key z, where $z.k = l.\mu(p)$, which is the property value from the property name p. The function returns $\varnothing$ if the property is not present in l.

lookupByKey $(c, l) \to z$, where $z.k = l.k$. The function returns $\varnothing$ if the key name is not present in c.

length $(l, p) \to i$ returns the last array index of the property name p in l. The property name p needs to contain a #, which indicates an array index. If no array index is found, a special value is returned that avoids iterations of a `for` loop. The loop `for (i: "#0" .. length (l, p))` iterates over all array indexes present in $l.\mu$.

The layer-based lookup is implemented as extension point `lookupByExtension` introduced in Section 3.1.5:

```
1 Key lookupByExtension (KeySet c, Key l, Key specKey)
2 {
3     if ((specKey == ∅) || !(l is of namespace ϵ)) return ∅;
4     Key k = lookupProperty (specKey, "context");
5     if (k != ∅)
6     {
7         k.k = context.evaluate (k.k);// evaluate property value
8         k   = lookup (c, k);    // recursion to lookup algorithm
9     }
10    return k;
11 }
```

The key `specKey` is the key spec `:/` l. In line 3 we handle invocations of the extension interface we do not need to implement for a layer-based lookup. In line 4 we check for the presence of property `context`. If the property is available, in line 7, the function `context.evaluate` replaces the context placeholders. Then we recursively descend with the new key name (line 8). In line 10 we return the found key or $\varnothing$, and let the caller continue with the cascading lookup [232].

3.3.2 Specification Lookup Algorithm

The algorithm `lookupBySpec` implements the search logic for the properties in the cascading lookup. Let us add further helper functions. The first helper implements the properties `override` and `fallback` (as specified with `type`):

```
1 Key lookupByLink (KeySet c, Key specKey, string type)
2 {   // type is either "override" or "fallback"
3     for (i: "#0" .. length (specKey, type ++ "/#"))
4     {
5         Key k = lookupProperty (specKey, type ++ "/" ++ i);
6         k = lookup (c, k); // recursion
7         if (k != Ø) return k;
8     }
9     return Ø; // not found
10 }
```

In the loop starting on line 3, we consider all array indexes of the links. If we find a link, we recursively look it up (line 6). If the lookup was successful, we return the found key (line 7).

We already discussed the exhaustive search of all namespaces in Section 3.1.5:

```
1 Key lookupNamespaces (KeySet c, Key l)
2 {
3     Key k = lookupByKey (c, "proc" :/ l);
4     if (k == Ø) k = lookupByKey (c, "dir" :/ l);
5     if (k == Ø) k = lookupByKey (c, "user" :/ l);
6     if (k == Ø) k = lookupByKey (c, "system" :/ l);
7     return k;
8 }
```

Evaluating the property `namespace/#` is similar to the algorithm `lookupByLink`. The behavior on absence of the property is different: Instead of doing nothing we exhaustively search all namespaces using the function `lookupNamespaces` specified directly above:

```
1 Key lookupByNamespace (KeySet c, Key l, Key specKey)
2 {
3     if (lookupProperty (specKey, "namespace/#0") != Ø)
4     {
5         for (i: "#0" .. length (specKey, "namespace/#"))
6         {
7             k = lookupProperty (specKey, "namespace/" ++ i);
8             k = lookupByKey (c, k.k :/ l);
9             if (k != Ø) return k;
10        }
11    }
12    else // if no property namespace exists
13    {
14        k = lookupNamespaces (c, l);
15        if (k != Ø) return k;
16    }
17    return Ø; // not found
18 }
```

To implement the properties defined in Section 3.2.4 (except properties `context` and `default`) we only need to call the functions in order of priority:

```
1 Key lookupBySpec (KeySet c, Key l, Key specKey)
2 {
3     Key k = lookupByLink (c, specKey, "override");
4     if (k == Ø) k = lookupByNamespace (c, l, specKey);
5     if (k == Ø) k = lookupByLink (c, specKey, "fallback");
6     return k;
7 }
```

The method `lookupBySpec` is only relevant within a *cascading lookup* and if a `specKey` is present.

3.3.3 Lookup Algorithm

```
1 Key lookup (KeySet c, Key l, Key specKey)
2 {
3     Key k = lookupByExtension (c, l, specKey);
4     if (k == ∅ && !(l is of namespace ϵ))
5     {
6         return lookupByKey (c, l); // non-cascading lookup
7     }
8     if (k == ∅ && specKey != ∅)
9     {
10        k = lookupBySpec (c, l, specKey); // cascading lookup
11    }
12    if (k == ∅) k = lookupNamespaces (c, l);
13    return k;
14 }
```

We see (because of the branch starting in line 4) that the function `lookup` supports the two already-discussed forms of lookups: cascading and non-cascading lookups. Because the function `lookup` calls `lookupByExtension` and `lookupBySpec`, all properties are handled recursively. As final helper function, we define `lookupPropertyAsValue` $(l, p) \rightarrow z$ that works similar to `lookupProperty` but with the property value used as value and not as key name. The record z has the following fields:

k is the name of l (i.e., $l.k$), and

v is the property value of the property name p as found by $l.\mu(p)$.

Now we have all functions ready to finally define the algorithm `ksLookup`:

```
1 Key ksLookup (KeySet c, Key l)
2 {
3     Key specKey = lookupByKey (c, "spec" :/ l);
4     Key k = lookup (c, l, specKey);
5     // <continues on the next page>
```

```
6      if ((k == ∅) && (l is of namespace ε) && (specKey != ∅))
7      {
8          k = lookupPropertyAsValue (specKey, "default");
9      }
10     return k;
11 }
```

The last step (line 6) of the lookup algorithm is to use the default value if everything else failed: The property default is exclusively considered on top-level of the recursion.

3.3.4 Abstraction of Metadata

Within ELEKTRA both configuration settings and specifications are represented by a key set. In Section 3.1.6 we introduced separated syntaxes for configuration specifications (with property:=value) and configuration settings (with key=value). Here we demonstrate why this separation of configuration settings and specifications is not visible to plugins and applications in ELEKTRA. We present an abstraction in which applications and plugins cannot distinguish between syntaxes. In particular, the abstraction obscures if metadata is separated or embedded.

Embedded Metadata

Many configuration file formats have metadata embedded. Often metadata is needed to properly reconstruct the configuration file [225]. ELEKTRA stores metadata within μ of the keys.

Example 3.52. Let us consider the following JSON file [227]:

```
1 { "key": true }
```

In JSON a non-quoted true is a boolean, which is different from the string "true". ELEKTRA's JSON plugin transforms this file into a key set, remembering JSON's type in the metadata type. As already mentioned, the values 0 and 1 represent a boolean in ELEKTRA. If we serialize this key set to XML syntax we get:

```
1 <?xml version="1.0" encoding="UTF-8" standalone="no" ?>
2 <key type="boolean">1</key>
```
▲

Abstraction over Embedded and Separated Metadata

In this book we keep configuration settings and specifications separated from each other. From the user's point of view the distinction is useful to easily get a grasp of the involved meta-level. From an application's point of view, however, it is useful if the metadata comes along with the configuration setting, for example, when using a context-aware lookup we do not know which key name we get. We do not burden applications and plugins to distinguish between the embedded or separated form.

To abstract over these two competing ways, we utilize the following concept: We copy all properties to the key's metadata in all other namespaces. ELEKTRA implements this concept in the plugin spec. The key name of the spec key is used as pattern to be matched against the other keys. Properties are copied to matching keys.

Example 3.53. Suppose we have the following configuration specification:

```
1 [slapd/threads/listener]
2    check/range:=1,2,4,8,16
```

And we have the following configuration setting mounted to namespace SYSTEM:

```
1 slapd/threads/listener=4
```

Because of the matching key name, the plugin spec assigns the metadata check/range :=1,2,4,8,16 to the key with the name system:/slapd/threads/listener. ▲

This abstraction makes it irrelevant for ELEKTRA's users if a specific configuration file format supports metadata. The user always has the configuration specification in namespace SPEC as place to add metadata. After the plugin spec has copied the metadata, it is indistinguishable to plugins if the metadata was already within the configuration file or if it was copied from the properties. The plugin spec rejects configuration settings and specifications if they are inconsistent.

Example 3.54. Suppose we have the configuration file from Example 3.52:

```
1 { "key": true }
```

And additionally we have the configuration specification:

```
1 [key]
2   type:=long
```

Then we have a conflict: The JSON plugin adds the metadata `type:=boolean` and the plugin `spec` tries to copy the property `type:=long`. The plugin `spec` rejects such a combination of configuration settings and specifications. ▲

3.3.5 Plugin Configurations

In Section 3.2.2 we introduced the key database and briefly mentioned that plugins implement the actual work of backends involved in `kdb.set` and `kdb.get`. The plugins process key sets, i.e., they have a key set as input and output. In LibElektra we linearly chain the plugins in a way that the output of one plugin is the input of the next. Within a backend all necessary plugins are ***instantiated*** and placed in the order of the instantiation within the chains for `kdb.set` and `kdb.get`. Plugins in the chain for `kdb.set` are executed in the opposite direction than plugins in the chain for `kdb.get`. Every plugin has a unique ***plugin name***.

Plugin configuration is an additional key set used for configuration settings passed to every plugin when it gets instantiated. Based on these configuration settings, plugins enable or modify features. Each plugin decides which plugin configuration it supports. We use the following grammar as compact syntax for plugin configuration:

$\langle$*plugin configuration*$\rangle$ ::= $\langle$*plugin configuration entry*$\rangle$
                           $\{$ '`,`' $\langle$*plugin configuration entry*$\rangle$ $\}$

$\langle$*plugin configuration entry*$\rangle$ ::= $\mathbb{R}$ '`=`' $\mathbb{C}'$

Example 3.55. The plugin `ini` is a feature-complete INI configuration file parser. The plugin configurations `delimiter` and `array` add support for INI dialects. To use + as delimiter and enable support for arrays, we pass the plugin configuration `delimiter=+,array=1` to plugin instantiation.   ▲

3.3.6   Plugin Contracts

We specify the plugin's behavior to guarantee that the plugin will work in a chain. **Contracts** specify requirements and possible effects of a plugin. A contract is a set of mostly formal **clauses** about plugins. Each clause is a mapping of a property name to a property value. The property values have a grammar assigned from Ψ.

Many clauses are used in two complementing scenarios:

1. A clause, used within SPECELEKTRA, indicates that functionality from the backend's plugins is required. We use configuration specification syntax for such key sets. Such a contract is valid between the user who wrote SPECELEKTRA and the plugins in the backend.

2. A clause being returned from a plugin indicates that a plugin has specific restrictions and requirements towards other plugins. We use configuration setting syntax for such key sets. The relative key name holds the property name and the key's value holds the property value. Such a contract is valid between the plugin itself and all other plugins in the backend.

In this book we rely on the following clauses:

infos/provides: Specifies an abstraction of the plugin's functionality. This clause is only useful within plugins, and not in SPECELEKTRA. We call plugins that offer an abstract functionality **provider** of this functionality. Plugins that provide the same functionality shall use the same plugin configuration. The syntax refers to the property value of the clause `infos/provides` and it is a grammar $\langle clause\ infos/provides \rangle \in G$ assigned by $\Psi(\texttt{infos/provides})$:

$\langle clause\ infos/provides \rangle ::= \langle provider \rangle \ \{\ `\sqcup' \ \{\ `\sqcup' \ \} \ \langle provider \rangle \ \}$

$\langle provider \rangle \qquad\qquad ::= \langle provider\ part \rangle \ \{\ `/' \ \langle provider\ part \rangle \ \}$

The / within a clause of `infos/provides` creates a hierarchy of providers where each part is also added individually as provider. The information we get from the clause `infos/provides` is a set of providers and provider parts. Each member of the set is an abstract functionality provided by the plugin, i.e., every provider part is also a provider.

Example 3.56. Plugins that parse and write INI files, have `storage/ini` in the clause `infos/provides` of their contract:

```
1  infos/provides=storage/ini
```

In this case the plugin provides the abstract functionality {`storage/ini`, `ini`, and `storage`}. Storage refers to the ability to parse and serialize configuration files, and INI is a concrete configuration file format provided by this plugin. We do not add `ini/storage` because storage is the more general term. ▲

infos/needs: Specifies which other plugins are needed for the plugin or SPECELEKTRA to work. For better abstraction such dependences are usually on providers, not on concrete plugin names. We use it in both SPECELEKTRA and plugins' contracts, with the grammar:

⟨*clause infos/needs*⟩   ::= ⟨*need*⟩ { '␣' { '␣' } ⟨*need*⟩ }

⟨*need*⟩   ::= ⟨*plugin name*⟩ | ⟨*provider*⟩

Example 3.57. The plugin `simpleini` is a plugin parsing and serializing a simple variant of INI configuration files. On its own, the plugin cannot handle values that are ϵ (ϵ indicates a missing value within a present key, see Definition 3.1 on page 84). The plugin `simpleini` needs the plugin `null`, which transparently transforms ϵ to strings; thus the plugin `simpleini` specifies in its contract:

```
1  infos/needs=null
```

During run-time, the plugin `null` escapes all values that are ϵ so that for the consecutively executed plugins all values are strings. The plugin `simpleini` then processes strings, and does not need to be aware of ϵ. ▲

As we see later, it is unwanted to have the clause `infos/needs` within SPECELEKTRA. Nevertheless, we sometimes need it to work around incomplete contracts of plugins.

Example 3.58. To manually add the plugin `range` to the backend, a system administrator writes:

```
1 [slapd/threads/listener]
2   check/range:=1,2,4,8,16
3   infos/needs:=range
```

Here we make sure that the plugin range is part of the backend.   ▲

The clause infos/needs has no effect if the plugin or a provider of this plugin is already part of the backend.

infos/plugins: Specifies which additional plugins shall be instantiated in the backend. We use it to manually specify complete backends. This clause is useful for both SPECELEKTRA and plugins' contracts. Different from the clause infos/needs plugins are instantiated regardless of earlier instantiations.

$\langle$*clause infos/plugins*$\rangle$ ::= $\langle$*plugin specification*$\rangle$
                            { ' ␣ ' { ' ␣ ' } $\langle$*plugin specification*$\rangle$ }

$\langle$*plugin specification*$\rangle$ ::= ($\langle$*plugin name*$\rangle$ | $\langle$*provider*$\rangle$)
                            [' ␣ ' { ' ␣ ' } $\langle$*plugin configuration*$\rangle$]

Example 3.59. Given the configuration specification:

```
1 [slapd/threads/listener]
2   infos/plugins:=ini delimiter=+,array crypto
```

We instantiate the INI plugin with the plugin configuration of Example 3.55. With this plugin configuration, the plugin parses and serializes configuration files like:

```
1 key+value
2 key+value
3 key2+value
```

The duplicated key from lines 1 and 2 is treated as an array. We use the array indexes as defined in Example 3.1.7 on page 96. The resulting key names are key/#0 and key/#1. Furthermore, the plugin crypto ensures that the configuration values are encrypted on the hard disk.   ▲

infos/status documents the development status and quality of the plugin in its contract, for example, how well it is maintained, documented, reviewed and tested. It is a sequence of qualitative attributes that are added or subtracted to a total score:

⟨*clause infos/status*⟩ ::= ⟨*Status*⟩ { '␣' { '␣' } ⟨*Status*⟩ }

⟨*Status*⟩ ::= ⟨*number*⟩ | ⟨*status name*⟩

A ⟨*number*⟩ is interpreted as number. The meta-specification globally maps each ⟨*status name*⟩ to a number. We add these numbers for the total score of a plugin.

Some of the statuses in the map are objective (such as if a plugin has dependences) and are tested automatically but most statuses are at least partly subjective. For subjective criteria, the status is considered to be in comparison with the other plugins providing a similar functionality.

Example 3.60. Given the following mapping of status names to scores: {nodep ↦ 250, unittest ↦ 1000, maintained ↦ 4000}, let us assume the plugin `simpleini` has the clause `infos/status = nodep unittest -500`. We get the total score $250 + 1000 - 500 = 750$. ▲

infos/metadata: Specifies which metadata is handled by the plugin. Because of the metadata abstraction it does not matter if the metadata is directly present in the configuration files or copied from the configuration specification. The clause specifies a list of metadata the plugin handles, enforces, or executes:

⟨*clause infos/metadata*⟩ ::= ⟨*metadata*⟩ { '␣' { '␣' } ⟨*metadata*⟩ }

Example 3.61. The plugin `range` has the clause `infos/metadata=check/ range`. Let us recall the specification of our running example:

```
1 [slapd/threads/listener]
2   check/range:=1,2,4,8,16
```

At run-time the plugin `spec` copies metadata from the namespace SPEC to the other namespaces. Thus the metadata `check/range` is present in the configuration settings with the same key name:

```
1 slapd/threads/listener=5
```

The plugin `range` guarantees to reject configuration values which are not in the range given by `check/range`. Assuming that the plugin `range` is present in the backend, the above configuration setting is being rejected.   ▲

infos/ordering: Specifies a (possibly empty) list of plugins, which must not already have been instantiated at the time when the plugin is instantiated for a backend. Instead the specified plugins must be instantiated later. This clause is only useful within plugins' contracts and has the following grammar ⟨*clause infos/ordering*⟩ ∈ *G* assigned from Ψ(`infos/ordering`):

⟨*clause infos/ordering*⟩ ::= { '␣' { '␣' } ⟨*plugin*⟩ }

⟨*plugin*⟩   ::= ⟨*plugin name*⟩ | ⟨*provider*⟩

In Example 3.62 we give a more complete example of a plugin's contract and in Example 3.63 we explain how we use the plugin within a configuration specification.

Example 3.62. The plugin `rename` renames key names to upper-case or lower-case characters. It enables system administrators to use any capitalization for relative key names in configuration files. The plugin `rename` has the following clauses in its contract:

```
1 infos/provides=filter/rename
2 infos/needs=
3 infos/status=maintained unittest nodep
4 infos/ordering=logging
5 infos/metadata=rename/toupper rename/tolower
```

In line 1 (i. e., the first clause) the contract states that the plugin *provides* `rename` and it acts as filter, i. e., it transforms a key set. In line 2 the plugin states it does not need other plugins to work correctly. Line 3 describes the development status, i. e., the maturity of the plugin. With the mapping of Example 3.60 we have a score of $4000+1000+250 = 5250$. Line 4 specifies that logging plugins must be instantiated later in the chain. In the next section, we describe how we assemble plugins in a backend using the clause `infos/metadata`, as shown in line 5, which specifies which properties the plugin is able to handle: The plugin `rename` enumerates `rename/toupper` and `rename/tolower` as supported properties [230].   ▲

Example 3.63. With the plugin `rename`, we specify a mountpoint using:

```
1 [slapd]
2   mountpoint:=slapd.conf
3   infos/plugins:=rename
4 [slapd/threads/listener]
5   rename/tolower:=
```

With this specification, system administrators can write the key `threads/listener` with any capitalization in the configuration file `slapd.conf`:

```
1 ThreaDs/LisTeneR=5
```

The configuration setting above leads to a key with the name `/threads/listener`. ▲

3.3.7 Automatic Assembling of Plugins

The specifications in Example 3.63 and Example 3.58 are not as minimal as we would like them to have. A system administrator would need to maintain a list of plugins in the clauses `infos/plugins` and `infos/needs` for every mountpoint, which would be cumbersome with non-trivial configuration specifications. In the following part, we introduce automatic assembling which allows us to avoid these clauses in configuration specifications. ELEKTRA automatically assembles plugins by evaluating the properties contained in the mountpoint's configuration specification.

We use the following algorithm to return a valid set of plugins (a backend), which fulfills all properties of a mountpoint [230]:

```
1 Backend assemblePlugins (KeySet keys)
2 {
3     Plugin plugins [] = {}; // <continues on the next page>
```

```
4      for (key: keys)
5      {
6          for (prop: allProperties (key))
7          {
8              Plugin p;
9              p = findBestPlugin (prop); // see Section 3.3.7
10             addIfMissing (plugins, prop, p);
11         }
12     }
13     topologicalSort (plugins, cmpBy ("infos/ordering"));
14     return Backend (plugins);
15 }
```

The function `assemblePlugins` is called with the mountpoint's keys. The for loop in line 4 iterates over all keys of the specification. For each key we iterate over the key's properties (line 6). In line 9 we find the best suitable plugin. If no plugin is found, we abort the process because of an unhandled exception from `findBestPlugin`. In line 10 we add the plugin `p` to `plugins` if the plugin's property `prop` is not already handled by one of the other plugins. The function `addIfMissing` needs to take care of properly adding all dependences (i. e., as specified in clauses `infos/needs` and `infos/plugins`), thus it can add more than one plugin to `plugins`. Line 13 ensures that plugins are in correct order when instantiating them into the chain of plugins [144, 230]. In the topological sort an exception is thrown if there is no valid order (circular dependences).

Example 3.64. With this approach to assemble plugins, we can simplify the specification of Example 3.63 to:

```
1 [slapd]
2   mountpoint:=slapd.conf
3 [slapd/threads/listener]
4   rename/tolower:=1
```

Because we only have one plugin `rename`, this plugin is chosen.   ▲

Find Best Plugin

To select the best suitable plugin handling a property, we facilitate the clause `infos/status` in the following algorithm [230]:

```
1 Plugin findBestPlugin (Property prop)
2 {
3     Plugin plugins [] = {};
4     plugins = findPluginsWithClause ("infos/metadata", prop);
5     if (plugins.empty ()) throw NoPluginFound ();
6     return max (plugins, cmpByScore ("infos/status"));
7 }
```

The function `findPluginsWithClause` invoked in line 4 finds all suitable plugins, i. e., those which have the property `prop` in their clause `infos/metadata`. In line 6, we return the plugin with the highest ranking compared by the score of the contract's clause `infos/status`. We refrained from having a concept in which a hard-coded default plugin (known beforehand) is returned in order to avoid assumptions about availability of plugins. Our algorithm always determines the plugin that scores best among the currently available plugins [230].

Example 3.65. ELEKTRA has two plugins that have the clause `infos/metadata` $\mapsto$ `check/network`: the plugin `ipaddr` and the plugin `network`. They both implement validation of IP addresses: plugin `ipaddr` using regular expressions, and plugin `network` using the network resolver of the operating system (i. e., `getaddrinfo`). We use the mapping of status names to scores from Example 3.60. The clause `infos/status` for the plugin `ipaddr` is `nodep` (score: $500 + 250 = 750$), and for the plugin `network` is `maintained unittest` (score: $4000 + 1000 = 5000$). Furthermore, we have the following configuration specification given:

```
1 [slapd]
2   mountpoint:=slapd.conf
3 [slapd/ipaddr]
4   check/network:=
```

Then `findBestPlugin("check/network")` returns the plugin `network` (which has the maximum score), except on operating systems that do not have `getaddrinfo`. On such operating systems the plugin `ipaddr` is used instead. In both cases, the resulting plugin is chosen to be included for the mountpoint of `slapd`.   ▲

3.4   Frontend

We elaborate on the abstraction to represent key sets in different ways. The abstraction allows us to generate source code from configuration specifications. We start by creating source code that instantiates in-memory, hard-coded key sets. Then we further extend GENELEKTRA until we are able to generate contextual values, as already introduced from the user's point of view in Section 3.2.6.

3.4.1   C Syntax

It is straightforward to define an alternative syntax for configuration settings and specifications. Different from our previous syntax for configuration settings and specifications in Section 3.1.6, we want the configuration settings and specifications to be valid C/C++ code. When compiled and executed, the result is an in-memory key set identical to the one the source code was generated by. We keep the grammar shorter by having strict spaces, assuming strings to be valid C strings, and not supporting comments:

⟨*KeySet*⟩   ::= 'ksNew␣(' { ⟨*Key*⟩ ',↵' } { '␣' } 'KS_END);'

⟨*Key*⟩   ::= 'keyNew␣("' ⟨*key name*⟩ '",↵' [⟨*Value*⟩] ⟨*properties*⟩ 'KEY_END)'

⟨*Value*⟩   ::= { '␣' } 'KEY_VALUE,␣"' ⟨*configuration value*⟩ '",↵'

⟨*properties*⟩   ::= { { '␣' } ⟨*property*⟩ ',↵' }

⟨*property*⟩   ::= 'KEY_META,␣"' ⟨*property name*⟩ '",␣"' ⟨*property value*⟩ '"'

Example 3.66. Given the key `spec:/slapd/threads/listener`, with the configuration value 4 and the property `default` ↦ 1, GENELEKTRA emits:

```
1 ksNew (keyNew ("spec:/slapd/threads/listener",
2              KEY_VALUE, "4",
3              KEY_META, "default", "1",
4              KEY_END),
5      KS_END);
```

Let us assume the content of this source code is stored in `config.c`. Although we specified a grammar for configuration settings and specifications, we got valid C/C++ code. We use this syntax to hard-code configuration settings and specifications in the frontend:

```
1 KeySet conf =
2 #include <config.c> // include above listing
3 kdb.get (conf);
```

If `kdb.get` in line 3 fails, the application nevertheless continues with the built-in configuration settings and specifications from the generated file `config.c`.   ▲

3.4.2 Contextual Value with Policies

The key set is a generic and widely useful data structure, but for most applications it is too low-level to be directly used. Here we present an API for configuration settings by providing configuration settings as if they were contextual values. As first step, we create a user-defined type that emulates the common behavior of built-in, native data types. We implement common behavior in the class `Value`, which is a part of LIBELEKTRA:

```
1 template <typename Type, Policies ...>
2 class Value
3 {
4     Type cache;   // the configuration value
5     KeySet & ks; // the connected key set
6     // connected context; specified via policies:
7     typename Policies::ContextPolicy & context;
8     ... // <continues on the next page>
```

```
 9 public:
10      Value const & operator= (Type n);      // assignment
11      Type operator++ (); // ... and all other operators
12      ...
13 };
```

The first template parameter of the class `Value` specifies the data type the contextual value shall implement. Instances of the class `Value` can be used wherever this data type is expected because of the operators defined in the lines starting at line 10. The handle `ks` points to a connected key set to be used for `ksLookup`. The member variable `cache` avoids repetitive use of `ksLookup`. When a class inherits from the class `Value`, instances of the inherited class act like variables of native types.

The other template parameters are needed for `Value`'s policies. Policies is a mechanism to specify extensions resolved at compile-time. Instead of hard-coding behavior, policies determine behavioral variations. Different from aspect-oriented programming (where behavior is changed globally) every object of class `Value` can be instantiated with different behavior. We use the C++ template mechanisms [6, 142] but the idea is applicable to other programming languages that provide generic programming features. The use of policies is an implementation detail, but we extensively utilize this extension mechanism throughout Chapter 4.

Instead of emitting nearly-identical source code for every configuration setting, the code generator only defines the policies if non-default behavior is specified via SPECELEKTRA. Other policies (not fixated by the code generator) are chosen by the developer. With the policies correctly implemented, instances of the class `Value` are contextual values. The following policies are the most important extension points in the class `Value`:

LockPolicy determines locking behavior of the class `Value` to support concurrent access from several threads. In the default case, no locking occurs.

WritePolicy implements the property `readonly`. It specifies read-only restrictions for a `Value`. All operations that change the value of `Value` are guarded by static asserts. If the policy is changed to be `ReadOnlyPolicy`, the compiler rejects source code that tries to modify contextual values. `ReadOnlyPolicy` is a trivial class defining a variable as `true`. If the variable is set, the static assertions fail. To prohibit any changes to a particular configuration setting, users set the property readonly $\mapsto$ 1 (i.e., true) as already discussed in Section 3.2.5.

SetPolicy defines how the cache of the class Value's instances is synchronized with the key set. One of the design decisions of applications is the namespace of newly-created configuration settings. This policy supports developers to select the namespace they prefer for their application.

ContextPolicy determines the class Context to be used. The class Value directly uses context.evaluate from this policy. The other methods of this policy are intended for users as already discussed in Section 3.2.6. To give the user access to context, the method context () of the class Value returns the context connected to the respective Value. The return type of this method is a class representing the context as specified by the policy ContextPolicy.

The policies mainly exist to implement properties, and for our extensions towards thread safety and context awareness. Nevertheless, developers can take advantage of the policies:

Example 3.67. If developers instantiate a contextual value to be read-only, developers specify the policy WritePolicy within the source code of the application:

```
1 Key k = keyNew ("/wrong/key/name", KEY_END);
2 Value <bool, WritePolicyIs<ReadOnlyPolicy>> value (ks, c, k);
3 value = true; // compilation error (value is readonly)
```

In line 2 we see that the CORBA data type boolean is mapped to the C/C++ type bool. Line 3 causes a compilation error because in line 2 the ReadOnlyPolicy was specified. The policy statically prohibits the use of the operator =. ▲

The class Value gives us already an improvement to directly using ksLookup. The user does not have to fiddle with raw strings and thus gets some type safety. The class Value alone, however, does not ensure to be consistent with the configuration specification. The user can use Value differently than specified:

- connect key names with the wrong key names ("/wrong... in Example 3.67),

- use the wrong type (**bool** in Example 3.67), or

- use the wrong policies (ReadOnlyPolicy in Example 3.67).

3.4.3   Generated APIs

We use the following generative grammar to generate code for every configuration specification. Here we use a simplified, non-hierarchical version and focus on solving the mentioned problems about type safety. The nonterminal ⟨*KeyName*⟩ is the relative key name, without the slashes, written in CamelCase with capitalization for every hierarchy level:

⟨*simplified generated code*⟩ ::= { '**class**␣' ⟨*KeyName*⟩
                              '␣:␣public␣Value<' ⟨*property value of type*⟩ ⟨*Policies*⟩
                              '>␣{' ⟨*implementation of the class*⟩ '};' }

For brevity we left out the ⟨*implementation of the class*⟩, which is responsible for connecting the correct key name. We use the idea of Section 3.4.1 and generate source code containing the configuration specification. When constructing an object of Value, an instance of the hard-coded specification is passed to the constructor.

Example 3.68. Given the configuration specification:

```
1 [slapd/threads/listener]
2   type:=long
3   readonly:=1
4   default:=1
```

The following source code is generated. The implementation includes a hard-coded copy of the configuration specification passed to the constructor:

```
1 class SlapdThreadsListener : public Value<long,
2         WritePolicyIs<ReadOnlyPolicy>> {
3    ... keyNew ("/slapd/threads/listener",
4             KEY_META, "type", "long",
5             KEY_META, "readonly", "1",
6             KEY_END) ...
7 };
```

Generated APIs ensure:

- Users cannot connect the wrong key names (line 3 of Example 3.68).

- Users cannot use the wrong type (`long` in line 1 and 4 of Example 3.68).

- Users cannot use the wrong policy (line 2 of Example 3.68).

Example 3.69. Developers still need to manually instantiate every contextual value:

```
1 KeySet config;
2 Context c;
3 long foo ()
4 {
5     // manual instantiation necessary:
6     SlapdThreadsListener slapdThreadsListener (config, c);
7     slapdThreadsListener++;
8     return slapdThreadsListener;
9 }
```

Afterwards, developers directly use the variable `slapdThreadsListener` as if it were of type `long`. ▲

Another downside—next to the manual instantiation—is that the class and variable names become too long.

3.4.4 Hierarchy

We extend GENELEKTRA to generate nested classes and namespaces for every hierarchy level of the configuration specification. We aim at a hierarchy of classes that are instantiated at a single place—all with the same key set and context. In the following grammar we use the nonterminals ⟨*Hierarchy level*⟩ and ⟨*hierarchy level*⟩. They are used to denoting one non-contextual hierarchy level from a key name capitalized or non-capitalized, respectively.

Example 3.70. Given the key name `[foo/%bar%/test]`, we have two strings for a ⟨*hierarchy level*⟩: the strings 'foo', and 'test'. Furthermore, we have two strings for a ⟨*Hierarchy level*⟩: the strings 'Foo', and 'Test'. The string `%bar%` is a contextual hierarchy level not included. ▲

⟨*generated code*⟩   ::= { '**namespace**␣' ⟨*hierarchy level*⟩
                              '↵{↵' ⟨*generated code*⟩ | ⟨*class*⟩ '↵}↵' }
                              '**class**␣Environment␣{' { ⟨*class content*⟩ } '};'

⟨*class*⟩   ::= '**class**␣' ⟨*Hierarchy level*⟩
                              '␣:␣public␣Value<' ⟨*property value of type*⟩ ⟨*Policies*⟩
                              '>' ('␣' | '↵') '{' { ⟨*class content*⟩ } '};'

⟨*class content*⟩   ::= { ⟨*hierarchy level*⟩ '::' } ⟨*Hierarchy level*⟩
                              '␣' ⟨*hierarchy level*⟩ ';'

The root of the hierarchy is the class Environment, which is always generated. For
code generation, we recursively walk through all hierarchy levels in all configuration
specifications. We generate a class for every hierarchy level and a namespace for every
non-leaf hierarchy level. If a configuration specification for a hierarchy level is missing, we
use the special type Value <none_t>. These classes are placeholders for configuration
specifications to be introduced later. For every configuration specification with a subtree
containing more than itself, we create a ⟨*class content*⟩. For brevity, we left out details
of the ⟨*class content*⟩, such as constructors and public modifiers.

Example 3.71. Given the configuration specification:

```
1 [slapd/threads/listener]
2     type:=long
3     default:=1
```

We emit the following code structure:

```
1 namespace slapd
2 {
3 namespace threads
4 {
5 class Listener : public Value<long> {};
6 }   // <continues on the next page>
```

```
 7 class Threads : public Value<none_t>
 8 {threads::Listener listener;};
 9 } // end namespace slapd
10 class Slapd : public Value<none_t>
11 {slapd::Threads threads;};
12 class Environment {Slapd slapd;};
```

Developers only need to instantiate the whole `Environment` `env` and then directly use the variable `env.slapd.threads.listener`. The hierarchical nesting enables them to pass any subtrees of the hierarchy to functions:

```
 1 long foo(slapd::Threads const & threads)
 2 {
 3     threads.listener++;
 4     Context & c = threads.context (); // access context
 5     return threads.listener;
 6 }
 7
 8 int main()
 9 {
10     KeySet config;
11     Context c;
12     Environment env (config, c);
13     long x = foo (env.slapd.threads);
14 }
```

Here we only need a single instantiation of `Environment` to get access to the whole execution environment (line 12). ▲

3.4.5 Contextual Substitution

Here we describe how the frontend takes care of replacing layer names. We use the syntax as specified in Definition 3.47 on page 111. Layer names are written as part of the key name, for example:

```
1 [foo/%bar%/hey]
2   type:=long
3   default:=Hello
```

By the use of the class `Context` (see Section 3.2.6), we define dynamic scopes specifying the presence of layers. The layers influence `context.evaluate`:

```
1 Context context;
2 assert (context.evaluate ("foo/%bar%/hey") == "/test/%/foo");
3 context.activate ("bar", "baz");
4 assert (context.evaluate ("foo/%bar%/hey") == "/test/baz/foo");
```

The parameters for `context.activate` here are the layer name and the layer value.[6] We will discuss different mechanisms for layer specifications in Chapter 4. Whenever the class `Value` synchronizes its cache, instances of the class:

1. call `context.evaluate` to get the key name from the contextual key name, and

2. call `ksLookup` using the key name resulting from Step 1.

Context Changes

We eagerly update the caches within the `Value` on context changes. We use the observer pattern to push notifications regarding context changes to the contextual values [98]. The class `Context` acts as subject and the class `Value` (the contextual value) acts as observer. Contextual values choose notifications they subscribe to. They do so by checking for layer names in their specifications [235].

Example 3.72. The configuration specification `[foo/%bar%/hey]` specifies the contextual value `hey` and uses layer name `bar`. The configuration specification causes a subscription to the class `Context` for changes of the layer `bar`. If a user calls `hey.context().activate("bar", ...)`, the contextual value `hey` will be notified.

Layer switches notify all contextual values that have a layer name in their key. At context changes, the context placeholders are substituted.

---

[6]We omitted the template parameters.

Example 3.73. We use the contextual value hey, specified as before with [foo/%bar%/hey]:

```
1 assert (hey.getKeyName () == "/foo/%/hey");
2 hey.context ().activate ("bar", "baz");
3 assert (hey.getKeyName () == "/foo/baz/hey");
4 // value of "hey" can have changed here
```

In line 2 we activate the layer name bar with the layer value baz. Thus the context placeholder %bar% is substituted with baz as shown in line 3. ▲

Assignment

The assignment of contextual values obey the expected semantics of variables. Additionally, the contextual values are keeping the underlying key set up to date.

Example 3.74. Given the contextual value hey as specified in Example 3.73, we write:

```
1 assert (hey == ks.get<long> ("foo/%/hey"));
2 hey=3;
3 assert (hey==3);
4 hey++;
5 assert (hey==4);
6 kdb.set (ks);
```

We assume ks to be a key set and kdb to be an instance of KDB. The assertion of line 1 is valid as long the layer bar does not change (bar is the only layer influencing the contextual value hey). The convenience wrapper ks.get does a ksLookup and lexically casts the found value to the type given in <>. With kdb.set in line 6 we synchronize the changed configuration setting foo/%/hey=4 to a configuration file using the key database kdb. ▲

Identity

For contextual values we mainly use semantics as defined for variables in the respective programming language. Usually contextual values are passed by reference. Then contextual values have the same identity and they refer to the same instance of a KeySet and

`Context`. We have an intuitive definition of identity: Two contextual values are identical if they have the same memory address.

As explained by Tanter [275], the goal is to avoid side effects on copies of contextual values visible to the rest of the system. To achieve that behavior, we need to construct a new contextual value with a copy of the previous key set. The disadvantage is that copying the key set disconnects the contextual value from the synchronization with the execution environment. Thus ELEKTRA does not support copy semantics.

We have an alternative with context-oriented programming. Users define new dynamic scopes and layer names for every place where side effects must stay local.

Example 3.75. Given the contextual value `local`:

```
1 [%infunc%/local]
2   type:=long
3   default:=1
```

We define a dynamic scope:

```
1 int foo (Local & local)
2 {
3     local.context ().with ("infunc", "foo") ([&] {
4         // work with "local" in private scope
5     });
6 }
```

With C++ lambdas (the `[&] {...}` construct), we activate the unique layer value `foo`. Then changes of the contextual value `local` are not visible outside the function `foo` although we share an object (with the same identity passed by `Local & local`). ▲

3.4.6   Guarantees for Configuration Access

The set of ***validation specifications*** is a subset of configuration specifications. Validation specifications are properties that put constraints on keys. A ***validated key*** is a key that complies with all its validation specifications. In a ***validated key set*** all keys are validated.

In the case of the absence of a key, `ksLookup` can return ∅. Most applications cannot deal with ∅ and thus this return value is often unwanted. Instead applications want to have guarantees that they receive configuration settings required by them. Guarantees for the presence of a configuration setting is given by the property `default`. Thus the property `default` is a validation specification. As already discussed in Section 3.2.5, the property `default` specifies a default value to be used if otherwise no configuration value of the given key name can be found.

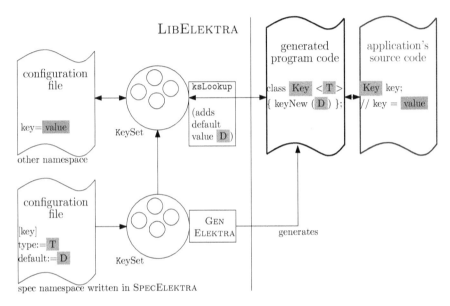

Figure 3.9: The guarantees for configuration access are given by `ksLookup`, although the specifications from generated source code might be used (if the configuration files are not available on the system). Only the generated high-level frontend uses `ksLookup` but not the user's code. The blue part needs to be supplied by the user. The arrows indicate data flow of key sets.

As we see in Figure 3.9 the property `default` (grey box D) influences `ksLookup` (shown on the left side, implemented in LIBELEKTRA) and frontends (shown on the right side, generated by GENELEKTRA). Usually, the default value is dynamically read from a configuration file. If the backend or configuration file is not available or is inconsistent, however, the hard-coded specification within the generated source code is used instead. By comparing the built-in specification with the specification we got from the configuration file we can easily detect problems—such as missing default values.

The introduced operations on the key database (implemented in LIBELEKTRA) guarantee:

kdb.set: to write only validated key sets into the key database (see Section 3.2.2). Keys not adhering to the validation specification are rejected with an error.

kdb.get: to only return a validated key set. Keys not adhering to the validation specification are dropped.[7]

The code generator GENELEKTRA guarantees for high-level APIs that:

- The configuration specifications are always available (see Section 3.4.3).

- Only cascading lookups are used to look up contextual values.

- For every generated contextual class the property `default` is present.

Lemma 3. When looking up keys in the high-level API, `ksLookup` never returns $\varnothing$.

Proof. To be able to look up a key in the high-level API, by definition the property `default` must be present and a cascading lookup is used. As we see in the algorithm `ksLookup` (Section 3.3.3), to use the property `default` three conditions need to be true:

`k == `$\varnothing$`:` can be false but then we already have a key and do not need the default.

`l `**`is of namespace`**` `ϵ`:` cannot be false because the code generator guarantees that only cascading lookups are used.

`specKey != `$\varnothing$`:` cannot be false, because the code generator ensures that the configuration specification is always present. The `specKey`'s presence (i.e., `spec` $:\!/\, l$) is implied due to the presence of the property `default`.   □

Default values are robust against context changes and reloading of configuration settings. We are resistant against missing configuration settings: Even if the backend cannot be used at all, we still have the specifications compiled in the application.

Example 3.76. We continue with Example 0.6 from page 16:

---
[7]This only happens if `kdb.set` is bypassed.

```
1 [slapd/threads/listener]
2   check/range:=1,2,4,8,16
3   context:=/slapd/threads/%cpu%/listener
4   default:=1
5   description:=One thread is adequate for up to 16 CPU cores.
6   type:=long
```

Because of the presence of the property default the key slapd/threads/listener can be looked up safely. The following values are tried in the given priority:

- Use the contextual value with the layer name cpu resolved in the backends. After checking the specifications of the resulting key name, we look it up in any namespace:

    - For 32 CPUs, the key name is /slapd/threads/32/listener.

    - If a specification for this configuration setting exist, it will be considered.

    - Otherwise, we try all namespaces for /slapd/threads/32/listener.

- Use the configuration setting /slapd/threads/listener in any namespace.

- Otherwise, the lookup returns the default value 1. ▲

CHAPTER 4

Frontends

As far as the laws of mathematics refer to reality, they are not certain; and as far as they are certain they do not refer to reality.

— Albert Einstein

A reusable way to provide functionality to different applications is via *APIs*. API design is known to be important and challenging [38, 47, 108, 253, 278]. For developers, ideally the visible part of configuration access is reduced to an API. In this chapter, after a short discourse of the history of ELEKTRA's APIs, we present three high-level, type-safe, and context-aware APIs. Furthermore, we elaborate on design choices, discuss extensions, find rationales for requirements, and tackle the research question:

RQ 5. Which concepts are needed for context-aware frontends to fulfill the requirements as unveiled in Chapter 2?

4.1 History of Elektra's APIs

Here we describe earlier versions of ELEKTRA's APIs and strive to answer **RQ 5.1**:

RQ 5.1. What is the design space for context-aware frontends?

Similar to programming languages [164] and data description languages [93] the design space for configuration access is vast. Here we discuss design choices of ELEKTRA's API and observations that lead us to the high-level APIs presented in this chapter.

Let us start with API functionality that survived unchanged for 13 years (2004–2017):

1. It is useful to pass to the user only data structures exclusively accessible via API. Among many advantages, the data structure allows internal reorganizations and optimizations without changes visible to the user.

   Example 4.1. The configuration access API `getenv` that does not prohibit direct access to `environ` is a negative example. Because of direct access to `environ`, `getenv` invocations give neither guarantees with respect to thread-safety nor about availability of the pointer passed back. Furthermore, `environ` is easily tricked into having duplicated entries.   ▲

2. ELEKTRA's data structure is a set composed of individual records (and not only strings) throughout the whole API's lifetime. Doing so had many advantages for advanced lookup strategies and for providing metadata.

3. It is a good idea to fully take control over memory management and always provide pairs of functions for opening and closing resources. Even though the details changed completely, all attempts to do otherwise failed completely. The abstraction proved to be useful, for example, when introducing an `mmap` cache.

4. ELEKTRA always emitted a data structure and never was event-driven [162]. Since later versions, hooks for updates on changes have been possible via plugins. With ELEKTRA, applications do not have to implement their own data structure for configuration settings. Other reasons for the data structure are its need for plugins, conversions, and frontends.

4.1.1   Abstraction

The first API of ELEKTRA offered operations that supported modifications of both persisted single keys and persisted key sets. From an implementation point of view this duality complicated the implementation of backends: Backends needed to implement both ways. It is, however, difficult to partially serialize configuration files, as it would be needed for setting a single key. We decided to put a focus on supporting configuration files by only supporting key set (and not key) operations in the backend. Modifications of single keys were moved to convenience APIs.

In ELEKTRA 0.6 released on 30th March, 2006, ELEKTRA described changes that shall be applied to the current configuration settings. For example, the API user had to explicitly remove keys if they were no longer wanted. This behavior was problematic for configuration files.

In ELEKTRA 0.7 released on 17th October, 2008, we used a hybrid approach [225]: In a key set we described the complete configuration settings as they shall be applied. Furthermore, we described the differences of which keys were removed since parsing the configuration files. This was an efficient method for configuration files as well as other backends. Unfortunately, the API was not intuitive: To remove a key, one needed to mark the key for removal instead of removing it from the key set. When simply removing keys from the key set, it would not necessarily be removed in the backend. Furthermore, this API required us to sort keys in the `KeySet` specially: The keys marked for removal had to be separated from the other keys.

Since ELEKTRA 0.8.0 [225] implemented in 2010, released on 5th May, 2012, we fully migrated to a system, where the key set contains the complete configuration settings. The correlation of in-memory key set and configuration files is an instance of the view-update problem [94]. The state represents a view of the configuration files. Changes in the state must be translated back to configuration files.

API evolution: To mitigate many problems of API evolution a proposal process proved to be helpful. Instead of directly adding to the API, developers first need to propose their change. This change is only accepted in a library that is specifically marked to contain proposed enhancements. When the demand is clearly given and no further improvements to the API are suggested, the API is moved to the core. The API stagnated and stayed minimal, which eased the development of the bindings for C++, Python, Haskell, Lua, Shell, Ruby, and Java; and we fulfilled the requirement:

Requirement 8. *The configuration access API must be minimal and crafted carefully.*

4.1.2 Context

Already before starting with the dissertation we had the intuition that key-value-based configuration access APIs alone had limitations in combination with some requirements. We wanted to implement a software stack for an embedded computer with a connected camera. The cameras needed various non-trivial configuration settings in order to work, for example, shutter speed and sensor sensitivity.

The challenging part was to easily switch connected cameras and add new cameras without changing the source code. Every camera needed different configuration settings but also had substantial overlap with configuration settings of other cameras.

The naïve object-oriented way is to implement the configuration procedure of every camera as subclass of a camera class. The configuration settings are for the camera objects to be instantiated. This solution fails in the requirement of the ability to add new cameras without source code changes. Furthermore, these classes would hardly describe any behavior; They mostly describe different values for different cameras, which is not the strength of object-oriented programming.

In an abstract viewpoint the connected camera is part of the configuration setting. But from the viewpoint of the application it is not configuration settings: It is something given from the outside world. We have to adapt our configuration settings to the constraints we have from the environment. We did not find an elegant solution within object-oriented programming for such constraints from the environment.

We came up with a solution by introducing an extension of *profiles*. In our extension, developers specify several profiles: If a configuration setting is not found in the first profile, the search continues in the second profile, and so on. So instead of looking up configuration values directly, profiles determine which value we shall use. In retrospect this feature has been a cascading lookup with manually specified namespaces. For example, if we use `ksLookup("shutter_speed", {"model","manufacturer"})` we look up the shutter speed:

1. accounting for the profile `model`, and

2. if the `shutter_speed` was not found, we use the `manufacturer` profile as fallback.

The API for profiles created a usability problem for developers because:

- Developers were directly confronted with this concept when using the API.

- One always had to remember to pass the list of profiles to the correct places.

- The combination of different profiles was hard to understand due to its flexibility.

- It inherently has the limitation that profiles are exclusively clustered in a single dimension.

Some time after the camera project, we found context-oriented programming to be a perfect fit. Instead of writing a list of profiles in every configuration access point, we write contextual specifications. The developers specify all dependences towards context in one place. Instead of the error-prone combination of profiles, we would activate layers. The environment would be modeled by layers as context-oriented programming proposes. In this chapter we discuss this idea in detail.

4.1.3 Decisions

Table 4.1 gives a summary of various decisions in ELEKTRA and shows which of them were reverted in the current version.

Decision	Earlier versions (< 0.8)	Current version (≥ 0.8)
data structure	list	custom
opaqueness	partly	fully
linear search	yes	no
metadata	fixed number	arbitrary
memory	open&close	ref-counted
hooks on access	no	via plugins
XML streaming	built-in	via plugins
process for API changes	no	yes
high-level API	in core	separated
focus in support of storages	no focus	configuration files
sorting	manual	always (at insert)
context-aware lookups	no	via plugins
configuration specification	informally	yes
object-oriented API	yes	yes
code-generated API	no	yes
context-oriented API	no	yes

Table 4.1: Decisions for an API. The version 0.8.0 was released on 5th May, 2012.

4.2 Execution Environment as Contextual Values

We suggest facilitating *execution environments* as *contextual values*. For example, let us employ external configuration settings via `getenv` to query the execution environment. We need to be careful: After dynamic reconfiguration the settings valid in the new context differ from those obtained with `getenv` [235].

Next to external context changes, we face another problem: In some parts of the program the context is more specific than in other parts of the program. For example, a Web browser has opened private and history-aware tabs at the same time. Although we want to run the same source code for all tabs, the differences are important for the user. To reduce the danger of applying wrong context information it is desirable to ensure that access to execution environments always considers context [235].

Contextual values allow us to safely interact with an execution environment. They ensure that the context is taken into account when accessing the execution environment [231].

We propose to specify the contextual values connected with the execution environment as part of a separate unit. The separate unit is the configuration specification and consists of external configuration files containing specifications for contextual values. Such specifications facilitate context placeholders, each representing a dimension of the context awareness of the contextual value [235].

Example 4.2. To greet in different languages, we would specify a contextual value:

```
1 [%language%/person/greeting]
2   type:=string
3   description:=hello in all languages
4   default:=Hi!
```

The basename of the key name (`greeting`) is the name of a contextual value of the type `string`; and `%language%` is a context placeholder to be substituted in contextual interpretations. GENELEKTRA yields the contextual class `Greeting` using the contextual value specification above [235].   ▲

For contextual interpretations, we substitute these context placeholders with values given by layers. The resulting key name is used with `ksLookup`. In addition to the specification, we have a configuration file containing the greetings in different languages:

```
1 german/person/greeting=Hallo!
```

In the example above, the contextual value provides two different values with `%` for an empty layer.

4.2.1 How to use Context Information?

To work with ELEKTRA, developers need to specify the contextual values and layers. Then developers can immediately facilitate the contextual values in their source code in the same way as variables are used [235].

Example 4.3. We expand the Example 4.2 [235]:

```
1 [%language%/%country%/%dialect%/person/greeting]
2   type:=string
3   default:=hello
4 [%country%/person/visits]
5   type:=long
6   default:=0
```

We specify two contextual values: greeting and visits. They are implemented in code-generated classes called Greeting and Visits. The class Person exists as placeholder to avoid troubles if the contextual value person is specified later on. The class Person has the two contextual values greeting and visits as member variables [235]. ▲

The default value will be used if the execution environment does not specify a value in some context, for example, 0 in visits of Example 4.3. Otherwise, ELEKTRA uses the execution environment. The key database abstracting the execution environment can contain a key-value pair for each value in each context [235]. We represent these key-value pairs as configuration settings.

Example 4.4. Here we give some key-value pairs that can be used by the contextual value greeting as defined in Example 4.3:

```
1 german/%/%/person/greeting=Guten Tag!
2 german/austria/%/person/greeting=Servus!
3 german/austria/traditional/person/greeting=Griass enk!
```

Such a configuration file is loaded at the beginning of the program and on change notifications. Next, we have to specify layers as manually written *layer classes* like the following one [235]:

```
1 class CountryAustriaLayer : public Layer {
2 public:
3     string id () const { return "country"; }
4     string operator() () const { return "austria"; }
5 };
```

The method `id` returns a fixed string that gives the layer its name. To return the layer value, we overload the function call operator. We introduce such layer classes because the string can be computed and does not need to be constant. We assume similar layer classes are implemented for the other countries, languages and dialects as well [235]. ▲

In a later extension we will elaborate on a technique without the need of such boilerplate code and still avoid the error-prone strings we had in Chapter 3.

Example 4.5. The following function demonstrates the use of contextual values [235]:

```
1 void visit (Person & person)
2 {
3     person.context ().with<CountryAustriaLayer> ()
4                     .with<LanguageGermanLayer> ()([&] {
5         cout << "visit " << ++person.visits
6              << " in " << person.context ()["country"]
7              << ": " << person.greeting << endl;
8     });
9     cout << person.greeting << endl;
10 }
```

The only parameter passed to the function `visit` is a reference (written with `&` in C++) to the contextual value `person`. We realized the dynamic scope with C++ lambdas: The expression `[&]` captures all variables by reference, such as `person`. The layer activation happens at the next application of the context's function call `operator()` to the lambda expression. The block `{}` in lines 4–8 is executed in a different context in which `CountryAustriaLayer` and `LanguageGermanLayer` are active. Context activations facilitating the method `with` are limited within the dynamic scope of this block [146]. In line 5 we increment `person.visits`. This effect is only visible in its context. Line 6 introspects the value of the layer name `country`. While in line 7 we output a greeting in the specific context, in line 9 we output the greeting in the context the program had before executing the block. An execution of the function `visit` produces the following output [235]:

```
visit 1 in Austria: Servus!
Hi!
```

By looking at the source, we know which language and country is activated when producing the first line. For the dialect, however, we do not know the context from the function alone, it is decided somewhere else in the program. The function has a side effect: The value of `visits` is incremented by one in the context of Austria, German, and some dialect but not in any other combination of activated contexts [235]. ▲

4.2.2 More on Layers

Each *layer class* implements the following interface [235]:

```
1 class Layer {
2 public:
3     virtual string id () const = 0;
4     virtual string operator() () const = 0;
5 };
```

The method `id` returns the name of the layer name, i. e., the context placeholder without %. Developers must guarantee uniqueness of the return values from `id`: The method `id` of every layer class must consistently return the same string, and the method `id` of every different layer class must return a different string. During the context evaluation the method `operator()` returns the layer value [235].

Simple implementations of layer classes, for example `CountryAustriaLayer` as defined in Example 4.4, return a constant string. In other situations, we need to calculate the layer values dynamically.

Example 4.6. The country is determined by invoking `lookupCountry` (utilizing the current GPS position) whenever the layer is activated [235]:

```
1 class CountryGPSLayer : public Layer
2 {
3 public:
4     CountryGPSLayer () : m_country (lookupCountry ()) {}
5     string id () const { return "country"; }                        ▲
6     string operator() () const { return m_country; }
7 private:
8     string m_country;
9 };
```

The context itself often depends on contextual values. This is the case for *profiles* as contextual values. Then a set of other contextual values depends on the profile.

Example 4.7. A profile of mobile devices is called "airplane mode" and switches context-aware applications to be silent and to not try to start wireless transmission functions. All settings deciding about silence and wireless transmission depend on this profile. ▲

Profiles are specified as contextual values but additionally represent a layer.

Example 4.8. We specify the profile to be defined by the execution environment [235]:

```
1 [%application%/profile]
2   type:=string
3   opt:=p
4   opt/long:=profile
5   default:=
```

A profile is easily combinable with contextual values to use completely different groups of configuration settings. ▲

Instead of manually changing the complete configuration settings back and forth, we have all configuration settings persistently stored and easily switch between them.

Example 4.9. Because of the properties opt and opt/long (see Section 3.2.5) this contextual value is initialized from the command-line options -p and --profile with a higher priority than initialization from the configuration file. Then we use a layer class that returns the contextual value passed by the profile [235]:

```
1 class ProfileLayer : public Layer
2 {
3 public:
4     ProfileLayer (Profile const & profile) :
5         m_profile (profile) {}
6     string id () const { return "profile"; }
7     string operator() () const { return m_profile; }
8 private:
9     Profile const & m_profile;
10 };
```

Such a profile usually is activated for the whole application. ▲

The implementation of the function main demonstrates how to set up the whole system [235]:

```
1 int main (int argc, char** argv)
2 {
3     KeySet ks;
4     ksGetOpt (argc, argv, ks);
5     KDB kdb;
6     kdb.get (ks);
7     Context c;
8     Environment env (ks, c);
9     c.activate<MainApplicationLayer> ();
10    c.activate<ProfileLayer> (env.profile);
11    // the rest of the program
12    // for example, visit (env.person);
13 }
```

In lines 3 and 7 we instantiate a KeySet and the Context as provided by the ELEKTRA library. The key set is initialized with data specified in configuration files (automatically found by ELEKTRA), environment variables and command-line options (lines 4 and 6). The function ksGetOpt is either generated, or the specification is read at run-time.

Either way, we parse arguments as specified with `opt` and `opt/long`. GENELEKTRA yields (beside the classes corresponding to the names in the execution environment) the class `Environment`, which provides access to the top-level contextual values like `person` and `profile`. As we see in line 8, `Environment` depends on the key set and the context. The use of the context's member function template `activate` activates two layers [235].

4.2.3 Implementation Choices

We evaluate four competing implementation choices for our frontend. Every technique guarantees that whenever the contextual value is accessed it correctly delivers its value under the interpretation of the current context. In the comparison we do not consider the costs of layer switching but only accessing the contextual value. In all techniques, needed updates in the event of context changes use the observer pattern as outlined in Section 3.4.5 [235]. Then we answer the research question:

RQ 5.2. Which implementation technique for implementing context-aware frontends has the best trade-off for time versus space?

We executed the benchmarks on a hp® EliteBook 8570w using the CPU Intel® Core™ i7-3740QM @ 2.70GHz. The operating system was GNU/Linux Debian Wheezy 7.5. We used, unless mentioned otherwise, Debian's GCC compiler 4.7.2-5 with the options `-std=c++11`, `-O2`, and `-Dopt=unlikely`. We measured the time passed using `get timeofday`. We executed each benchmark eleven times but discuss only the median value (except in the boxplots, where all data are displayed) [235].

Our micro-benchmark facilitates an arithmetic calculation that frequently accesses contextual values [235]. We compare subsequent benchmarks with a function adding two variables passed by reference:

```
1 Integer::type add_native (uint32_t const & i1,
2                            uint32_t const & i2)
3 {
4     return i1+i2;
5 }
```

This function is called 100 billion times (`iterations=100000000000LL`) in a loop as shown below [235]:

```
1 for (long long i=0; i<iterations; ++i)
2 {
3     x ^= add_native (val, val);
4 }
```

The loop needs 27.16 seconds (see data labeled "native cmp noif" in figures 4.1 and 7.1[1]). Without the exclusive or (the ^ in line 3), for example, by adding up the results with x += add_native, the loop takes 0.00 seconds (see "native noif sum" in Figure 4.1) because the compiler replaces the loop by an arithmetical operation [235].

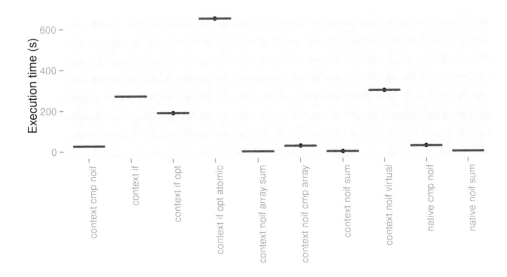

Figure 4.1: Benchmark of implementation choices [235]. The figure shows a boxplot with linear scale. Because of the large scale, the boxes are only (thick) lines. Figure 7.1 shows the boxes of the three fastest variants. Black dots indicate measurements not within 1.5*interquartile range [226]

For the next four microbenchmarks, we compare the performance on the contextual class Integer instead of the native value of type uint32_t using the following code [235]:

---

[1]The second figure compares the three fastest variants.

```
1 Integer::type add_contextual (Integer const & i1,
2                                 Integer const & i2)
3 {
4     return i1+i2;
5 }
```

To make above source code work, we overload the *type conversation operator*. The type conversation operator in C++ allows contextual values to be used whenever a type uint32_t is expected [235]:

```
1 operator uint32_t () const
2 {
3     /* Implementation of different access strategies
4         for contextual values*/
5 }
```

(Atomic) Branches

A naïve approach to update context changes is by checking a tidy flag on every access of the contextual value [235]:

```
1 operator uint32_t () const
2 {
3     if (m_context_changed)
4     {
5         update ();
6     }
7     return m_cache;
8 }
```

This specific implementation requires two additional branches for each call of add_contextual with devastating results: The loop then takes 271.62 seconds (it is ten times slower, see "context if" in Figure 4.1). The run-time is improved to 190.13

seconds (30 % faster, see "context if opt" in Figure 4.1) by giving the compiler hints which `if`-branch is taken more often [235]. Such improvements, however, do not change the overall outcome, the overhead is still high. Another major drawback of the solution with branches is that the compiler cannot optimize away arithmetic loops [235]. The use of branches for every access, however, yields benefits:

- It makes context changes lazy. Instead of looking up affected contextual value on every context change, we would only mark them as tidy (`m_context_changed` from above).

- When the contextual value facilitates `std::atomic<bool>` instead of `bool` for `m_context_changed`, the contextual values are multi-thread safe. Unfortunately, atomicity adds extra costs: The resulting run-time of 651.92 seconds is more than doubled if we use an `atomic` type (see "context if opt atomic" in Figure 4.1). With clang (version `3.5-1~exp1` using option `-O3`) the run-time is 81.42 seconds both for `std::atomic<bool>` and `volatile bool`. Nevertheless, the results are still far from desired [235].

Virtual Function Calls

The next implementation technique we discuss is switching objects at run-time. The only change needed is to provide a base class and add the C++ `virtual` modifier [235]:

```
1 virtual operator uint32_t () const
2 {
3     return m_cache;
4 }
```

Virtual function calls are generally believed to outperform switch statements. Virtual function tables, a possible implementation technique, received attention of the research community, particularly for super-scalar processors [22, 48, 78]. But, virtual function calls (where it is not known which class be called) make some optimizations (especially inlining) impossible [78]. In our case, virtual function calls even perform poorer than an `if`-branch, leaving us with a run-time of 298.8 seconds (see "context noif virtual" in Figure 4.1). Optimizations that avoid the whole loop are impossible, too [235].

Member Array

The next method is a member array containing values for every context. Context changes are represented by modifying the array index `m_index`, again using the observer pattern. On access of the contextual value, we return an element of the array [235]:

```
1 operator uint32_t () const
2 {
3     return g_arr[m_index];
4 }
```

Such member arrays yield promising results: 27.16 seconds (see "context noif cmp array" in Figure 4.1 and later in 7.1). Additionally, optimizations can completely eliminate arithmetic loops [235].

An array with elements for every combination of activated layers has a drawback: Done in a naïve way it needs a large amount of memory for each contextual value because the number of layer combinations easily gets huge. We left optimizations of this technique as a future work [235].

Member Variable

The most efficient implementation is the use of one memory cell per contextual value and returning its content directly [235]:

```
1 operator uint32_t () const
2 {
3     return m_cache;
4 }
```

With this technique we measured a median of 27.16 seconds (see "context cmp noif" in figures 4.1 and 7.1). We got the same result as with the native variable access ("native cmp noif"), which means that we did not measure any overhead. Furthermore, the technique requires only minimal memory for caching (one native type per contextual value). Of course, we must look up values on layer activation [235].

Discussion

It is not surprising that such a simple variable access performs well. Nevertheless, we cannot claim that the optimizations (we rely on) are done by every compiler for every program. We answer our research question:

RQ 5.2. Which implementation technique for implementing context-aware frontends has the best trade-off for time versus space?

Finding. *Both member arrays and member variables have no overhead in our benchmark. The use of member variables has minimal space requirements.*

We decided to use the member variable implementation technique because it had no run-time overhead in the benchmark on read-only access. Furthermore, the technique has minimal memory overhead, fulfilling our requirement:

Requirement 10. *Developers must have guarantees that read-only configuration access is fast and updates only happen if wanted.*

We will elaborate on this benchmark, and evaluate the costs of layer activations much later in Section 7.1.2.

4.3   Multi-threaded Contextual Values

In this section we extend ELEKTRA to ubiquitous computing. We found a combination of three problems in this domain:

Context awareness aims to impress users by letting devices react in smart ways. Devices shall consider properties of their physical environment and information users gave them. For example, if a smart phone is taken out of the pocket, the phone does not measure body temperature anymore. In this situation, the phone turns off vibration because the user would not feel it anyway [226].

Customizability aims to give end users the opportunity to modify unwanted default values and context awareness, hence bringing the behavior in line with their needs. For example, if users are deaf, turning off vibration is not a good solution [226].

Performance on multi-core processors bear new challenges and are accepted as an upcoming trend for embedded computing. Multi-threading is an attractive technique to more thoroughly facilitate multi-core processor resources [226].

In the previous section we mainly addressed context awareness and customizability. In this section we extend LIBELEKTRA with support for multi-threading. We aim at context activations across threads. For example, if context sensors detect that the battery is low, we want to have a mechanism that notifies all threads of each running application [226].

4.3.1   Introduction of Embedded Use Case

We describe an embedded use case as often found in ubiquitous computing. Let us consider a ubiquitous computing device that shall be protected via a watchdog:

```
1 [watchdog/%security%/enabled]
2    type:=boolean
3    default:=1
```

In the example above, we specify enabled as contextual value. We use boolean as its type. GENELEKTRA generates the source code implementing the contextual values. GEN-ELEKTRA reads the specification above and emits the classes Environment, Watchdog, and Enabled [226].

A single contextual value has a countable, infinite number of values: one value for every relevant context. These values are available in a key set. The unique key name required to look up individual values is resolved by substitution of the context placeholders [226].

```
1 void printWatchdogStatus (Watchdog::Enabled const & e)
2 {
3     if (e) { cout << "Watchdog is enabled"; }
4 }
```

In ELEKTRA, contextual values are only subject to be changed iff at least one of the context placeholders in the specification coincides with the layer name [226]:

```
1  void enableWatchdogInHighSecurity (Watchdog::Enabled & e)
2  {
3      bool originallyEnabled = e;
4      assert (e.getName () == "/watchdog/%/enabled");
5      e.context ().with<Security> ("high")([&]{
6          e = true; // security context "high" active here
7          assert (e.getName () == "/watchdog/high/enabled");
8      }); // end of security context "high"
9      assert (e == originallyEnabled);
10     assert (e.getName () == "/watchdog/%/enabled");
11 }
```

In line 3, we see a read-access of the contextual value e. In line 4, we assert that no `security` context was set before, by checking that the context placeholder `%security%` is replaced by a `%`, i.e., an empty layer. In line 5, we activate the layer `Security` with the argument `"high"` for the layer construction. The lambda function (block after the capture list `[&]`) is executed in the same thread but in another context. In line 9, the contextual value e again has the value and context as before because we left the block where `Security` was activated. The function has a side effect: The contextual value e is modified in the security-context `high`. After calling this function and serializing the configuration settings, we get the resulting configuration setting [226]:

```
1  watchdog/high/enabled=1
```

4.3.2 Synchronization Points

In its essence, our extension defines *synchronization points* for multi-thread-safe synchronization of layers and contextual values. At these synchronization points global locks ensure sequential activations and deactivations. We leave priority concerns to threading facilities of the operating system [226]. We implement our extension as `ContextPolicy` (see Section 3.4.2) called `ThreadContext`.

Because programs access contextual values frequently but change context less frequently, ELEKTRA avoids overhead while reading the value. We achieve this behavior by demanding the introduction of synchronization points by the developer. Code executed at the synchronization points pushes new values to contextual values using the observer pattern. We gain two advantages:

- Performance overhead occurs exclusively during synchronization points and assignments. Reading contextual values still has the same overhead as accessing native variables [235].

- Another advantage of synchronization points is that the user has full control over resource consumption including battery drain that is important for most battery-powered devices [231].

The first synchronization point we introduce is `syncLayers`. The thread of execution uses `syncLayers` to have identical active layers to that it would have had if it had executed every `activate` and `deactivate` of the program itself. After every thread has called `syncLayers`, the whole process has the same active layers.

Example 4.10. Let us consider two threads with a `ThreadContext` c1 and c2, respectively:

```
1 c1.activate<BatteryLow> ();
2
```

```
1
2 c2.syncLayers ();
```

The `Context`'s method `syncLayers` updates the layers of the context c2 accounting for the `activate` in c1, which happened before. After execution of `c2.syncLayers`, the layers in c2 are at par to the context of the other thread c1.   ▲

The need of placing synchronization points seems to be cumbersome when programming. In practice, however, these places are usually evident—when users start new interactions. With a use-case-based approach to software engineering developers systematically find all such places. For optimization purposes, users can avoid synchronization points at less important places. Global optimizations are possible, too. For example, we can ignore synchronization points if we visited one a short time ago. In some architectures we completely remove synchronization points from the main concerns. For example, in architectures with short interactions and notifications on context changes [231]. In some situations this explicit definition of checkpoints yields an advantage. For example, if an algorithm assumes variables to be constant. Then the developer has a way to specify where updates are done safely [226].

Example 4.11. Consider an algorithm that must terminate sooner if the battery is low. Because of the reduction of computation, the device would consume less power. As a first step, we specify a contextual value that defines the accuracy for this algorithm [226]:

```
1 [algorithm/%batterylow%/accuracy]
2   type:=long
3   default:=100
```

As second step, we add a synchronization point before the algorithm. Afterwards, the algorithm calculates its task without any overhead [226]:

```
1 void userInteraction (Algorithm::Accuracy const & accuracy)
2 {
3     accuracy.context ().syncLayers (); // sync accuracy
4     for (long i=0; i<accuracy; ++i)
5     {
6         // calculate Task with given accuracy
7         // contextual value is not changed within loop
8     }
9 }
```

The method `context` returns the `ThreadContext` associated with the contextual value `accuracy`. Then we define a synchronization point using its method `syncLayers`. Every time a synchronization point is passed, all layer changes in other threads are taken into account [226]. The developer is certain that `accuracy` is not changed during the loop starting on line 4 at unwanted places [231]. ▲

4.3.3 Global Activation

We extend our frontend so that `activate` and `deactivate` work across threads [226]. Let us specify a contextual value that provides a security level based on the tampering of the device:

```
1 [security/%tampered%/level]
2   type:=long
3   default:=high
```

Then we share the contextual value in a multi-threaded program with two threads. The local variables c1 and c2 represent the context in the respective left and right thread. They keep track of the currently active layers of their own threads:

```
1 c1.deactivate<Tampered> ();        Security.Level sl (ks, c2);    1
2                                                                    2
3 // Security unchanged              c2.activate<Security> (sl);    3
4 // (missed update)                 // Tampered now deactivated    4
```

After *synchronization points*, contexts integrate layer switches that occurred in other threads. Every activate and deactivate works as synchronization point. On the left thread in line 1, we deactivate the layer Tampered. The change happens immediately in the left thread but needs till line 3 of the right thread because no synchronization point occurs earlier. The activation in line 3 pulls the deactivated layer to the context c2. Thus the contextual value sl (security level) is affected by the layer change of Tampered. ELEKTRA guarantees that sl gets aware of its new context before the Security layer gets activated. At the end of the left side's thread, the layer Tampered is deactivated and Security has the value it had in c1 from the beginning. At the end of the right side's thread, Tampered is deactivated and Security is activated. All contextual values connected with c2, including sl, are updated at that point.

We implicitly synchronize all layers with any activation to be sure that the activation is not using out-dated information. The synchronization of layers before layer (de)activations itself is a preferable property: This way we guarantee that every context in every thread consists of the same activated layers with the same layer values. This is essential if we activate a layer that internally uses contextual values. Without layer synchronization done first, the contextual values used during activations would have wrong values. We want to avoid that because of our requirement:

Requirement 6. *Configuration libraries must provide ways to keep transient and persistent views consistent.*

4.3.4 Coordination

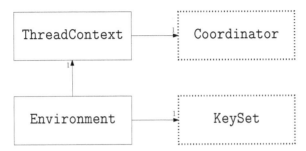

Figure 4.2: Coordination between threads, showing the major components involved. The dotted boxes are to be shared between threads. Arrows express a composition [226].

In Figure 4.2 we display the major parts necessary for coordination between contextual values. The key set is used as the set of all values in every context as needed for lookup and serialization. The class `Environment` is the generated class hierarchy's root. Objects of `ThreadContext` encapsulate all layers active in one thread. As the name suggests, every thread uses its own `ThreadContext`. Finally, the `Coordinator` guards coordination between `ThreadContext`. The boxes, which are drawn with the dotted dash style, are only instantiated once per process and are shared between all threads [226].

We do not need any locks or atomic values in `KeySet`, `ThreadContext` nor the `Environment` (the contextual values). Instead we delegate all coordination work to objects of the class `Coordinator`. Both `ThreadContext` and `Coordinator` employ the observer pattern internally. By the use of callbacks, we completely decouple the coordination and the key sets [226].

Applications do not have restrictions of how many objects of the class `Coordinator` or `KeySet` are used. They can be used within plugins or otherwise nested applications. Nevertheless, ELEKTRA imposes the following constraints: Every `Coordinator` is bound to exactly one `KeySet`, every `ThreadContext` is liable to exactly one `Coordinator`, and again every contextual value is accountable for exactly one `ThreadContext` [226].

Assignment

Suppose `value` is specified to be a contextual value of type long integer [226]:

```
1 [value]
2   type:=long
3   default:=0
```

Then we assign and use the contextual value as an integer in source code [226]:

```
1 value = 8;
2 assert (value == 8);
```

Different from reading contextual values, the assignment of contextual values has additional overhead. For every change of the value, next to the cache, the underlying key set needs to be updated in a thread-safe way. The design decision is because of the assumption that customization (assignment) occurs less often than accessing values and changing layers. The decision leads to desired properties:

1. Freshly created contextual values have an up-to-date value with respect to assignments, even across threads [226]:

```
1 value = 5;                      ThreadContext tc (c);         1
2                                 Value value (ks, tc);         2
3                                 assert (value == 5);          3
4                                                               4
```

2. The data structure key set is kept up to date and its serialization always contains the latest assignments [226].

Thread-based Layers

Layers, that compare the current thread identification with a selected thread identification, are a powerful technique. When these layers are activated globally, they selectively influence threads [226].

Example 4.12. We want to activate a layer only within a single thread specified with the thread identification `m_selected`. Implementing this layer is straightforward [226]:

```
1 class Thread : public Layer
2 {
3 public:
4     Thread (pthread_t selected) :
5         m_selected (selected) {}
6     string id () const { return "thread"; }
7     string operator() () const {
8         if (pthread_self () == m_selected) return "active";
9         return "";
10     };
11 private:
12     pthread_t m_selected;
13 };
```

At line 8, we have to check if the current thread identification is identical to the thread identification of a selected thread. The method `pthread_self` tells us the thread identification of the calling thread. If the current thread is the selected thread, we return that the layer is `"active"`. Otherwise, we return an empty string to tell that the layer is deactivated [226]. ▲

The same technique is applied to change the context for a pool of threads. Instead remembering a single selected thread, we remember a set of relevant threads [226].

4.3.5 Result and Use

Here we answer the research question:

RQ 5.3. How can we improve on the usability of context-aware frontends if being used concurrently from several threads?

> **Finding.** *We improve contextual values by defining synchronization points that allow thread-safe use of contextual values and layer activations across selected threads.*

We described an extension in which we use the policy implementation `ThreadContext` instead of `Context` (from the previous Section 4.2). For multi-threaded applications, we have to set `ContextPolicyIs` [226] (see Section 3.4.2 for details of `ContextPolicy`).

A function `main` that uses multi-threaded ELEKTRA can be written as follows [226]:

```
1  int main (int argc, char ** argv)
2  {
3      KeySet ks;
4      ksGetOpt (argc, argv, ks);
5      KDB kdb;
6      kdb.get (ks);
7      Coordinator c;
8      ThreadContext tc (c);
9      Environment<ContextPolicyIs<ThreadContext>> env (ks,tc);
10     // the rest of the program using env
11 }
```

The `ContextPolicyIs` in line 9 changes the policy class for all contextual values for this instantiation of the `Environment`.

4.4   Persistent Contextual Values as Inter-process Layers

While the manually written layers provide some opportunities as shown in Section 4.3.4, in nearly all cases the layers are boilerplate code pursuing the same goals:

1. Making activation of layers *context aware*: Here we need to take a contextual value as parameter for the layer.

2. Allowing *persistence* of layers: Doing so, we share layers across applications.

In this section we describe the novel idea to use contextual values for layer activation, avoiding manual implementation of layers. We aim at combining layer activations with contextual values fulfilling the goals above. We suggest to use contextual values as parameters to `activate` and `with`. Because contextual values are context aware, by definition, they always consider their context. By persisting contextual values we enable synchronization of layer activations between applications. We keep our previous performance properties: Reading contextual values is as fast as reading native variables [231].

Example 4.13. Let us consider internationalized software. As a prerequisite, we need a specification shared between applications:

```
1 [language]
2   type:=string
3   default:=english
4 [person/%language%/greeting]
5   type:=string
6   default:=hello
```

Using this specification a code generator yields the classes `Person`, `Greeting`, and `Language`. The classes ensure contextual value semantics.

Contextual values help us, for example, to easily display translated messages. Using the concepts as introduced before, it is difficult to ensure that every application has activated the same language. We would need to activate the correct layer in every application individually. There was no straightforward way for one application to tell all other applications that the language has changed. We propose to activate such layers with code-generated contextual classes (such as `Language`) [231]:

```
1 void greet (Person const & p, Language const & language)
2 {
3     p.activate (language);
4     cout << p.greeting << endl;
5 }
```

In line 3 we activate the contextual value `language`. The execution environment initializes contextual values at application startup, providing sensible default values changeable by settings for different contexts. The build-in persistence of key sets allows us to activate the same layer across applications [231]. ▲

The rest of the section is structured as follows:

Section 4.4.1: We describe the semantics of inter-process layers.

Section 4.4.2: An intra-process notification system is allowing us to update the context of contextual values when other contextual values, representing layers, change.

Section 4.4.3: An inter-process notification system is telling us when to reparse configuration files.

4.4.1   Inter-process Layers

Because we use contextual values as layers, all properties of context specifications are reused. The only missing information to enable activation of contextual values is the layer name. To make specifications more compact, we decided that by default the layer name is the basename of the contextual key names. This convention yields appropriate layer names for most contextual values [231].

Example 4.14. Let us define a contextual value to be used as layer:

```
1 [%language%/country]
2    default:=
```

The contextual value `country` has the layer name `country`.   ▲

Layer names, unlike contextual values, do not form a hierarchy. In some situations the basename does not present the right choice. In such situations we use the property value of `layer/name` to select a layer name.

Example 4.15. Let us facilitate a country code to identify countries [231]:

```
1 [country/%language%/code]
2    type:=string
3    layer/name:=country
4    default:=C
```

Because the layer name `code` (derived from the basename) would be too generic, we use property `layer/name` to rename it. Then activating the contextual value `env.country.code` activates the layer `country` [231].   ▲

We have a complete context specification as necessary for contextual values and layers, fulfilling the requirement:

Requirement 3. *A single configuration specification must be able to include all information to generate all artifacts needed for configuration settings.*

Context-aware Activation

With this extension, developers do not have to consider context when activating layers. Context-aware activations correctly consider up-to-date contextual values.

Example 4.16. Let us define some contextual values [231]:

```
1 [location]
2   type:=string
3   description:=GPS position in ??N??W
4   default:=
5 [%location%/country]
6   type:=string
7   default:=
8 [person/%country%/greeting]
9   type:=string
10  default:=Hello
```

To activate the layer `country` and `location` we use [231]:

```
1 void greet (Person & p, Country & country, Location & location)
2 {
3     p.context ().activate (location);
4     p.context ().activate (country);
5     cout << p.greeting << endl;
6 }
```

If `location` and `country` would be layers without contextual values as described in earlier sections, exactly these layers would be activated without influencing each other. This means that `activate` in line 4 would not take the location changed in line 3

into account. But since location and country are contextual values (implemented
by the contextual classes Location and Country), they factor in context and the
activations correctly influence each other. In the example above, after the activation
of the contextual value location, the position of the contextual value country is
updated. Line 4 updates the contextual value country as needed by the established
context [231]. Given the configuration settings:

```
1 location=48N16O
2 48N16O/country=austria
3 person/austria/greeting=Griaz enk!
```

The output of the program is:

```
1 Griaz enk!                                                                    ▲
```

Activation via Assignment

A not-so-obvious property of activating contextual values is that, after activation, developers control (de)activation via changing the values of contextual values [231].

Example 4.17. We deactivate the layer location by an assignment:

```
1 void emptyGreet (Person & p, Location & location)
2 {
3     location = "";
4     p.activate (location);
5     cout << p.greeting << endl;
6 }
```

After line 3, the contextual value location has an empty string in its current context.
In line 4 we activate the layer location. Despite the activation, because of the empty
value, the context placeholder location is replaced with %, i. e., it is deactivated. The
greeting in line 5 is according to a deactivated layer location.   ▲

Example 4.18. No layer switch occurs after we have done a deactivation of a contextual value:

```
1  void assignLanguage (Language & language)
2  {
3      language.context ().activate (language);
4      language = "";
5      // layer language deactivated
6      language = "spanish";
7      // layer switch to spanish
8      language.context ().deactivate (language);
9      language = "english";
10     // layer still deactivated
11 }
```

As precondition, to make contextual values act as a layer, we activate the contextual value (line 3). Layers with an empty value (line 4) impact contextual values in the same way as otherwise deactivated layers: Placeholders are replaced with %. Only after explicit deactivation in line 8, assignments of the contextual value `language` do not interfere with other contextual values anymore [231].   ▲

In summary we have two different ways to deactivate layers:

1. We call `deactivate` with the contextual value as parameter.

2. We activate a contextual value that contains an empty string or assign an empty value to an already activated contextual value.

The different deactivations have an important difference: A layer with an empty value can be activated by assigning a different string, which is not possible after calling `deactivate`.

4.4.2 Intra-process Notification

In previous sections we assumed that changes of a contextual value only happen by an assignment to a contextual value. In this extension we do not need this assumption anymore. We introduce a reloading mechanism for updates of the underlying key set [231].

For such in-memory synchronizations we provide the method `sync` [231]. Invoking `sync` updates all contextual values with the values the key set currently has and makes sure that correct layers are active afterwards.

Example 4.19. To fetch the latest configuration settings from the hard disk and update all contextual values according to the new configuration settings, we use:

```
1  void doSync (Context & c, KDB & kdb, KeySet & ks)
2  {
3      kdb.get (ks);
4      c.sync ();
5      // contextual values are updated;
6      // and layers are activated accordingly
7  }
```

In line 3 we update the `KeySet ks`, which is connected with the contextual values. In line 4 we execute the in-memory update to reload the contextual values [231].   ▲

The behavior of the synchronization via `sync` does not differ from performing `activate` or `deactivate` via assignment. Developers can think of `sync` as assigning all changed contextual values in the correct order [231].

Activation Order

For correct behavior of `sync` we need to consider the dependences between contextual values. Contextual values with context placeholders (`%...%`) depend on contextual values with a basename identical to the context placeholder's name. We use a topological sort based on Kahn to order according to the dependences [144, 231].

As long as layers and contextual values were completely separate concepts, we cannot build dependence cycles: It was not possible that layers depend on contextual values. Activation of contextual values, however, introduces the possibility of cyclic dependences.

Example 4.20. We need at least two contextual values to build a cycle [231]:

```
1 [%country%/language]
2   type:=string
3   default:=
4 [%language%/country]
5   type:=string
6   default:=
```

Then we need to craft configuration settings to make use of the cycle:

```
1 swiss/language=de
2 luxembourg/language=fr
3 fr/country=swiss
4 de/country=luxembourg
```

If the application activates the layer country, ELEKTRA would need the value of the language layer and vice versa. Activation of layers within such cycles lead to toggling values [231].

Luckily such cycles only stem from design errors and are unwanted. Thus we prohibit such cycles already in the context specification. These situations shall be detected early by checking the specification [231], following the requirement:

Requirement 5. *The specification must enable code generation and inconsistencies must be ruled out during compilation.*

4.4.3   Inter-process Notification

Because of diverse requirements in different applications and systems, we took care that ELEKTRA exhibits modular design principles [225, 230]. We decided to give applications different inter-process notification methods to choose from [231], complying with the Requirement **2**:

Requirement 2. *A configuration library must be able to integrate (legacy) systems and must fully support (legacy) configuration files.*

Whenever processes use kdb.set to modify the underlying configuration files the notification mechanisms fire. Every interested process listens to the notifications and then fetches the updated configuration settings using `kdb.get`. Once every thread has passed a synchronization point, the application is fully up to date [231], fulfilling the requirement:

Requirement 6. *Configuration libraries must provide ways to keep transient and persistent views consistent.*

As shown in Example 4.19, `kdb.get` updates the contextual values. On conflicts ELEKTRA supports a three-way merge [231]. A ***three-way merge*** implies that we consider the common ancestor next to our internal (the application's) and the external (the system's) configuration settings. Using a three-way merge, we avoid errors in situations where configuration settings are clearly changed by one party (either internal or external). If both sides change the same configuration value conflictingly, the three-way merge cannot help and we usually need to propagate the decision to the user.

With inter-process notification in place, we answer the research question:

RQ 5.4. How can we share context between applications?

Finding. *We found that most of the time, contextual values have the necessary information to be used as replacement to manual implementation of layers. As main benefit, we always get context-aware layer activation. Using persistence and inter-process notification, we share layer information between applications.*

CHAPTER 5

Backends

You are responsible for the predictable consequences of your actions.

— Noam Chomsky

System administrators are rarely confronted with the developer's frontends. They are concerned about making applications in the system work together as a whole. In this section we deal with modular and programmable backends. We explore extensions of SPECELEKTRA for these needs, answering the research question:

RQ 6. Which concepts are needed for context-aware backends to fulfill the requirements as unveiled in Chapter 2?

Only a hand-full factors determine how well an application is integrated into its system, for example: logging, available external interfaces, look&feel of the user interface, and user interaction (such as shortcuts and menus). In modern applications these aspects are configurable. We attempt to exploit already present configuration access points to make the system feel as if it was made from one piece [227].

Currently, such an endeavor requires a user to configure each application manually. We have an instance of the *configuration integration problem* as described in Section 0.1.4. In this chapter, we mitigate the configuration integration problem by introducing a system-wide, programmable *key database*. The key database can be accessed by any of the frontends described earlier.

In Section 5.1, we describe how abstractions help in solving the configuration integration problem. We describe the history of earlier failed attempts to create a universal backend and show how modularization of backends helped to overcome the challenges. Then we elaborate on the current state of how to integrate already existing configuration files into the system-wide key database using backends.

In Section 5.2, we elaborate on context-aware lookups in the key database. We describe how layers are integrated in the backend. We assume that applications use one of the frontends discussed in the previous chapter.

In Section 5.3, we get rid of the assumption that application's source code needs to be modified and integrate already existing frontends. We show how the key database helps us to integrate applications without compromising modularity. We demonstrate improved modularity in the areas of suitable configuration settings and configuration validation.

In Section 5.4, we elaborate on how to adapt widely used frontends. We present a solution of how to improve context awareness of applications without any modifications in the source code.

5.1 Configuration Abstractions

In this section we describe different levels of configuration abstractions, exploring the research question:

RQ 6.1. What is the design space for abstractions of context-aware configuration in backends?

5.1.1 History

As in the frontend, also in the backend the most problematic part was too weak or wrong abstraction. In particular, passing out internals about the backends caused many hard-to-fix problems.

In the first versions of ELEKTRA, every key had a direct relation to a file in the file system. The metadata of the key was the metadata of the file, for example, access permissions. Soon we realized that this abstraction is poor. Limitations of file systems directly affected ELEKTRA. For example, every persisted key in its own file needed the block size of the underlying file system. At that time, the block size usually was 4 kilobytes, but many configuration values only have the size of a few bytes.

Out of necessity, we enabled system administrators to choose between different backends. We implemented a Berkeley DB backend to avoid the mentioned waste of resources. In these backends, the leaky abstractions were troublesome: The metadata and the direct relation to files was not useful anymore.

Even more problematic was the semantics to get or set individual keys. It was time-consuming to implement backends, which serialized configuration settings to configuration files: It was a complicated endeavor to modify a single `Key` in the middle of the configuration file efficiently. We have to check if a different process modified the file (conflict-detection), parse the file, do the necessary modifications, and write the changes back. This implementation has to be repeated for every configuration file parser.

For ELEKTRA 0.7, released on 17th October, 2008, we thought of the following solution: We wanted to use capabilities to describe what a backend is able to do. If a backend cannot change individual keys within the file, its capabilities would say so. The capabilities were a way to describe that backends were incompatible to some file system semantics. Unfortunately every backend, except for file system backends, was incompatible in some way. The capability descriptions were long and complicated.

From the user's point of view, most of the backends were not an option: If a single application needed a specific capability, the user is already tied to the specific backend. To defuse the situation, we introduced a way to *mount* several backends into the system-wide key database. Hence, if an application had specific requirements for the backend, we mount this particular backend.

In ELEKTRA 0.8 released on 5th May, 2012, we implemented a full abstraction in that frontends are no longer able to distinguish between different kinds of backends. Backends only differ in:

- Their quality characteristics, such as their performance.

- The kind of configuration settings they accept and reject.

- Characteristics important for system administrators and legacy systems, such as the configuration file format.

This history resembles that of file systems. Our solution is similar to what modern virtual file systems provide. The main difference to file systems is that ELEKTRA:

- builds upon key-value pairs and not files, and

- provides configuration abstractions such as default values and transformation.

5.1.2   Key Database

Here we have a top-down discussion of the configuration abstraction included in the key database. The *key database* stores all configuration settings in configuration files. This way, the operating system takes care of security via file system permissions [232].

The bootstrapping (see Section 3.2.2) is important to fulfill Requirement **1**:

Requirement 1. *A configuration library must be simple to use, easily available, lightweight, efficient, and have an excellent out-of-the-box experience.*

It is a prerequisite to have a global view to enable sharing of configuration settings:

Requirement 4. *A configuration library must allow us to share configuration settings.*

Plugins

The backends delegate their complete work to plugins. We recently added many plugins to support even more functionality for configuration access. The figure on page 183 shows the current state of plugins with dependences. For some functionality, we are already aware of a saturation: Only small details are missing. For other functionality, such as supporting more configuration file formats and validation specifications, we currently do not see any limitation for the number of plugins that would be useful.

Implementing too many features in one plugin is problematic. Many aspects would clutter the source code, making the plugins difficult to maintain. To alleviate this problem, ***several plugins*** together build up a backend. Each plugin implements a single concrete requirement, as standard in many architectures [50, 185]. Hence, we ended up with the large number of 78 plugins as shown in full-page figure on the next page. Arrows indicate plugins that *provide* some abstract functionality. Square boxes are providers. Names in ellipses are concrete plugins not used as provider names. We did not include plugins without arrows.

The architecture allows plugins to have external dependences without adding the dependence to ELEKTRA's core. Not every plugin has the burden to be portable, instead highly-optimized plugins are useful alternatives to generic plugins. With this separation, each plugin and the core of ELEKTRA stays minimal.

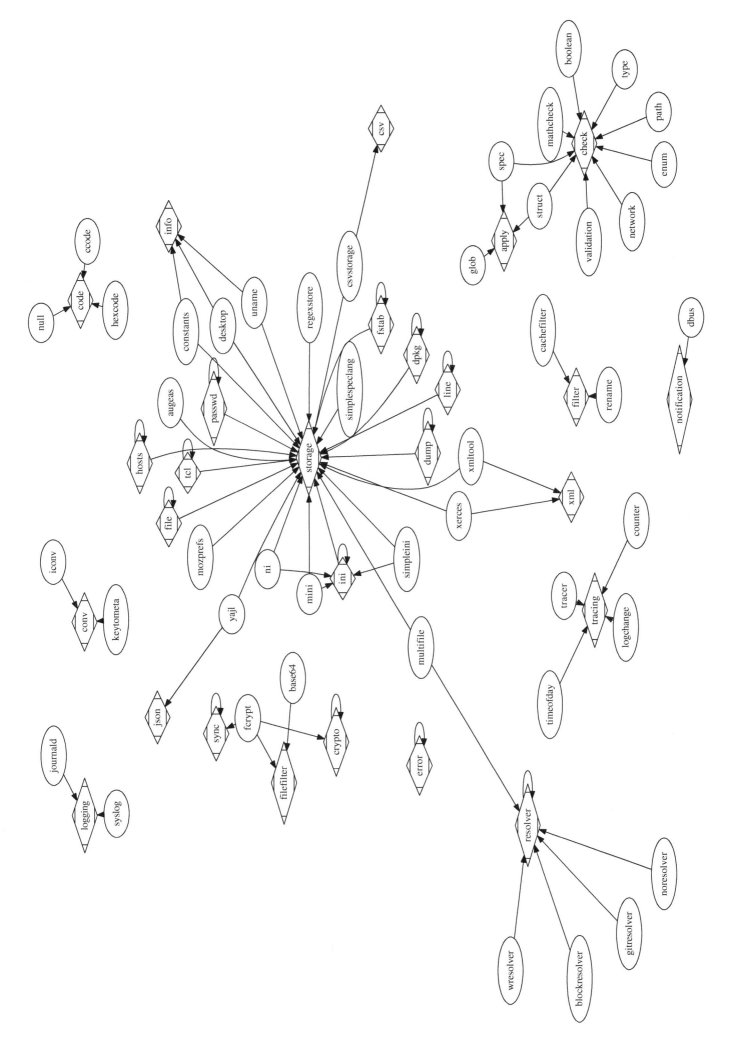

Storage Plugins

Configuration file formats have countless variations in their syntax. The repository of Augeas [177] (that covers a small part of GNU/Linux configuration files) already contains lenses for 181 configuration file formats. Plugins concerned with parsing and serializing configuration files are called ***storage plugins***. Metadata enables reconstruction of configuration-file-format-specific syntax and information, such as comments.

To better cope with the vast number of existing configuration file formats, ELEKTRA benefits from techniques to rapidly implement many formats. ELEKTRA currently supports more than 190 different configuration file formats, not counting the number of combinations the plugin configurations would allow. It has support for popular formats such as XML, JSON, INI, and CSV, but also many other file formats typically found in /etc, supporting Requirement **2**:

Requirement 2. *A configuration library must be able to integrate (legacy) systems and must fully support (legacy) configuration files.*

Resolver Plugin

Different operating systems and distributions have different locations for configuration files. ELEKTRA's configuration abstractions set aside these differences. During the installation of applications, ELEKTRA remembers the choice of the respective operating system and distribution in the key database. Some differences are not static but depend on calls to the operating system, for example, to locate the user's home directory. ELEKTRA handles these situations at run-time using ***resolver plugins***. Whenever ELEKTRA needs the name of a configuration file, the plugins resolve the path name from the static and dynamic information sources [227].

The plugin `resolver` is also responsible for all other non-portable tasks related to configuration access. These tasks include overwriting the configuration file atomically, detecting conflicts, and checking for updates. The plugin `resolver` provides the following guarantees[1]:

- Configuration files are only parsed by `kdb.get` again if they were modified.

- If any plugin fails during `kdb.set` (except of logging plugins that are executed after committing the changes), no backend will persist any changes.

---

[1] The guarantees depend on guarantees file systems offer. For example, if an uncooperative external write operation happens within one time unit of the file system, conflicts cannot be detected.

- If an external application modifies a configuration file, a subsequent `kdb.set` operation fails and a conflict will be reported.

The idea of extracting all the operating system-dependent parts from the storage plugins has advantages: An important benefit is that adding support for a new operating system is reduced to implementing a resolver plugin. Moreover, it enables the support for completely different ways to retrieve configuration files. For example, we implemented resolvers that directly work with Git repositories or fetch files from URLs.

5.2 Context-aware Lookup

In this section we elaborate on design, requirements, and the use of *context-aware lookup*. The context-aware lookup includes the layer-based lookup and the cascading lookup. We start with the *cascading lookup*, which supports namespaces (Section 5.2.1) and links (Section 5.2.2). Then we continue with the layer-based lookup in Section 5.2.3. In Section 5.2.4, we discuss the goals of such specifications to mitigate run-time errors. Overall, we answer the question:

RQ 6.2. How can we enable context awareness in backends without support from frontends?

5.2.1 Namespaces

One dimension of configuration settings in the cascading lookup is their **namespace**. We already mentioned that configuration settings and specifications are separated. Namespaces provide the way to separate keys of different locations, purpose, and importance from each other.

Applications aim to have no hard-coded namespace in their source code. This way applications are abstracted over the concrete configuration source. With namespaces, we are able to uniquely identify different sources of configuration settings [227]. Only system administrator tools directly work with namespaces because they need full control. For introspection system administrators prefer context-aware lookup as they are interested to see configuration settings exactly as applications see them. ELEKTRA supports the following namespaces with the given prioritization as default [227]:

SPEC for configuration files containing configuration specifications, stored in some system location such as `/usr/share`.

PROC for process-specific configuration settings, for example, command-line options and
environment variables, fulfilling the requirement:

Requirement 11. *A configuration library must support all three popular ways for
configuration access: configuration files, command-line options, and environment
variables.*

DIR for configuration files in a special directory, for example, `.htaccess` of the Apache
Web server or `.git` in the current working directory.

USER for configuration files in the user's home directory.

SYSTEM for configuration files located at positions of system-wide relevance, for example,
below `/etc`.

(DEFAULT) (as given from the property `default`) for default values that are directly
derived from the configuration specification.

Our justification for this fixed prioritization is: Most applications already use this order,
therefore system administrators expect it. Nevertheless, in some situations exceptions
are needed. Links and the property `namespace` define such exceptions.

5.2.2 Links

We designed the configuration specification to be extensible and independent of a concrete
programming language.

Example 5.1. Consider shortcuts of applications: Nearly every graphical user interface
has a shortcut for quitting the application. The default is often Ctrl+Q. Nearly every
application provides a way to change the default. But we miss a way to change the
shortcut for all applications [227]. Using ELEKTRA we specify how we share shortcuts
between editors by [227]:

```
1 [our_editor/quit]
2   fallback/#0:=/editorconfig/shortcut/quit
3   fallback/#1:=/kde/kate/ActionProp/Def/file_quit
4   fallback/#2:=/vim/map/:qa<CR>
5   fallback/#3:=/emacs/keyboard-escape-quit
```

The property `fallback` establishes a link to other configuration setting. The links are used if the key (here `our_editor/quit`) is not found. ▲

Using such simple specifications, we establish a single configuration setting to change shortcuts of all applications. The novelty is that these links are globally available and introspectable [227], complying with the requirement:

Requirement 7. *Configuration settings and specifications must be introspectable.*

This functionality is implemented in `ksLookup` because only then we are always consistent with the latest changes of the in-memory key set. Plugins can extend the lookup functionality. For example, with the help of plugins default values are derived from other values [227]. Using such links and transformations, we enable applications to use configuration settings of other applications, fulfilling Requirement **13**:

Requirement 13. *A configuration library must mitigate the configuration integration problem.*

Example

Suppose we have no configuration settings but only the following specification:

```
1 [our_editor/quit][morekeywords={namespace,fallback}]
2   namespace/#0:=system
3   fallback/#0:=/vim/quit
4   default:=Ctrl+Q
5
6 [vim/quit]
7   namespace/#0:=user
8   default:=:q
```

Then a `ksLookup` invocation, with the key name `/our_editor/quit`, conducts the following steps:

1. it looks up the key `spec:/our_editor/quit` successfully,

2. it skips the layer-based lookup (because no property `context` is present),

3. it calls `lookupBySpec` with the key from the step before,

4. it skips override (because no property `override` is present),

5. it fails in searching for the key in the namespace SYSTEM (because no configuration file is present), and

6. because of the property `fallback` it recursively continues with the steps:

    a) it looks up the key `/vim/quit` in namespace SPEC successfully,

    b) it skips the layer-based lookup,

    c) it calls `lookupBySpec` with this key,

    d) it skips properties `context` and `override` for `/vim/quit`, and

    e) it fails in searching for the key `/vim/quit` in the namespace USER, and

7. it uses the default value `Ctrl+Q` (but not the default value `:q`, because we only consider top-level default values).

5.2.3   Layer-based Lookup

Here we discuss the generalization of namespaces, called **layer-based lookup**, that avoids some limitations of the cascading lookup:

- Instead of fixed namespaces, arbitrary layer names are used.

- Instead of having a single dimension (one namespace per key), an arbitrary number of context placeholders are used to look up a single key.

Layer-based lookups implement *contextual values* [275]. The layer-based lookup shall return the correct variables with respect to the currently active layers. As running example, we use vibration of mobile phones. Let us start by considering if a mobile phone is in the pocket:

```
1 [phone/call/vibration]
2   type:=boolean
3   context:=/phone/call/%inpocket%/vibration
```

In this example, `vibration` is a contextual value. Because the specification is configurable, users naturally have a chance to modify the behavior regarding their needs. To turn on vibrations for phones in a pocket, we would use [232]:

```
1 phone/call/inpocket/vibration=on
2 phone/call/notinpocket/vibration=off
```

Context Sensors

To make the layers work within any frontend, we use out-of-process layer activation and deactivation by facilitating the key database. We call processes actively changing the key database to update layer values **context sensors**. A context sensor changes configuration settings named as /env/layer/<layer name> to reflect the current situation of layers. This change in the key database influences all processes across the whole system and can change contextual values [232]. We identified three different kinds of context sensors:

Information within the key database: In some cases the wanted information is already present in some other parts of the key database. Plugins read context information and integrate this information into the key database. In such situations, we create a link from /env/layer to the already-present key [232]. For example, we mount the plugin uname to /env/uname and create a link from /env/layer/nodename to /env/uname/nodename. Then the layer value of nodename contains the nodename.

Hooks: Some systems provide hooks to be executed on context changes. For example, if new software is installed or the network connection changes, often custom hooks are provided. In these custom hooks, we update /env/layer according to the state change.

Context sensor daemon: In the other cases, we facilitate daemons (active processes). They observe changes of the system, accumulate and interpret the data, and finally write the condensed layer information into /env/layer. Doing so, they implement value transformations, hysteresis, and even feedback control systems [232]. For example, an active process combines different temperature and proximity sensors. When a context sensor detects that the device is outside the pocket, it changes /env/layer/inpocket to notinpocket. Then the layer name inpocket of the contextual value vibration is changed accordingly.

Example

We want to complete the example `inpocket` to demonstrate recursion and several layers.
Think of a mobile phone lying on a table during a meeting inside a building, i. e. [232]:

```
1 env/layer/inpocket=notinpocket
2 env/layer/inmeeting=inmeeting
3 env/layer/inbuilding=inbuilding
```

Context sensors continuously update these values but we assume them to be static during
a lookup. Similar to the layer `inpocket`, the layer `inbuilding`'s value can be derived
from physical sensor values. Such context is usually derived from GPS or in-door location
services [198]. The layer value `inmeeting`, however, cannot be derived from physical
sensors. Instead the context sensor needs to query the person's schedule to get to the
relevant data. Such context sensors's data sources are called *virtual sensors* [24].

Suppose the application on the mobile phone executes the following non-context-aware
source code [232]. We show the source code someone who avoids type-safe frontends
would use:

```
1 Key * vibration = ksLookup (ks, Key ("/phone/call/vibration"));
2 if (!strcmp (keyString (vibration), "1"))
3 {
4     /* commence vibration */
5 }
```

Then we need a context specification [232]:

```
1 [phone/call/vibration]
2   type:=boolean
3   context:=/phone/call/%inbuilding%/vibration
4 [phone/call/inbuilding/vibration]
5   type:=boolean
6   context:=/phone/call/%inpocket%/%inmeeting%/vibration
```

And we need configuration settings [232]:

```
1 phone/call/inpocket/inmeeting/vibration=on
2 phone/call/notinpocket/inmeeting/vibration=off
3 phone/call/notinpocket/notinmeeting/vibration=on
4 phone/call/inpocket/notinmeeting/vibration=on
5 phone/call/notinbuilding/vibration=on
```

When the mobile phone gets a call, `ksLookup` performs the following steps [232]:

1. It starts to look up `/phone/call/vibration` and finds the property `context` in the context specification.

2. It finds the property value `/phone/call/%inbuilding%/vibration`, and replaces `%inbuilding%` with `inbuilding`.

3. In the next recursion step, it looks up `/phone/call/inbuilding/vibration`, in which we find the context specification `/phone/call/%inpocket%/%inmeeting%/vibration`.

4. It replaces the two layer names `inpocket` and `inmeeting` with the layer values `notinpocket` and `inmeeting`, respectively.

5. In the last recursion step, it looks up `/phone/call/notinpocket/inmeeting/vibration`.

6. It does not find a context specification for `/phone/call/notinpocket/inmeeting/vibration`. Hence, the layer-based lookup returns the configuration setting for this key name that has the configuration value `off`.

7. As a result, the phone does not vibrate.

Discussion

Compared with activating layers in the frontend, the solution implemented in the backend has different qualities:

1. We avoid hard-coded context specifications within the key names that are only working with support from frontends.

2. We are more flexible in changing context specifications, and avoid recompilations.

3. We enable other applications to access the context specifications.

4. We do not have ways to express dynamic scoping within the program. Context sensors only have the equivalence of an `activate` construct. We have to dispense the power of the `with` construct.

Finding. *Context awareness, implemented in a backend, allows us to share context in the form of layers across applications. Compared to a solution in context-aware frontends, we lose dynamic scopes, but we gain links and recursion.*

5.2.4   Configuration Specification Checking

One of the essentials of configuration specification languages is their capabilities to thoroughly validate configuration settings. They have the benefit that inconsistencies within the configuration settings and specifications can be found. We have two different kinds of type checking, taking place at different stages:

1. While accessing configuration specifications, we can type check if the configuration specification SpecElektra uses its types consistently.

2. While accessing configuration settings, we must type check if the configuration settings adheres to the configuration specification to prevent misconfiguration.

Here we discuss the type checking of configuration specifications, which means to check SpecElektra for internal consistency.

Goals of Static Checking

Lamport and Paulson [163] summarize debates about static typing of specification languages. They suggest that it *"may be possible to have the best of both worlds by adding typing annotations to an untyped specification language"*. Elektra follows this recommendation: We use properties to add types to an otherwise untyped language.

For lookups, more static checking is preferable because errors at lookup-time cannot be handled properly. The developer expects that every lookup terminates and returns a configuration value of the correct type.

The goals of checking SPECELEKTRA are:

- Defaults must be present for safe lookups (see Section 3.4.6). This goal also implies that there must be at least one valid configuration setting.

- Layer dependences must not build cycles (see Section 4.4.2).

- Links must not refer to each other in cycles.

- Types of default values must be compatible with the types of the keys.

- Every link and the pointee must have compatible types.

- Every contextual interpretation of a key must yield a compatible type.

Currently, most parts of the specification checker are not implemented in the public repository and static type checking remains future work. The implementation is expected to be straight-forward but unfortunately we lacked the time. Some of the goals are part of a not-yet-included type-checker for SPECELEKTRA.

5.3 Modular Abstractions

Up to now, we discussed context-aware configuration. In this section, we will enhance our ideas to *suitable*, context-aware configuration. To recognize suitability of configuration settings, we need to enable users to specify their requirements. We explain the modular abstractions of the specification language SPECELEKTRA to improve modularity, and integrate more applications. We focus on the research question:

RQ 6.3. Which abstractions retain and improve modularity of configuration access in FLOSS applications?

The section is structured as follows:

1. By unifying configuration access, we put ourself in danger of coupling applications and reducing modularity. As first step in Section 5.3.1, we investigate how we retain modularity between applications.

2. As next step in Section 5.3.2, we elaborate on abstractions that improve modularity beyond the current situation.

3. With these modular abstractions, we have the potential to connect any configuration settings within the system, without unwanted coupling. In Section 5.3.3, we will use the modular abstraction to express requirements and derive suitable configuration settings from it.

4. In Section 5.3.4, we demonstrate the need of the modularity as introduced before. We will focus on the area of configuration validation.

Systems become increasingly complex and their requirements more fluid. Only with highly adaptable systems we have a chance to fulfill user requirements, we did not anticipate during development. Modularity presents a confirmed mechanism to cope with complexity. Instead of rebuilding every system from scratch, we aim towards configuring existing systems to create new systems [19, 230].

Unfortunately, most software does not yet consider to be part of an integral whole. Most software, however, provides run-time configurability. To integrate an application into a system, it usually needs to be configured individually. When user requirements change, many configuration files need to be adapted, which is an error-prone process: Configuration files differ in their format, and software to access them is implemented in many languages. To mitigate this problem we introduce modular abstractions, which enable encoding requirements uniformly as configuration settings to tune the whole system. These high-level configuration settings automatically influence configuration settings of every individual application as specified [230].

As running example we use a location-tracking device. On the location-tracking device we install `ntpd`. The time synchronization daemon `ntpd` reads a configuration file named `ntp.conf` at startup. In system-wide context changes, such as when the device switches to battery, the user wants to modify many configuration settings in order to save energy. One possibility to save power is the reduction of NTP-polling frequency. Some software directly supports changes of these settings via inter-process communication. To make changes persistent, however, we have to change the poll settings in `ntp.conf`. After changes in `ntp.conf`, we notify `ntpd` to reparse its configuration settings without the need for other inter-process communication. The same steps are applied to other applications, for example, to reduce the frequency of polling GPS data [230].

In the previous Chapter 4, we introduced techniques that required developers to make decisions about contexts at design time. Such techniques are not suitable for context and requirements not known during implementation. We investigate in postponing decisions about context until deployment or even run-time. We aim at a language that externally specifies configuration settings and its context: By specification changes we adapt our system to the users requirements—even after deployment [230].

Two major directions for configuration accesses are [230]:

1. Some proprietary and embedded systems already have system-wide key databases. Then every application easily interacts with all configuration settings of the whole system. Such systems often already employ parts of the suggestions we initially made.

   The downside is the strong coupling of all applications to such a platform. Developers need to rewrite applications to work with the key database. We want to avoid such coupling.

2. In other systems, such as most FLOSS applications, every application uses its own configuration file. Every application has full control over every aspect of its configuration accesses. We gain a fully modular system without compromise. Although the fully modular approach has some advantages, it completely fails with our Goal Abstraction: In such a system, it is practically impossible for an application to access configuration settings and context of all other applications.

   Such systems suffer from the *configuration integration problem*, making it difficult to share configuration settings. Applications cannot access other's configuration settings for better integration at a large scale. If we want to adapt a system better to its context, for example, to make it more energy efficient, we need to tinker with the configuration settings of each application.

We want systems using ELEKTRA to retain current FLOSS applications' modularity. The aim is to keep unrelated applications unrelated. SPECELEKTRA shall provide a way to bring in coupling between configuration files, but in a wanted, specified and controlled way.

For our approach to work we only have two assumptions. Applications shall be:

- configurable to achieve the requirements, and

- provide a way to trigger reloading of their configuration settings.

Modularity is the degree of how well a program is split up in independently reusable modules [19]. We distinguish two dimensions of modularity in configuration libraries: vertical and horizontal modularity. We make the distinction in the following way [230]: *Vertical modularity* describes how strongly separated the configuration accesses of different applications is. *Horizontal modularity* describes how strongly separated modules implementing configuration access for a single application is. Approaches trying to unify configuration libraries endanger both kinds of modularity [230]:

- They might couple previously unrelated applications. For example, a configuration library writing to a non-modular key database couples applications performance wise: If one application stresses the key database, other applications can have troubles with their performance.

- They might couple specifics of configuration accesses to applications. For example, if an application has hard-coded information for how to validate its configuration settings, the application is coupled to a particular validation method in a particular configuration library.

In the next two parts of the section, we demonstrate mechanisms of SPECELEKTRA that preserve both dimensions of modularity.

5.3.1   Vertical Modularity

" ***Vertical modularity*** is the degree of separation between different applications." [230]. If all applications use the same key database with a single backend or a single configuration file, applications would be coupled tightly. For example, as shown in Figure 5.2, the applications `gpsd` and `batteryd` both employ the configuration library L1. Here we cannot deploy `gpsd` nor `batteryd` without L1. We prefer high vertical modularity: We want applications to stay independent of each other. If coupling between applications is low, for example every application uses a different configuration library or a different backend, we have a high degree of vertical modularity [230].

ELEKTRA provides two mechanisms to retain vertical modularity:

- Mounting configuration files facilitates different applications to use their own backend and their own configuration file. Furthermore, mounting enables integrating

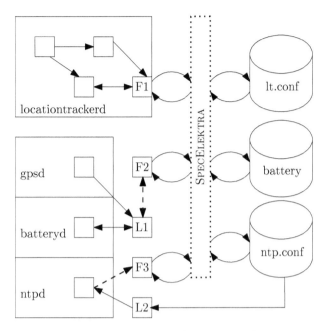

Figure 5.2: Vertical modularity of locationtracker device. Boxes are applications, cylinders are configuration files, F? are frontends or frontend adapters, L? are configuration libraries [230].

existing configuration files into the key database. Configuration specifications written in SPECELEKTRA allow different applications to share their configuration files with each other in a controlled way.

- Having frontends that implement existing *application programming interfaces (API)* decouple applications from each other. These applications continue to use their specific configuration accesses, but ELEKTRA redirects their configuration accesses to the shared key database. Because of the underlying shared key database these frontends improve on the configuration integration problem.

Mechanism 1: Mounting

Mounting allows applications to directly access the configurations settings in configuration files of other applications. The coupling happens in a controlled way within the configuration specification. We avoid coupling from applications to configuration files. We use the following specification to define a mountpoint [230]:

```
1 [ntp]
2   mountpoint:=ntp.conf
```

The property `mountpoint` (line 2) specifies the configuration file `ntp.conf` to be mounted at `/ntp` influencing the subtree with the root `/ntp`. In Figure 5.2 the application `ntpd` accesses its configuration file `ntp.conf` using the library L2, bypassing SPEC-ELEKTRA. This application is strongly coupled with `ntp.conf`. The same configuration file, however, is also accessible through the mountpoint within SPECELEKTRA, which provides a more modular configuration access [230].

If the configuration specification does not refer to any configuration settings outside of `/ntp`, only the configuration file `ntp.conf` will be loaded. Thus, from the view of system calls, we retain the same situation as if the applications would directly parse the configuration file `ntp.conf`. For performance-wise decoupling, we rely on the capabilities of the file system.

The reason for the improvement in modularity is that mounting avoids coupling from applications to specific backends or to specific configuration files. Applications using configuration settings below `/ntp` (possibly also indirectly via transformations and links) retain their independence from the concrete configuration file `ntp.conf`.

Mechanism 2: Frontends

Providing different frontends decouples implementation internals of different applications. In the spirit of the adapter design pattern [98] such frontends implement the need of the application. In the case of F1 in Figure 5.2, the frontend is part of `locationtrackerd`, providing a better modularity of the system. ELEKTRA eases creating new frontends by providing access to configuration settings via lookups in the key set. Frontends only need to access and update the key set and call `kdb.get` and `kdb.set` accordingly.

Such frontends are used without any knowledge and concession of applications. For example, L1 tries to open a configuration file with the system call `open`. Because F2 intercepts this system call (dashed line), L1 uses ELEKTRA instead. Then the library L1 parses a configuration file dynamically serialized by LIBELEKTRA [234]. Therefore indirectly, `gpsd` and `batteryd` participate in SPECELEKTRA. Modern operating systems provide ways to intercept library and system calls without modifications in the source code. Neither `gpsd`, `batteryd` nor `L1` need any coupling to a configuration library in the source code [230].

The power of such frontends is not limited to system calls: We extend it to library invocations, for example `getenv`. In Figure 5.2, `F3` implements the `getenv` interface. Whenever `ntpd` calls `getenv`, `F3` redirects the invocation and requests configuration settings from ELEKTRA instead. Again, even though `ntpd` has no source code modifications, `F3` makes `ntpd` participating in a unified configuration system.

Finding. *Due to the use of application-specific frontends and backends,* ELEKTRA *does not endanger vertical modularity.*

Because the key set allows us to support many frontends, we do not have the necessity to have a single API fulfilling all needs, supporting the requirement:

Requirement 8. *The configuration access API must be minimal and crafted carefully.*

5.3.2 Horizontal Modularity

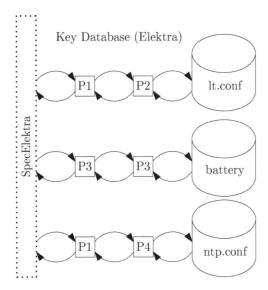

Figure 5.3: Horizontal modularity of locationtracker device. Cylinders are configuration files, P? are plugins [230].

In earlier work we defined ***horizontal modularity*** to be "the degree of separation in configuration access code" [230]. A higher degree of horizontal modularity allows us to better separate configuration access code and plug the code together as needed. SPEC-ELEKTRA employs the pipes-and-filters architectural pattern (see P1–P4 in Figure 5.3). *Plugins* are pieces of configuration access code that share the same interface. Three factors of SPECELEKTRA improve horizontal modularity:

1. Using SPECELEKTRA, applications are completely decoupled from configuration specifications.

2. The plugin assembling algorithm described in Section 3.3.7 abstracts the specifications written in SPECELEKTRA over concrete plugins. ELEKTRA has no dependence to other libraries but only concrete plugins introduce dependences. We achieve a system-level dependence injection.

3. The *provider* abstractions in the dependences between the plugins abstract over concrete implementations of configuration access code. Here we reduce the coupling between plugins.

Finding. *Moving configuration specifications and dependences from the applications' source code to configuration specifications and plugins improves horizontal modularity.*

We improve on Requirement **12**:

Requirement 12. *Dependences exclusively needed to validate configuration settings must be avoided.*

Generic Plugins

Here we describe a technique how we facilitate a single implementation of a plugin to create different plugins with different features sets. By making plugins more fine-granular, we achieve better horizontal modularity.

We say a plugin is ***generic*** if its feature set cannot be described in a single contract. We distinguish between static and dynamic generic plugins. Dynamic generic plugins have non-trivial plugin configuration such as behavioral descriptions, programs, or scripts. For example, the script plugin `lua` is a dynamic generic plugin. The plugin configuration `script` specifies a Lua-script [230]:

```
1 [locationtrackerd]
2   infos/plugins:=lua script=batterytotracker.lua
```

Different scripts cause the dynamic generic plugins to require different contracts. We need to take care about not confusing such plugins: They have the same plugin name but otherwise are hardly related [230].

The static type of generic plugins facilitates compile-time conditionals, which we call **compilation variants**. They can only be used if the plugin is written in a programming language that supports compile-time decisions, for example, macros in C. Here the compiler resolves variability. Compilation variants are beneficial if [230]:

1. We need performance, which conflicts with flexibility.

2. We need the plugin during *bootstrapping*, where we cannot provide plugin configuration [227].

3. We need nearly-identical plugins depending on different APIs, which cannot coexist in the same plugin.

We compile the plugin's code with requested combinations of defined and undefined macros. Different combinations of macros then can yield different contracts. For example, the plugin `crypto` decides which cryptography library should be used via compilation variants [230].

5.3.3   Suitable Configuration Settings

We propose to use configuration settings to encode requirements. Other configuration settings derive information from these configuration settings. We aim at *suitable* context-aware configuration.

Example 5.2. A software running on different devices with different requirements would use the following specification as requirement [230]:

```
1  [device]
2    check/enum/#0:=wearable
3    check/enum/#1:=smartphone
4    check/enum/#2:=car
```

The configuration setting `device` can have three different configuration values: wearable, smartphone, or car.   ▲

To map the configuration settings encoding information for requirements to concrete configuration settings, configuration value transformations are needed. The most important transformation is assignment between configuration settings:

Example 5.3. As discussed in [230]:

```
1  [powersaving/gps]
2    assign/condition:=(device != 'car') ? (battery/level) : ('0')
3  [gps/resolution]
4    assign/condition:=(device == 'car') ? ('high') : ('low')
```

We facilitate the plugin `conditionals` that allows us to specify conditions with two branches. SPECELEKTRA ensures that the keys `powersaving/gps` and `gps/resolution` are always set according the requirements defined in `device` [230].   ▲

We are not limited to transformations from configuration settings encoding requirements.

Example 5.4. We want a device with a low battery to stop polling GPS. Again we use conditionals [230]:

```
1  [gps/status]
2    assign/condition:=(battery/level > 'low') ? ('on') : ('off')
```
▲

5.3.4   Modular Type Checking

Compared to checking of configuration specifications, type checking of configuration settings has a more direct impact on the system. If the validation is not rigorous enough, misconfiguration is not caught. A too complicated specification language, however, would be avoided by developers. No further dependences shall be added to the application if new validation specifications are added:

Requirement 12. *Dependences exclusively needed to validate configuration settings must be avoided.*

To fulfill these diverse requirements, ELEKTRA does not have a single way to validate configuration. Instead ELEKTRA provides a *modular configuration specification language* that enables developers to create their own validation languages. One rationale is that ELEKTRA validates configuration values to be consistent with their context, even if the context is not encoded as configuration setting. Here we might need language constructs for every kind of context. For example, users not only need validations whether a configuration setting contains an IP address but they also need validations whether the address points to a reachable service. We got the following feedback during the survey described in Chapter 2: *"There are variables which have a huge list of possible values. These lists are taken from databases. So at the end we have two sources for the possible values: the configuration specification and the database"*.

We could integrate file system metadata, the surrounding network topology, and other databases within the key database. Then we would exclusively validate data without external factors. Integrating all data in ELEKTRA crosses the border of having a tool that is specific enough to be useful. Integrating huge databases, as requested in the survey, conflicts with other requirements of ELEKTRA.

We propose to have a modular configuration specification language in which users add their own configuration specification constructs and implement them as plugins. Users shall be able to combine already existing validation plugins with their own validation plugins. For example, a user writes a validation plugin querying large databases.

Pluggable Type System

We extend on the ideas of pluggable type systems [12, 115, 209]. The idea of pluggable type systems is to guarantee the absence of additional errors that would not be detected by the built-in type system. Users *"should be able to choose the kind of static checks one would like to perform"* [115]. This way, we do not introduce problems if we add an exotic type system for a single application.

For SPECELEKTRA, we decided to adapt such a flexible approach and users can plug in arbitrary type checkers. Papi et al. [209] suggested to use annotations for additional type information. Based on the idea, we use properties of keys to describe data types:

```
1 [slapd/threads/listener]
2    check/type:=long
3    check/range:=1,2,4,8,16
```

In line 2, the property check/type states that we use the CORBA data type long. Different to specifications with the property type, we use the data type only for validation and not for code generation. In line 3 we further restrict the configuration setting to some specific values. Because line 3 specifies the configuration setting in a stricter way, line 2 does not have an influence on the configuration validation. SPECELEKTRA's syntax is verbose but with the advantage that adding extensions never causes conflicts because our model requires us to always use fresh property names.

Two-phase Checking

To provide maximum flexibility and modularity, the checking of the structure and data types is separated. This separation establishes a ***two-phase type checking***:

Checking structure: For some applications, missing keys is as fatal as non-validated keys. In a first phase, the structure of the specification is enforced. The phase makes sure that keys (not) allowed to occur are (not) present. Additionally, it applies concrete dynamic type information as properties to keys by matching key names with *glob* expressions.

Example 5.5. The plugin spec is a plugin that checks structure and supports following glob expressions:

  _ denotes an arbitrary hierarchy level, and

  # denotes an arbitrary array index.

Thus the specification [a/_/key/#] will match keys such as:

```
1 a/simple/key/#0=
2 a/nother/key/#_12=value not part of match
```

The plugin spec also copies metadata to every matching configuration setting.   ▲

Checking values: In a second phase, the checks given by metadata copied in the first step are checked for each key. These two phases are independent of each other and have their own use cases. For the second phase, many data types are supported.

Data Types

We already introduced `check/type` and `check/enum` which are two of the data types. ELEKTRA supports many other data types, each implemented in its own plugin(s):

check/type allows us to specify CORBA data types, as already listed in Example 3.15 on page 87. Checking `any` is always successful. The record and enum types defined by CORBA are not part of this plugin but of others as explained below.

check/enum supports a list of supported values denoted by array indexes.

check/bool transforms specific strings, for example `true` and `false`, into the canonical boolean representation, i.e., `0` and `1`.

check/ipaddr checks if a string is a valid IP address.

check/path checks presence, permissions, and type of paths in the file system.

check/date supports to check date formats such as POSIX, ISO8601, and RFC2822.

check/validation checks the configuration value with regular expressions.

check/condition checks using conditionals and comparisons.

check/math checks using mathematical expressions.

check/range allows us to check if numerical values are within a range.

trigger/error allows us to express unconditional failures.

ELEKTRA supports binary and string types. Binary configuration values can include null characters in their string and can have the special value ϵ. Because binary is only used on special occasions, for example to represent encrypted values, all validations are only against string types.

The data types form a lattice, with `error` as bottom and `any` as top element [115, 118]. By default, every key has the type `any` regardless if it is specified using `[]` or not. Adding specifications without any properties is useful: It tells the user which of the configuration settings are relevant for an application. Every property that additionally specifies a type restricts the range of allowed values.

Discussion

Up to now, we used type restrictions, also known as **subtype** in Ada. In ELEKTRA the specifications are even more flexible than in Ada: They allow a type to be a list of any checkers. Each of these checkers make the type stricter. This fact makes the types in ELEKTRA safe to use, even though ELEKTRA's types do not have a closed model (and thus can be neither sound nor complete). The trouble-free combination of many checkers is a pragmatic decision.

To define a structured type, we use the ideas of Relax NG [56]. Our language, defined by the plugin `spec`, is simpler because neither attributes nor XML namespaces exist. Instead of repeating key names, we make key names unique by adding array indexes. A specification without any property, for example `[x]`, is equivalent to Relax NG's `zeroOrMore` which is the same as Relax NG's `optional` in our case. In the area of structured types, the lack of a closed model is problematic as features can have unnecessary overlap. The advantage of our open model is that every developer can participate and applications can choose to use completely different models for their validation specifications.

5.4   Context awareness without Source-code Modifications

Instead of improving configuration access APIs as done in the previous Chapter 4, in this section we focus on providing the best user experience with existing configuration access APIs. The idea is to facilitate *configuration access points* present in applications. We retrofit legacy applications by combing the already introduced:

- context-aware lookup from Section 5.2 (as specified in Section 3.3.1), and

- modularity and adaptation of frontends from Section 5.3.

Such a functionality is important because rewriting all applications to new configuration access APIs is unrealistic. Legacy applications will always play an important role: What we implement today, will be legacy tomorrow. We want to improve on the requirement:

Requirement 2. *A configuration library must be able to integrate (legacy) systems and must fully support (legacy) configuration files.*

We focus on free and open source software (FLOSS) and configuration access APIs usually present there. We claim that it is feasible and practical to use software without source code modifications, and by run-time reconfiguration, upgrade their context awareness. We aim at exploiting already existing configuration access points in free and open source software [234], answering:

RQ 6.4. Which techniques enable applications to become more context aware without any changes in the source code?

5.4.1 Demand

As already stated, context awareness is not an absolute measure. Instead *viewpoints* always create demand for more context awareness. We usually do not learn about such situations before we discuss them with a user. These conflicts with current ideas of *context-oriented software engineering* where context needs to be considered already at design time [145]. Hence, context-oriented software engineering is not applicable to existing large software projects where context is not known beforehand, neither for legacy software [234].

To improve on this problem, we propose to delay context-oriented software engineering to deployment-time. This way we move decisions about supported contexts to a time when more about the required contexts is known. We classified three *stakeholders* [234]:

- the developers, who implement programs with variations useful for context awareness, without defining which variation is used in which situations,

- the system administrators, who enable context awareness in their systems with our novel context-oriented software engineering during deployment, and

- the end users, who enjoy better context awareness in their systems and can report missing context awareness to system administrators.

As running example in this section, we use mobile workplaces. For browsers the network connection is an important context. With different network connections, we require different proxy settings. We aim at browsers automatically adapting themselves to the current context. We want browsers to be aware of the current network connection, of the nearest printers, etc. [232].

5.4.2 Configuration Access APIs

To avoid any source code modifications, applications must fulfill the following assumptions to be suitable for ELEKTRA:

1. The applications must have configuration access points present in the source code.

2. Without extensions, we require the use of configuration access APIs at configuration access points. For example, configuration access points that access data structures and variables are currently not supported. We do not impose restrictions on the gestalt of the configuration access APIs.

3. For flawless context awareness the configuration access points must be triggered perpetually; and not only once at start-up.

Assumption 3 is not strictly necessary, but without it, dynamic adaptation is not possible. Instead we would need to restart applications on context changes. We focus on situations where such restarts are not necessary.

Based on our earlier studies in Chapter 2 these assumptions are reasonable. Applications have plenty of configuration access points, often in the form of an API, which are called repeatedly. We did not show, however, whether configuration access points control behavior that is of interest for context awareness.

getenv

The `getenv` API enables developers to query environment variables. ***Environment variables*** live in a data structure called `environ` within the processes. They are initialized once at program startup. In the current implementations, only the process itself can update `environ`.

If the user changes an environment variable, for example `PATH`, only new subprocesses see the change. This can be wanted, for example, if choosing which compiler to be used for the next compilation process. Most often, however, this is unwanted and a major usability problem. For example, a user modifying `http_proxy` needs to logout and restart all relevant daemons.

We include `getenv` for our investigations because it [234]

- is widely standardized, including SVr4, POSIX.1-2001, 4.3BSD, C89, C99 [1],

- and is supported by many programming languages.

open

Applications use the `open` API to open configuration files. Its return value is a file handle, which is processed by further system calls. Usually, applications use it indirectly via some higher-level API, such as `fopen`. Different from `getenv`, the file system is designed for inter-process communication. Hence, applications can implement reloading of configuration settings on configuration file changes.

The `open` system call is

- standardized by SVr4, 4.3BSD, POSIX.1-2001, POSIX.1-2008 [2],

- and available in every relevant programming language, although sometimes with restrictions for security reasons.

5.4.3 Approach

To make applications use ELEKTRA without any source code modifications, we hijack their API calls. For example, Web browsers contain code such as [234]:

```
1 getenv ("http_proxy");
```

Conventional implementations of `getenv` would return an outdated proxy after network changes because environment variables cannot be corrected from outside of processes. We interpret such `getenv` accesses as reading a contextual value [234]. Replacing the `getenv` implementation with ELEKTRA's context-aware lookup, unmodified applications will use context-aware configuration. Contrary to standard `getenv`, the configuration setting are consistent with the content of configuration files, fulfilling the requirement:

Requirement 6. *Configuration libraries must provide ways to keep transient and persistent views consistent.*

Interception

ELEKTRA with interception works as follows:

- We intercept a pre-main method. In it ELEKTRA *bootstraps* itself with the help of initial configuration files. The initial configuration files contain both the configuration settings and specifications for the contextual values [234]. At this early stage we will pass command-line options to ELEKTRA.

- If the application calls open with its configuration file as argument, ELEKTRA serializes a configuration file on-the-fly and returns a file handle to it.

- If the application calls getenv with a parameter specified in SPECELEKTRA, ELEKTRA's context-aware lookup is invoked.

Unfortunately, interceptions of library invocations are platform-dependent. But every major operating system provides some techniques for interceptions. We implemented the interception techniques for GNU/Linux using LD_PRELOAD and /etc/ld.so.preload [234]:

- The environment variable LD_PRELOAD allows us to preload libraries. Then the symbols of the preloaded library are preferred. This technique does not work during boot-up of the system.

- The configuration file /etc/ld.so.preload has the same purpose but does not have LD_PRELOAD's restriction. Libraries mentioned in this file are automatically preloaded for every process. We prefer this method, and registered our library, which implements getenv and open, in this configuration file.

Context Specification

In SPECELEKTRA, the user has to define which getenv parameters and configuration files shall be controlled by ELEKTRA. In our approach, the frontend responsible for the interception reads the layers and configuration specifications from keys below /env:

/env/layer contains the layers to use.

/env/override contains the keys that shall be preferred to environment variables.

Example 5.6. Let us specify the return value of getenv("http_proxy") [234]:

```
1 [env/override/http_proxy]
2   context:=/http_proxy/%interface%/%network%
```

Then ELEKTRA takes control over every `getenv` invocation that has the parameter `http_proxy`. Line 2 is the specification as defined in Section 3.3.1. The context-aware lookup ensures that the contextual value recursively considers context specifications. After layer switches, the same requested key name can yield different values. We use a configuration file containing the mapping to concrete values [234]:

```
1 http_proxy/wlan/home=proxy.example.org
2 http_proxy/eth/work=proxy.example.com
3 http_proxy/%/%=default.example.com
```

If *interface* changes to `eth` and the *network* to work, the next invocation of `getenv("http_proxy")` returns `proxy.example.com` [234].   ▲

Context Changes

To always reflect external changes of the context, we have two options. We either pull changes, or a *context sensor*, as introduced in Section 5.2.3, pushes changes to all applications. We implemented both approaches to support more applications and APIs.

Pulling changes works well for configuration access APIs that are called repetitively, such as `getenv`. ELEKTRA's `getenv` implementation uses the following algorithm [232]:

```
1 KeySet conf; // global variable used by reload* functions
2 char * getenv (const char * key)
3 {
4     if (reloadNeeded ())
5     {
6         reloadConfiguration ();
7         reloadLayers ();
8     }
9     return ksLookup (conf, Key ("/env/override/" ++ key));
10 }
```

The continuous polling makes sure that every `getenv` considers the latest layers and configuration settings.

For other configuration access APIs polling does not work. For example, most applications call `open` already at startup but provide a way to trigger reinitialization. In such situations, we use a plugin that triggers application on configuration changes.

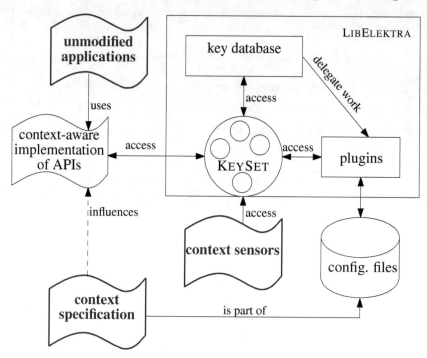

Figure 5.4: Architecture of ELEKTRA if used with interception. The common data structure is the key set (shown in the middle). Bold, blue boxes need to be provided by the users of ELEKTRA [232].

This architecture shown in Figure 5.4 ensures complete decoupling between context sensors and applications. Thus the same context sensors are reused for many applications.

In the running example, users change their location or connect a network cable. A context sensor recognizes such changes and modifies the key database accordingly. The key database executes the plugins that trigger the applications to reparse their configuration files when using `open` interception. For `getenv` interceptions the triggering is not necessary because of the polling.

5.4.4 Context-oriented Software Engineering Process

Here we describe a process of how our approach is applied. We expand on our running example, and show how to use ELEKTRA to enable flexible workplaces. The requirements were that applications such as Firefox shall automatically use (1) the nearest printer, and (2) the correct proxy.

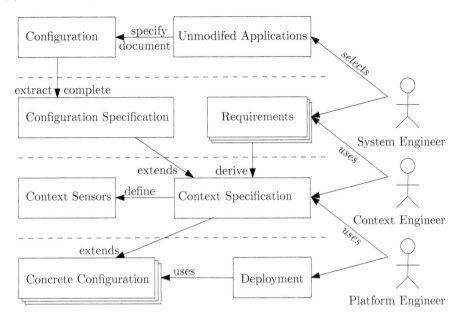

Figure 5.5: Context-oriented software engineering process.

As shown in Figure 5.5 we split up the engineering team into the roles of system, context, and platform engineers. In large organizations these roles are implemented by different teams. Otherwise, different persons act according to the role they get assigned.

System engineers first define the requirements. Then they decide which applications shall be used. They document their decisions and complete the specification of relevant configuration settings.

In our running example, one of our requirements is that the browser picks up proxy settings automatically. Then the system engineers investigate if Firefox has all needed settings and find it is enough to intercept getenv. They choose Firefox as the unmodified application to use.

In the role of context engineers we extracted relevant contexts from the previously constructed requirements. Context-oriented software engineering works with the hypothesis that *"The factors dynamically changing the system behavior are candidates for contexts"* [145]. They consider "changing of workplace" as context. Based on the context, engineers specify the layers. We decided the relevant context consists of two layers: The layer *network* differs for every workplace. The layer *interface* distinguishes how someone is connected to the workplace's network. This permits a user in the same location, but connected via a wireless network, to see different printers and use a different proxy as someone connected via cable. We specified `http_proxy` and `PRINTER_LIST` to automatically use the nearest printer:

```
1 [env/override/http_proxy]
2   context:=/http_proxy/%interface%/%network%
3 [env/override/PRINTER_LIST]
4   context:=/printer/%interface%/%network%
```

The context engineers then implement a context sensor that updates the layers *interface* and *network*. The context engineers adapt their network scripts such that the layers are always set according to the workplace in use. In the example, the context sensors are trivial one-line hooks in the `/etc/NetworkManager` scripts.

In the last step, the platform engineers deploy the applications on the organization's platforms. They enrich the configuration settings with platform-specific configuration settings such as concrete proxies and printers. Finally, they install the artifacts and configuration files produced in the previous steps.

CHAPTER 6

Implications and Open Topics

*Freedom only remains healthy if we think about the implications of what we
do on a day-to-day basis.*

— Rebecca MacKinnon

In this chapter we evaluate the risks and implications on systems that use ELEKTRA,
answering **RQ 7**:

RQ 7. What are the risks and implications of introducing ELEKTRA?

Our main concerns are the topics effected most by ELEKTRA. We look into impact on
users. We rely on case studies, experience, and ideas—fully conducted experiments and
benchmarks follow in the next chapter.

In Section 6.1, we look into the administration of the key database. We present implications and risks of SPECELEKTRA for system administrators.

In Section 6.2, we discuss the impact ELEKTRA has on tooling and show user interfaces.

In Section 6.3, we consider implications on development. In a case study, we found
that development time is reduced and quality improved. We look into maintenance of
applications using ELEKTRA.

Finally, in Section 6.4, we reflect on the security, safety, and quality of ELEKTRA. We
present some metrics of ELEKTRA's source code and then discuss implications concerning
security and misconfiguration.

6.1   Administration

One of the main goals of ELEKTRA was to make administration of configuration settings easier in order to avoid misconfiguration. Here we answer **RQ 7.1**:

RQ 7.1. Which risks and implications does ELEKTRA have for administrating configuration settings?

6.1.1   Sharing of Configuration Settings

As discussed so far, context awareness across applications implies sharing of configuration settings between applications. Sharing is not always a good idea and imposes risks: Sharing creates dependences between different communities. Because communities can independently change the semantics of configuration values, sharing introduces co-evolution, which can lead to breakage.

A countermeasure in place is that we provide transformation of configuration values. Using the transformation, we decouple applications from the exact configuration value other applications have. But whenever an application changes its configuration settings, we need to update the transformation logic. Supporting different versions of configuration specifications can lead to a complex transformation logic.

We suggest another solution: Instead of directly sharing configuration settings between applications, we propose to use agreed shared places. From these agreed shared places, applications transform their configuration settings, as hinted in Example 5.1. There does not need to be a single central organization for such reusable configuration settings. Instead projects like `EditorConfig.org` specify configuration settings to solve specific configuration integration problems. This way, the risk of changes in the configuration specification is reduced and configuration specifications have clear ownerships.

Because of the configuration specification, `/etc` can be left completely empty by default. A system administrator only needs to add settings to the agreed shared places. Applications would calculate their default values from these agreed shared places. Using this procedure, ELEKTRA fulfills Requirement **13**:

Requirement 13. *A configuration library must mitigate the configuration integration problem.*

It is future work to evaluate the efficiency of mitigation strategies to co-evolution.

6.1.2 Documentation

Documentation is a valuable artifact. To enable social coding and to understand the intention of the specifications, we need further properties that document the specification, contributing to the requirement:

Requirement 14. *There must be a support for shipping correct documentation and examples generated from the configuration specifications.*

Even though some tools infer validation specifications [157, 194, 304], most parts of the configuration specification must be populated and maintained manually [55, 187]. This applies in particular to documentation. While the type and defaults are already part of the configuration specification in ELEKTRA, other documentation needs additional properties. We explain some further properties improving documentation with the aid of an example extending on Example 0.1:

```
1 [slapd/threads/listener]
2   check/range:=1,2,4,8,16
3   default:=1
4   description:=adjust to use more threads
5   rationale:=needed for many-core systems
6   requirement:=1234
7   accessibility:=platform engineers
```

The first line contains the most important information: It specifies the existence of a configuration setting and its name. The second line tells the system administrator which configuration values are permitted to be present. Line 3 is already less important for system administrators. It is more reliable to introspect configuration values because this reduces the danger of oversight.

The property `description` in line 4 contains only as much information as necessary and focuses on behavioral descriptions. It does not repeat other parts of the specifications. In particular, it does not repeat other specifications, such as default values. Hand-written documentation that duplicates information from the source code is known to be error-prone [252]. Instead the description should describe the configuration setting from the application's perspective.

The property `rationale` is an explanation of why the configuration setting is needed and why it is specified as it is. Following the concept of documenting architectural decisions [120], only configuration settings are added if a clear demand for them exists. Possible reasons for adding a configuration setting are:

1. a requirement,

2. an architectural decision,

3. a technical need, and

4. an ad hoc decision.

For the first three reasons the configuration settings need revalidation on influencing events, for example, on changes in requirements, decisions and technology. Traceability links [241] are useful to detect influencing events. Ad hoc decisions need to be revalidated periodically. If customers never change configuration settings—because the default value is already the optimal solution—the configuration setting and specification shall be removed.

For most stakeholders only some configuration settings are relevant. The property `accessibility` defines who is responsible for a particular key in the configuration specification. Tools filtering for this property present only relevant configuration settings to the respective stakeholders. For example, in a graphical user interface the visibility of a configuration setting is directly derived from accessibility levels.

The risks of these suggestions are:

- That important documentation is missing because no property is obligatory.

- That unnecessary documentation is added for the sake of having a complete set of documentation properties.

- Enforced properties might have more severe effects than wrong documentation. For example, the property `accessibility` can cause problems: If the property is assigned too strict, some stakeholders will not find the configuration setting they are looking for.

Thus configuration specifications need to be subject of maintenance by the application's developer. Bugs in the configuration specification need to be handled like other bugs.

6.1.3 Validation

In ELEKTRA, configuration specifications are not hard coded in applications and can be extended by system administrators. Because `kdb.set` always enforces validation, system administrators that only use tools based on LIBELEKTRA, fulfill the requirement:

Requirement 9. *Validation of configuration settings must happen systematically before the application is even started.*

Without configuration specifications, ELEKTRA works completely without any configuration validation. Every configuration value is either a string or binary data with any content. This behavior addresses the need to have a low barrier for ELEKTRA's adoption. On the downside, the behavior adds the risk that system administrators forget adding configuration specifications.

Introducing the **two-phase type checking** has important consequences for the daily work. It separates checks intended to be extended by developers and system administrators. The first phase (structure check) is usually tightly interwoven with the application's configuration settings. Writing such plugins is a challenging development effort and thus usually is not done by system administrators.

System administrators usually know pattern-matching languages such as globs and regular expressions well. Thus they can employ the plugin `validation` to strengthen checks for their purposes:

```
1 [slapd/logfile]
2   check/validation:=/var/log/.*\.log
3   check/validation/match:=word
4   check/validation/message:=Policy violation: must be /var/log
```

Other plugins check if configuration settings are consistent with the context. Such plugins can check the validity of network addresses and the existence of paths in a file system. For example, to check if the configuration setting points to a existent file, system administrators use:

```
1 [slapd/logfile]
2   check/path:=file
```

Because of the vast amount of possibilities for checking values to be consistent with context, it is essential that system administrators are able to invent new kinds of consistency checks. In our design, system administrators combine their own checks with the application developer's predefined structure checks. It remains future work to evaluate up to what extent system administrators successfully combine different validation techniques.

6.1.4   Error Messages

Currently, system administrators are often confronted with applications behaving wrongly and not starting up. Employing ELEKTRA, they would instead encounter error messages from plugins rejecting their misconfigurations. To make their work easier, it is essential that the plugins give good error messages. Having human-friendly error messages is challenging [168, 174, 310]. Using ELEKTRA we have, however, a distinctive advantage: During execution of kdb.set plugins know which keys were changed.

We use information about last-changed keys (a modification bit in metadata μ) to improve error messages by a simple heuristic: If several keys are potential causers of an error, we prefer those in the error message that were changed by the user.

Example 6.1. Given the specification:

```
1 [a]
2   check/type:=long
3 [b]
4   check/type:=long
5 [c]
6   check/range:=0-10
7   assign/math:=../a+../b
```

If we change b to 10 and a remains unchanged with 5, we have in the following in-memory configuration settings to be processed by kdb.set:

```
1 a=5   ; unmodified
2 b=10 ; modification bit in metadata is only set here
3 c=15 ; unmodified by user but changed later by assign/math
```

ELEKTRA is capable to inform the user that b was set to an invalid value, even though the validation failed at c:

```
Sorry, I was unable to change the configuration settings!
Description: I tried to set a value outside the range!
Reason: I tried to modify b to be 10 but this caused c to be
        outside of the allowed range (0-10).
Module: range
At: sourcefile.c:1234
Mountpoint: /test
Configfile: /etc/testfile.conf
```

For the error message, we are only interested in keys changed by the user. This way we can pinpoint to a likely source of the error. Unfortunately, plugins need to implement this feature, and the heuristic can fail.

The error message is personalized and starts with "Sorry" and "I". This eye catcher is relevant to improve novice[1] programmers' learning. Lee and Ko [168] found in a study with a programming game that participants receiving personalized feedback *"completed significantly more levels in a similar amount of time"*. Future work is needed to evaluate the impact of such error messages on the daily work of system administrators.

6.1.5 Context-aware Lookup

If possible, we prefer tools to automatically avoid problems and not only to check for them. Here we consider implications of SPECELEKTRA as a high-level programming language with its context-aware lookup features.

Links already allow us to implement simple logics. We easily add new rules where configuration settings shall be searched for.

---

[1] And as we know, also expert developers and system administrators start as novice when using a new tool.

Example 6.2. Let us determine if one of the arguments is set to true, i.e., the string 1:

```
1 [sw/org/abc/has_true_arg]
2   type:=boolean
3   default:=0
4   override/#0:=/sw/org/abc/arg0
5   override/#1:=/sw/org/abc/arg1
```

Using `override` we specify a list of arguments that ensure that the key `/sw/org/abc/has_true_arg` yields true if one of the `argN` is true.   ▲

Cascading lookup requires all namespaces to be inquired exhaustively. Evard [87] proposes to use cascading lookup but only at configuration file level. ELEKTRA extends these ideas to individual keys. Administrators employ cascading lookups of applications to have different configuration settings:

- to try out new configuration settings via command-line options and environment variables (`proc` namespace),

- if the application is started from different directories (`dir` namespace), and

- for different users (`user` namespace).

System administrators facilitate the cascading lookup to know the configuration settings an application currently uses—without any manual calculations or guesswork. We fulfill Requirement **7**:

Requirement 7. *Configuration settings and specifications must be introspectable.*

A *layer-based lookup* includes even more possibilities to consider context. We gain flexibility but also make the introspection more difficult. With dynamic scoping, the configuration setting can even change for different parts of the same application. We are still able to introspect each of the possibilities but which of these is used depends on the layers within the threads and dynamic scopes.

Except for the layer-based lookup, we gain a futz-free system to introspect configuration values. It remains as future work to evaluate the layer-based lookup from the system administrator's viewpoint.

6.1.6 Discussion

Here we conclude the answer to **RQ 7.1**:

RQ 7.1. Which risks and implications does ELEKTRA have for administrating configuration settings?

Evard [87] said: *"A good abstraction model changes the way in which one thinks."* Allowing programming of configuration access widens the spectrum of how system administrators control their systems. Instead of seeing configuration access as a black box, with SPEC-ELEKTRA they get possibilities to introspect and even program configuration access. System administrators finally get ways to:

- share configuration settings,

- document configuration settings at specified places,

- make configuration validations stricter with more specific error messages, and

- derive configuration settings from context and requirements.

SPECELEKTRA blurs the line of responsibility between developers and system administrators, which involves risks:

- System administrators need to learn more concepts and need more programming background. Some of ELEKTRA's concepts are difficult to grasp, for example, the context-aware lookup.

- System administrators can loosen or change validation specifications in wrong ways. Such actions not only open doors for misconfiguration but the tools even give wrong statements about valid configuration settings.

- System administrators can use wrong plugins, or can implement plugins wrongly.

- System administrators might get even less help in case of misconfigurations because developers may suspect system administrators to have failed in one of the points above.

- Layer-based lookups in frontends are too flexible to fully cover Requirement **7**.

6.2   Tooling

A consequence of LIBELEKTRA is that configuration management tooling does not need to be bothered with mechanics how to manipulate specific configuration files. With respect to the parts that SPECELEKTRA dictates, the tooling has consistent behavior. In this section we discuss the implications on tooling.

6.2.1   Configuration Management

While many approaches for *configuration management* [58, 137] exist, they lack good support for consistent configuration file manipulation and introspection. In the current situation, the user of the configuration management tool is either severely restricted in which configuration settings can be changed, or needs to have a working knowledge about the syntax of involved configuration files. Configuration management tools have limited possibilities to detect syntactically wrong and non-validating configuration files, especially if the errors result from context.

ELEKTRA is a good fit for these problems. Using ELEKTRA

1. the mechanisms of how to manipulate configuration files is reduced to key-value manipulations,

2. with correctly-working storage plugins it is impossible to create syntactically incorrect configuration files (assuming every key name and every configuration value is representable in the respective syntax),

3. configuration settings are always validated before they are serialized to configuration files, and

4. via introspection the current state of the system can be queried.

The disadvantage is that ELEKTRA needs to be installed and all configuration files need to be mounted. Furthermore, some concepts such as cascading lookup is not needed for configuration management and introduces complexity.

6.2.2   Text Editor

Because ELEKTRA usually parses and serializes configuration files from the hard disk, system administrators can still access these configuration files with a text editor. Directly manipulating configuration files, however, does not respect validation, syntax, and notification constraints ELEKTRA otherwise would enforce. Hence, we do not recommend bypassing ELEKTRA. One solution is to consequently rely on `open` interception, i. e., configuration files are not present in the file system but always passed through ELEKTRA. In general, however, such a solution is too heavyweight.

As an alternative, ELEKTRA provides a small wrapper around text editors. The wrapper's functionality is that it exports the configuration settings to a temporary file and spawns the users' favorite editor with this temporary file. After the editor has terminated successfully, the wrapper tries to import the configuration file. During the import ELEKTRA enforces correct syntax and validation. This way, we provide a work flow and user experience almost identical to directly editing configuration files.

6.2.3 Command-line Interface

We created a command-line tool `kdb` that maps all features of the configuration access API to the command-line. It is straightforward to transform the declarative syntax we used in this book to imperative `kdb` commands.

Example 6.3. Suppose we want to have the configuration settings:

```
1 a=5
2 b=10
3 c=15
```

We apply these configuration settings using:

```
1 kdb set /a 5
2 kdb set /b 10
3 kdb set /c 15
```

And we list them with `kdb ls /`.   ▲

Example 6.4. For specifications such as:

```
1 [slapd/threads/listener]
2   check/range:=1,2,4,8,16
3   default:=1
```

We use:

```
1 kdb setmeta /slapd/threads/listener check/range 1,2,4,8,16
2 kdb setmeta /slapd/threads/listener default 1
```

And we list them with kdb **lsmeta** /slapd/threads/listener.   ▲

Given a specification we explore which key names exist with tab completion (implemented
for bash, zsh, and fish, or use kdb **complete** otherwise). For debugging purposes,
the complete trace of which keys are considered by ksLookup are printed (-v option of
kdb **get**). This functionality is implemented by using the hook lookupByExtension.

6.2.4   Graphical User Interface

Figure 6.1 shows a screenshot of the graphical user interface. It was the second user
interface after the command-line interface and provides undo functionality.

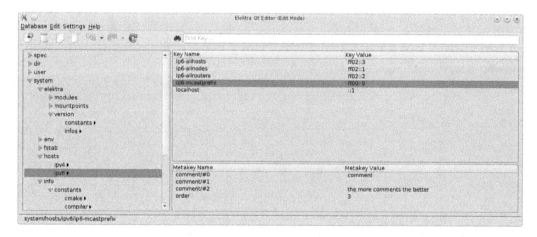

Figure 6.1: Graphical User Interface of ELEKTRA.

Figure 6.2: Web user interface of ELEKTRA.

6.2.5 Web User Interface

Figure 6.2 shows a screenshot of the Web user interface. During the still ongoing implementation of the Web user interface, we explore to what extent a user interface can avoid misconfiguration even earlier. The idea is to avoid text fields but instead let the user choose between known-to-be-valid configuration settings inferred from SPECELEKTRA.

Example 6.5. Suppose the administrator wrote the specification:

```
1 [hello/pk/student/registered]
2   check/type:=boolean
```

Here the user interface provides a checkbox, making it impossible to enter anything except true or false.   ▲

6.2.6 Converting Configuration Settings

Another implication of the common data structure is that we can freely convert between any of two converted formats in ELEKTRA as shown in Figure 6.3. This is useful for im-

porting and exporting configuration settings. It can help for upgrades if the configuration
file format changed.

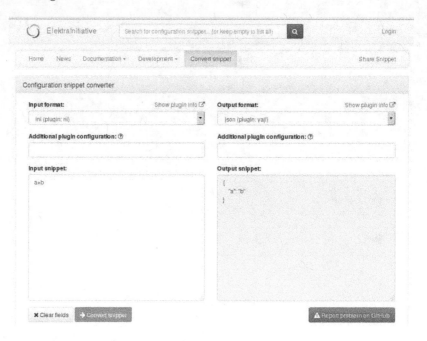

Figure 6.3: Convert configuration settings with ELEKTRA.

The conversion enables us to integrate configuration settings as source code. We wrote
the plugin c that outputs the configuration settings as C code. Applications include and
compile these files to have built-in configuration settings.

6.2.7   Discussion

ELEKTRA has advantages for tooling:

- System administrators use configuration management tools easier with and more
  confidence: Configuration files automatically use the correct syntax and invalid
  configuration settings get rejected.

- User interfaces utilize information from SPECELEKTRA: They show descriptions
  and even restrict input fields to improve usability.

Using ELEKTRA involves risks:

- If system administrators or applications forget to mount a configuration file, configuration settings are serialized to unwanted places.

- The user is dependent on plugin's decisions with respect to the formatting of configuration files. Some plugins reformat to consistent but potentially unwanted style. Other plugins aim at preservation of the original format, which is not ideal if configuration files are formatted in a chaotic style.

- System administrators might get careless when they edit configuration settings because they expect their errors to be caught.

- New tools may be refused by system administrators who are used to manipulate configuration files with their self-written tools. Depending on the setup, bypassing ELEKTRA by directly modifying configuration files is possible, but it is never recommended.

6.3 Development

In this section, we give experience reports with the lessons learned in software projects using ELEKTRA.

6.3.1 RQ 7.2: Case Study: Development Time

We investigate **RQ 7.2**:

RQ 7.2. How does ELEKTRA influence risks of development and time effort if used in a large real-world project?

Method

We developed an integrated camera system in a one-year engineering project. The project combined development of software and hardware components. The staff of the software team varied between three and five full-time software developers. We wrote about 50,000 lines of C and C++ code. We used Scrum [247] as agile development method [227].

The project aimed to engineer a platform for integrating different software applications. The platform offered more than 200 configuration settings via ELEKTRA. The configuration settings affected both the platform and integrated applications [227]. Many of these configuration settings were relevant for system administrators.

Unfortunately, we did not do time measurements during the project. Thus we redid the parts of the project relevant to configuration access in ELEKTRA's public repository [227]. We measured the time using stop watches or by calculating time from Git commits. We argue that these time measurements are more realistic because of the background from a real-world project. The shown source code is representative for what we did during the project.

Case Study

We got the basic setup for ELEKTRA running within a day. Hindering factors were that ELEKTRA was not packaged everywhere and features for unusual requirements were missing. The basic setup in the main program only consisted of the following lines [227]:

```cpp
1  #include <camera.hpp>
2
3  int main ()
4  {
5      using namespace kdb;
6      KDB kdb;
7      KeySet conf;
8      Context c;
9      Environment env (conf, c);
10     std::cout << env.camera.name << "\n";
11 }
```

In the first line, we include the source code generated by GENELEKTRA. After creating a handle to the key database (line 6), we create a `KeySet` for configuration specifications, settings (line 7), and a `Context` (line 8) [235]. Then we create an instance of the generated class `Environment` (line 9). In line 10, we access a configuration setting. Within minutes new developers started using these configuration settings [227].

To add a configuration setting is also simple. We only needed 2 minutes to specify a new configuration setting and to use it in the application. Because of this effort being so little, it is important to take care not to introduce unnecessary configuration settings [305]. Adding the ability to accept command-line options for the configuration setting was done within 6 minutes [227].

We heavily relied on the extensibility of ELEKTRA, for example we invented new properties. These properties are not described in this book because they are specific to requirements of that project. Extending code generators and plugins to support the new properties had acceptable effort [227].

Within the same project we had difficulties to extend ELEKTRA to further configuration file formats. For example, to implement the NTP configuration file format, we estimated the implementation to need more than a week. To improve on that situation, we evaluated different ways to implement new configuration file formats more quickly [227]:

Existing Libraries: Integrating existing libraries requires low effort. We must transform ELEKTRA's data structures to the data structures the existing library uses.

> **Example 6.6.** The INI plugin `ni` (it implements the syntax of the examples in this book) had 158 lines of C code and was implemented within less than a day (10:41:54–16:22:01). For parsing the properties of configuration specifications, in essence, the following source code suffices [227]:

```
1 Ni_node mcur = NULL;
2 while ((mcur = Ni_GetNextChild (current, mcur)) != NULL)
3 {
4         keySetMeta (k, Ni_GetName (mcur, NULL),
5                         Ni_GetValue (mcur, NULL));
6 }
```

> The code parses a configuration specification in the syntax as used in this book.▲

For low-level, event-driven APIs the required effort is higher, even more than one week, for example, to parse JSON. The main effort for the JSON plugin was to remember in which (sub)array and (sub)object the key currently is because the events do not give such hints.

A vast amount of configuration libraries suitable to be integrated in ELEKTRA exist, and it is usually easily possible to avoid APIs causing extra effort.

Using Grammars: Implementing storage plugins with grammars took us more time than using typical configuration libraries. Grammars only mitigate the problem of how to parse but the serialization of the configuration files still needs to be done manually. For parsing and serializing a TCL format we needed about three days (9th August, 2010 12:54:44–12th August, 2010 13:37:35). The advantage of grammars is that changing the parsing code is as straightforward as changing the serializer code [225].

Example 6.7. Using Boost.Spirit [225], we needed the following parsing code:

```
1 query = '{' >> *(pair) > '}';
2 pair = '{' >> key_name > '=' >> key_value >>
3        *('{' >> metakey_name > '=' >> metakey_value > '}')
4        > '}';
```

Hand-written parsers: It is the most effort to implement a configuration file parser by hand. For example, it took about *one month* to implement a fully-fledged INI parser that preserves order and comments. Adding many features needs considerable time—even for seemingly trivial parsers like CSV and hosts.

For extending GENELEKTRA with new features we noticed a similar variety as in parsing. The one extreme is that adding long option parsing support required less than one hour implementation time (10:53:30–11:33:04) [227]. The other extreme is implementing support for contextual values, which took many months and needed research to do it efficiently. The entry barrier to support new properties turned out to be minimal. Someone unfamiliar with ELEKTRA wrote support for new properties within several days.

Code generation sometimes drastically reduces efforts. In particular, many artifacts can be easily kept in sync by generating them from a single specification. GENELEKTRA currently allows us to generate code in C and C++ and documentation as man pages, Doxygen, and HTML.

Sometimes refactoring was needed when the hierarchy of the configuration settings was not adjusted to the features anymore. In this situation, GENELEKTRA was especially useful because we got immediate compilation feedback of all places that needed adjustment. Developers easily forget where a configuration setting is used otherwise.

Discussion

We answer **RQ 7.2**:

RQ 7.2. How does ELEKTRA influence risks of development and time effort if used in a large real-world project?

Finding. *We were able to use* ELEKTRA *within a large real-world project successfully. Many otherwise time-consuming tasks could be done within minutes or hours; in other cases* ELEKTRA *did not help. We did not have any requirement that could not be solved by extending* ELEKTRA. *Due to time reduction,* ELEKTRA *increases risks that developers introduce too many configuration settings. We are positive that the generation of artifacts related to configuration settings reduces co-evolution.*

6.3.2 RQ 7.3: Case Study: Embedded Web Server

We implemented a Web server on an embedded hardware using the high-performance C++ Web development framework CppCMS [31]. As target platform we chose a Raspberry Pi® Model B because of its low prize and power consumption. In this case study we answer **RQ 7.3**:

RQ 7.3. Which features are elegantly realizable in ELEKTRA to configure non-trivial embedded systems?

Case Study

The configuration specification of all contextual values was only 83 lines long. The specification contained basic settings needed to run a Web server, to work with hardware profiles, and to output tampering events. Some of these contextual values are shown below. From the configuration specification we generated 3500 lines of policy-based, nested C++ classes and command-line option parsing code [226, 235].

Contextual values are well suited to represent server side knowledge about an HTTP session. We facilitated a specification that used the context placeholders %session% and %language% [226]:

```
1 [sw/pi/%session%/language]
2   type:=string
3 [sw/pi/%language%/hello]
4   type:=string
```

In the first version of the Web server, we manually implemented the layers [226]. In a second version, we instead used contextual values [231].

Example 6.8. One of the first steps was to implement the HTTP request handler. The object out is a stream to write the HTTP response [226]:

```
1  tc.with<Session>(sessionid)([this]()
2  {
3      out << "<html>\n"
4              "<body>\n";
5      out << "<p>Language: " << language << "</p>";
6      tc.with<Language>(language)([this](){
7          out << "<p>" << hello << "</p>";
8          //...
9      });
10     out << "</body>\n"
11             "</html>\n";
12 });
```

We use with to have the current session as thread-local context during the HTTP request handler. ELEKTRA changes all contextual values according to the session including the contextual value sessionid. Then we can activate the other layers, for example, language. When we output the contextual values, for example hello, the output will match with the user's session and language settings [226].   ▲

We want to avoid losing session information, for example, the selected language. ELEKTRA satisfies such persistence requirements by using the following two lines of source code [226]:

```
1  {
2    std::unique_lock<std::mutex> l = c.requireLock();
3    kdb.set(ks);
4  } // automatic unlocked at end of scope
```

In the source code above, we require a lock using the Coordinator interface accessed with c. Afterwards, we use kdb.set to serialize the data structure KeySet ks. The key set ks contains all values for every context [226].

In our study we were able to elegantly represent device-wide changes of contexts. For example, our device was able to report tampering events using motion detection within an enclosure. When opening the enclosure, the motion detection would trigger. We used an infrared sensor HC-SR501 connected via the general-purpose input/output (GPIO). On tampering events, we included the information on the delivered Web pages. To implement this use case we specified a contextual value [226]:

```
1 [sw/pi/tamper/%tamper%]
2   default:=0
```

We used one thread to wait for tampering events via the system call `select`. If a tampering event occurs, `select` returns and we activate the layer `Tamper`. Eventually the contextual values in the other threads are updated. We use the contextual value `t` (short for `tamper`) to notify users via the delivered Web pages [226]:

```
1 select (fd+1, 0, 0, &fds, 0);
2 context.activate<Tamper> ();
3
4
```

```
1
2
3 t.context ().syncLayers ();
4 if (t) out << "tampered!";
```

Finally, ELEKTRA enabled us to arbitrarily multiplex GPIO via layer activations. We call the according layers *hardware profiles*. A hardware profile is a layer that distinguishes between different hardware setups [226].

Example 6.9. An excerpt of the configuration specification is [226]:

```
1 [hw/pi/pi/%profile%/folder]
2   type:=string
3   check/path:=directory
4   default:=~
5 [hw/pi/pi/%profile%/tamper]
6   type:=string
7   default:=tamper.txt
```

We used the specification with configuration settings such as [226]:

```
1 hw/pi/pi/gpio/folder=/sys/class/gpio/
2 hw/pi/pi/gpio/tamper=gpio7
3 hw/pi/elitebook/gpio/folder=~/context/pi
4 hw/pi/elitebook/gpio/tamper=tamper.txt
```

With the hardware profiles, we were able to use ordinary files on our development laptop while using kernel interfaces on the embedded hardware. Apart from simplifications during development, the hardware profiles enabled us to have different hardware setups with the same firmware image [226].   ▲

As we see from the example, layer activation works without having the target hardware available: We achieve a hardware abstraction [226].

Contextual values easily emulate the functionality of profiles as described in Section 4.1.2. Different from profiles, we are:

- not limited in the number of dimensions due to layers, and

- not confronting every developer with the concept; without a need of layers activation, API users do not need to know about it.

Discussion

We answer **RQ 7.3**:

RQ 7.3. Which features are elegantly realizable in ELEKTRA to configure non-trivial embedded systems?

Finding. *We wrote a multi-threaded embedded Web server without having to take care about context and synchronization with the execution environment. Instead all context specifications were short and located at a single place. Hardware profiles implemented with contextual values enabled easier embedded development.*

Manual implementation of layers was only needed in rare occasions, for example, to restrict contextual values to specific threads and processes.

6.3.3 RQ 7.4: Debugging Support

We discuss improved ways to debug and test context-oriented programs answering **RQ 7.4**:

RQ 7.4. How can we improve debugging support of context-oriented programs?

The uniqueness of layer names emerged to be valuable debugging information [235]:

Logging facilities know the context under that a contextual value is used [235].

Backtraces are augmented by telling us unique names [235]:

```
1 #3   0x0000000000407a56 in operator() at first.cpp:1521
2     i = @0x7fffe36b69a0: { ...
3       m_evaluated_name = "/german/germany/%/test" }
```

Breakpoints use the context as condition [235]:

```
1 break 1520 if i.getEvaluatedName()
2             .compare("/german/germany/%/test") == 0
```

Assertions satisfy that a contextual value is in a correct context [235]:

```
1 assert (i.context ()["language"] == "german");
2 assert (i.getEvaluatedName () == "/german/%/%/test");
```

The second assertion is more precise. It makes sure that *all* other layers influencing the contextual value are deactivated. If the specification is changed, the assertion triggers instead of covering potential problems [235]; answering **RQ 7.4**:

RQ 7.4. How can we improve debugging support of context-oriented programs?

Finding. *Context-aware logging, backtraces, breakpoints, and assertions helped for debugging. The unique layer names turned out to be valuable.*

Implication. *Due to run-time introspection of context,* ELEKTRA *provides helpful debugging experience.*

6.3.4   Reduction of Configuration Settings

An important goal of maintaining configuration settings is to reduce their number [305]. In this section, we present an algorithm that provides feedback about the use of individual configuration settings in source code and tests.

Motivation

Using ELEKTRA's abstractions, some decisions can be delayed. For example, developers do not decide which configuration sources and which configuration file format shall be used. Postponing decisions often have benefits, for example, it avoids going back and forth. But postponing decisions also includes risks, for example, keeping the system too flexible leads to higher complexity. Thus it is important to reduce unwanted complexity whenever possible. Because it involves so little time to add configuration settings using ELEKTRA, there is a high risk that developers add too many configuration settings.

To improve maintenance beyond manual checks, we introduce a continuous feedback mechanism. It assumes that high-level APIs with GENELEKTRA are used. We want to obtain information whether configuration settings are used and tested. We propose an algorithm that processes line coverage information in two steps.

Algorithm

The first (optional) step of the algorithm is:

- Run all tests with code coverage.

- Check if generated code, implementing the contextual value, is executed.

- If it is, we know that the configuration setting is used in a test case. Otherwise, we know it is not tested by the test suite. All these untested configuration settings are remembered as candidates for the second step.

The second step `findUnusedSettings` uses mutation testing. We remove one of the candidates from the configuration specification and try to recompile the software. If it still compiles, we know that the configuration setting is not used at all. This action is done for every candidate of the first step. Alternatively, we are pessimistic and assume that all configuration settings are untested. Here is the algorithm of the second step:

```
1 KeySet findUnusedSettings (KeySet untestedSettings,
2                            KDB kdb,
3                            Builder build)
4 {
5    KeySet unusedSettings = {};
6    KeySet configurationSpecification;
7
8    kdb.get (configurationSpecification);
9
10   for (candidate: untestedSettings)
11   {
12       configurationSpecification.remove (candidate);
13       kdb.set (configurationSpecification);
14       build.recompile ();
15
16       if (build.wasSuccessful ())
17       {
18           unusedSettings.append (candidate);
19       }
20
21       configurationSpecification.append (candidate);
22   }
23
24   kdb.set (configurationSpecification);
25   return unusedSettings;
26 }
```

We assume that `kdb` parses and serializes the configuration specification as used by the software project. The `Builder` allows us to recompile the software project and check if the compilation was successful.

Using this algorithm developers get feedback about which configuration settings are untested and unused. These metrics are valuable for cleanups of configuration specifications and source code.

Evaluation of this algorithm in practice is left as future work.

6.4 Security, Safety, and Quality

We answer **RQ 7.5**:

RQ 7.5. What are the risks and implications on security, safety, and quality in systems using ELEKTRA?

6.4.1 Elektra's Metrics

We start with **RQ 7.5.1**:

RQ 7.5.1. What are the source code metrics of ELEKTRA and who develops ELEKTRA?

The author of this book developed most parts of ELEKTRA (including all relevant parts related to the contributions of this book) by himself. The other parts of ELEKTRA were developed by many other persons. Here we discuss, who contributed which parts and give statistical data and software metrics.

Method: The data collected here refers to ELEKTRA's Git repository (`https://git.libelektra.org`) till commit 599fc45b4bf9957e and data from OpenHub and GitHub as found on 21st August, 2017. Most stats were collected by running Git commands, and then validated with information from OpenHub and GitHub. We used Sloccount 2.26 and Cloc 1.60 [66] to measure lines of code. Furthermore, code complexity was measured with Pmccabe 2.6 with "Modified McCabe Cyclomatic Complexity". We rendered Figure 6.4 with `ggplot2 geom_smooth` using `gam` with the formula: $y \sim s(x, bs = "cs")$.

As we see in Figure 6.4, ELEKTRA started in 2004 and we removed some source code around 2012. This was mainly a cleanup of obsolete bindings (for example, python, which was reintroduced later), patches for other applications (for example, KDE and Xserver), and plugins (for example, gconf and filesys [225]). Since then, the lines of code continuously grew on average.

In total, ELEKTRA has 308,875 lines in all files. Sloccount reports 128,735 lines of code, while Cloc finds 158,679 lines of code. Sloccount gives an estimation that developing ELEKTRA from scratch would cost \$4,434,280.

About 40 people participated in the development of ELEKTRA, 26 of them have their names in the credits. Using `git blame` we found that the author of this book is responsible for 145,534 lines. This is the highest number from all contributors, the next person

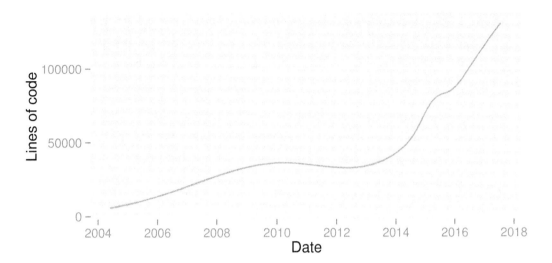

Figure 6.4: History of lines of code in Elektra as counted with Sloccount and visualized with smoothed conditional means.

following with 41,166 lines. The author of the book contributed 5,234 commits. In total he added 502,833 lines, and removed 574,261 lines[2].

The author reviewed at least[3] 726 patches for ELEKTRA. In the reviews we sometimes had lengthy discussions, in one review we wrote 287 comments. In the bug tracker, ELEKTRA had 223 open and 616 closed issues. The most commented issue was about the build server with 152 comments.

The mostly used languages are C with 63,299 lines of code, C++ with 35,521 lines of code, and C/C++ header with 27,488 lines of code. The core is exclusively in C. C++ was used for tooling and some plugins.

According to Sloccount, most of the lines of code are for tests: about 50,877 lines of code[4]. The testing source code contains about 10,179 assert statements. Non-testing source code in LIBELEKTRA has 103 assert statements and 137 logging statements.

Of the remaining 77,858 lines of non-testing code 32,429 are for the 79 plugins.[5] Looking in more detail at the lines of non-testing code for the individual plugins, most plugins

---

[2]The small difference is caused by removing source code of others, mainly done in 2012.
[3]On GitHub alone, not counting emails and previous source code collaboration tools.
[4]Estimated with Sloccount by counting folders called `tests` and files called `testmod*`.
[5]The plugin `ipaddr` was not merged at that time.

are fairly small: The mean is 410 lines of non-testing code, the median is 239 lines of non-testing code. The source code size is within the suggested optimum of 200–400 lines of code for modules [124]. Our largest plugins are `ni` with 3,474 lines of non-testing code, `crypto` with 2,393 lines of non-testing code, and `ini` with 1,997 lines of non-testing code. Our smallest plugin is `journald` with 53 lines of non-testing code.

ELEKTRA is packaged for most GNU/Linux distributions. Current packages (ELEKTRA version 0.8) are known to exist for at least 10 distributions. The maintainers of these distributions sometimes use distribution-specific tools that improve the quality of packages, which sometimes improves ELEKTRA. For example, on Debian's infrastructure most of ELEKTRA's unit tests run at many architectures which unveiled architecture-specific problems. In particular, the Debian maintainer found that the source code for intercepting the function `pre-main` (to hijack command-line arguments) needed to be different on the Powerpc architecture.

ELEKTRA's official build server has about 40 build jobs and 8 build agents. It builds with three different compilers (GCC, Icc, Clang). The build times are from ten minutes to half an hour if also memory leak checks are done. We run about 8 build jobs for every patch under review and nearly all build jobs for every accepted patch.

Pmccabe reported code complexity metrics for 4,121 C/C++ functions in the 546 ELEKTRA's C/C++ source files. The median for the code complexity is 1, and the mean is 3.7. Two functions were extreme outliers in terms of code complexity. They were independently developed but both in plugins related to INI parsing. These outliers had code complexity 76 and 131.

No vulnerabilities against ELEKTRA were reported.

The author of the book developed the following parts of ELEKTRA by himself:

Core of LIBELEKTRA contains mounting logic, lookup algorithms, and delegation of the work to plugins. The `KeySet` has origins in earlier source code. Most parts of the data structure, such as `ksLookup` as described in Section 3.3.3, were completely redesigned by the author.

Libtools contains algorithms assembling plugins as described in Section 3.3.7.

Plugins of the author include many small plugins (logging and encodings), some larger plugins (resolvers and validations), and some storage plugins (C, INI and JSON).

GenElektra is a prototype with rudimentary error reporting.

Kdb-tool is the command-line tool suite as described in Section 6.2.3. Some commands of the command-line tool suite were contributed by others.

Interception of `getenv` and `pre-main` (for command-line arguments).

The following parts were mainly developed by students of the author:

Augeas is a plugin using lenses as described in Section 1.1.1.

Crypto enables the encryption and signature of configuration files.

Puppet integrates ELEKTRA into Puppet. It supports to mount backends and to set keys using Puppet.

User interfaces of ELEKTRA that include a website with snippet sharing functionality, a graphical user interface implemented using Qt, and a web user interface implemented using Node.js (see Section 6.2).

3-way merge improves merging of configuration settings as described in Section 4.4.3.

ELEKTRA has other contributors, mainly people who are users of ELEKTRA. For example, people from Oyranos (a color management framework) and Machinekit (a framework for machine control applications) have contributed to ELEKTRA.

6.4.2 Security Considerations

Here we discuss if it is more secure to implement a configuration file parser (which is still a popular way, as our survey suggests) or to use ELEKTRA.

From the security perspective LIBELEKTRA provides a lightweight solution. LIBELEKTRA does not spawn new threads or processes, nor does it need any special privileges. LIB-ELEKTRA is only a library that parses and serializes several configuration files. Thus by design, ELEKTRA does not make any privilege escalation possible—at least not beyond the privileges of the application. Implementing access control checks within ELEKTRA is less useful, as they are easily circumvented. Instead isolation techniques of the file system shall be used [170].

A project we started to *elektrify* is LCDproc, a software to drive liquid-crystal displays. Measured with Cloc, LCDproc 0.5.8 has 76,552 lines of code in total. Configuration access code is at least 1,652 lines of code (2 %) which can be fully replaced by ELEKTRA. Additionally, LCDproc's modules have even more lines of code that parses configuration values. This source code is a candidate to be replaced by source code in plugins.

We found three important security considerations:

1. If a parser within ELEKTRA is known to be problematic, applications can immediately switch to others, without having to wait for upstream changes. Adding the property `mountpoint` to the configuration specification and reimporting configuration settings suffices. Other configuration libraries do not have this capability.

2. ELEKTRA has more lines of code than a single configuration file parser. For example, LCDproc's configuration file parser has 1,652 lines of code, while the core of ELEKTRA has 6,103 lines of code. From the system's perspective, however, a solution with ELEKTRA can still lead to less exploitable code because ELEKTRA intends to replace all other configuration file parsers, too. Another aspect is that SPECELEKTRA's specifications have less source code and are easier to understand than configuration validation code written in low-level languages.

3. Instead of many mostly unmaintained and untested parsers in every application, ELEKTRA's parsers are maintained by the ELEKTRA initiative. The ELEKTRA initiative uses full-automatic checkers to find security problems within the library. We elaborate on memory safety in ELEKTRA in Section 6.4.3.

6.4.3   Memory Safety

ELEKTRA is mostly implemented in the programming language C, which is an unsafe programming language [182]. The ELEKTRA initiative uses several techniques to mitigate the problems coming from this programming language [281]:

Code sanitizers make sure that ELEKTRA does not have undefined behavior while executing the tests [263].

Static analysis tools such as Cppcheck reparse the source code and yield useful additional warnings but are inherently incomplete.

Valgrind finds memory and data-race errors [196].

C Bounded Model Checker (CBMC) [161] proves that assertions always hold with a source code where the loops are unrolled to a specified depth. Because not everything is specified using assertions and because of the limitations with loops, CBMC is incomplete.

American Fuzzy Lop (AFL[6]) is the state of the art of mutational fuzzer tools [52]. We use it to mutate configuration files and kdb scripts. While it is a highly effective solution, it is incomplete.

Code complexity tools tell us the code complexity of functions. We use it to decide about refactoring.

API design is essential to make sure that memory-safety is not circumvented by API misuse. Unfortunately, despite its design goals, the C API has potential to be misused because pointers are needed. In the high-level APIs and bindings of ELEKTRA, however, which are the only recommended ways to use ELEKTRA, we are not aware of design flaws.

Code reviews have some chance to find anything else or at least increase the chances that the tools are not cheated.

Unfortunately in practice, errors slip through despite all these counter-measures. Nevertheless, it is unlikely that applications put such efforts into their configuration access code. So ELEKTRA can increase security, despite being implemented in an unsafe language.

6.4.4 Misconfiguration

We continue with **RQ 7.5.2**:

RQ 7.5.2. What are the implications of ELEKTRA on misconfiguration?

In the introduction, we claimed that ELEKTRA helps in reducing misconfigurations. Here we discuss in which situations we expected or observed reduction of misconfigurations. We discuss misconfigurations specific to security later in Section 6.4.5. We report on misconfigurations mentioned by Xu and Zhou [303], Nagaraja et al. [195], and Keller et al. [154].

Whether ELEKTRA is resilient against spelling mistakes in configuration files, depends on which plugins are used. For example, different configuration file syntaxes or capitalization

---

[6]A technical whitepaper on details of AFL-fuzz (American Fuzzy Lop) is found here: http://lcamtuf.coredump.cx/afl/technical_details.txt.

allowance (using the plugin `rename`) has effects on acceptance of spelling mistakes. The largest class of spelling mistakes is covered by the extensive set of data types ELEKTRA provides. We listed all plugins implementing data types in Section 5.3.4. Using these plugins, we were able to restrict configuration settings to exactly the allowed characters and canonicalize different allowed spellings if confusion is unlikely. These features are beyond the features of other configuration libraries, so ELEKTRA improves the situation.

For structural errors a similar reasoning is applied. One of ELEKTRA's contributions is that different user interfaces are available. If the tool shows the structure more clearly and gives better feedback, we increase usability. For example, a tool suggests to change settings relevant within a hierarchy. By design the constraints from the key set—as discussed in Chapter 3—cannot be violated. The user cannot

- add keys into the key set with the same key name,

- create syntactically invalid configuration files by persisting a key set, and

- create a situation where a key is not found by the application (see Section 3.4.6).

Misconfigurations that stem from unawareness of the configuration file syntax should be greatly reduced. Such misconfigurations should not reach applications anymore because they are already eliminated during `kdb.set`, i. e., before serializing the configuration files (see Section 3.2.2).

With SPECELEKTRA system administrators avoid duplication of configuration settings. They use the properties `override` and `fallback` instead. We are positive that a reduction of duplication reduces misconfiguration because it eliminates a source of inconsistency. Furthermore, system administrators do not need to set configuration settings that can be derived by default value calculations.

For semantic errors, the plugin system is essential. In plugins, we check for success using the exact same APIs the application uses later. This way we exclude whole classes of errors such as:

- Invalid file paths using the plugin `path`.

- Invalid IP addresses or host names using the plugins `network` or `ipaddr`.

Because the checks occur before the resources are actually used, the checks are subject to race conditions. For example, a path that was present during the check, can have been removed when the application tries to access it. In some situations facilities of the operating system help,[7] in others we have fundamental problems.[8]

Beyond misconfigurations impossible due to ELEKTRA's design, the rejection rate of misconfigurations depends on the effort put into writing SPECELEKTRA specifications. While most of the misconfigurations described above are reliably rejected after adding a single property, sometimes more elaborate specifications are needed. For example, Nagaraja et al. [195] discussed two errors (both with mod_jk):

- A name was added at one place, but forgotten at another place.

- A uniqueness constraint was violated.

While such errors can be checked by configuration validations, a redesign of the key names can lead to a system where wanted constraints are always implicitly fulfilled. For example, we designed the plugin hosts so that the canonical host name is part of the key name. With such a design, violation of uniqueness is impossible due to the key set semantics. It remains to be seen if thinking about how to write validation specifications (and trying to avoid complicated validation specifications) will lead to better design overall.

For some errors, ELEKTRA needs additional information next to the specifications. For example, Nagaraja et al. [195] described a situation where the file path was valid but pointed to a slower hard disk. To detect such situations, we would need performance requirements encoded as configuration setting and plugins that check the performance of individual folders. It is unclear if the effort to implement such a plugin is worthwhile. If we had such a plugin available, however, including such a check would be easy.

It is likely that ELEKTRA helps in situations where users want to share configuration settings. The presence of key names referring to configuration settings has certainly benefits compared to manually locating and manipulating configuration files. Tutorials can use configuration settings in a format for which ELEKTRA provides a reliable import.

We are positive that ELEKTRA yields better error messages than most of the previous configuration libraries. Even more important, ELEKTRA provides diagnostics and trouble shooting support. ELEKTRA enables throughout introspection of all configuration settings.

---

[7]For example, we open the file during the check and pass /proc/<pid>/fd/<fd> to the application. This file cannot be unlinked, but unfortunately the file descriptor requires resources.

[8]For example, if the host we want to reach has gone offline after validation.

We do not know yet if ELEKTRA helps with compatibility problems. Some misconfigurations are out of scope for ELEKTRA. For example, installation of applications needs to be done by configuration management tools on top of ELEKTRA.

A quantitative evaluation showing significant reduction of misconfiguration, is still missing. Nevertheless, as discussed above, ELEKTRA helps in many cases of misconfigurations.

In particular, we can facilitate the main contribution of our book, i.e. context-aware configuration, to reduce misconfiguration. We can use the configuration settings and hardware information of the system to derive configuration settings. Ideally, the configuration settings are also automatically adapted to new situations as shown in the use case of flexible workspaces in Section 5.4.4.

6.4.5　Secure Configuration Settings

Currently, in FLOSS ecosystems security patches are unable to efficiently enforce presence of specific values in configuration files. Completely patching the insecure functionality away, however, breaks some legacy systems. We propose to use configuration settings as requirements that specify security levels. Once the user tries to configure the application to be too insecure, the validation checker fails. ELEKTRA guarantees that the application only receives data as specified in the configuration specification. Distributions change the specification to enforce that insecure configuration settings are avoided. System administrators that need to maintain legacy systems can weaken the security levels. We do not recommend exposing the security levels to end users.

Using the introspection ELEKTRA enables monitoring of security relevant configuration settings. Tools are able to warn users about non-recommended configuration settings. For example, Nagaraja et al. [195] described a case where a study participant forgot assigning a password for the MySQL root user. Using ELEKTRA, we easily integrate checks that warn on such situations.

ELEKTRA supports signing and encryption of configuration settings. This way, unwanted tampering of configuration settings is detected. The encryption is particularly important for configuration settings that contain passwords as often found in `.netrc` (a configuration file containing login data). ELEKTRA relies on security and key management of `gpg`, which is an encryption and signing tool.

Further work is required to evaluate the security implications in more detail.

6.4.6 Discussion

We answer **RQ 7.5** and its subquestions:

RQ 7.5. What are the risks and implications on security, safety, and quality in systems using ELEKTRA?

Finding. Security: *The metrics show that* ELEKTRA *has more lines of codes than a configuration parser by itself. Implications and risks on security are manifold: Some risks may be higher but* ELEKTRA *gives more ways to deal with them.*

Safety: ELEKTRA *avoids several classes of misconfiguration and enables us to deal with other classes, sometimes with little effort.*

Due to ELEKTRA*'s flexibility and configurability,* ELEKTRA *might introduce new kinds of misconfigurations. Problems that might occur during writing the specifications were discussed in Section 6.1.*

Quality: *Users might not be aware of individual's plugins low quality. We mitigated this issue by automatic selection of plugins.*

ELEKTRA *makes complexity—that previously has been resolved manually by system administrators—explicit. Potential bugs in manual configuration processes are moved to potential bugs in* ELEKTRA*.*

CHAPTER 7

Evaluation

Courage doesn't happen when you have all the answers. It happens when you are ready to face the questions you have been avoiding your whole life.

— Shannon L. Alder

In this chapter, we evaluate ELEKTRA. In Section 7.1, we benchmark the frontends. In Section 7.2, we compare solutions of a cascading lookup implemented in a frontend and in a backend. In Section 7.3, we evaluate the overhead of ELEKTRA's modularity in backends. Finally, in Section 7.4, we conduct a large-scale evaluation of introducing context awareness in software without source code modifications using ELEKTRA. Overall, we strive to answer **RQ 8**:

RQ 8. Which software characteristics change if ELEKTRA is applied?

7.1 Performance of Frontends

We benchmark the frontends in the order as they were introduced in Chapter 4, answering **RQ 8.1**:

RQ 8.1. What are the performance characteristics for applications specifically programmed for ELEKTRA?

7.1.1 Method

We measured the performance of applications using ELEKTRA on two devices:

- Raspberry Pi® Model B using the ARMv6 architecture. We will refer to the device as "Raspberry Pi" in later text.

- Hp® EliteBook 8570w using the central processor unit (CPU) Intel® Core™ i7-3740QM @ 2.70GHz. We will refer to the laptop as the "EliteBook" in later text.

We used the operating system Debian GNU/Linux Wheezy 7.8 with the architecture `armhf` (Raspbian) and `amd64`, respectively. We did not change the default compiler GCC 4.7.2-5 (+rpi1 on Raspbian). The systems were not altered for performance improvements, for example, the maximal number of file descriptors remained unchanged with its default 1024 [226].

For measurements we used `gettimeofday` with the following `Timer` implementation:

```
1  #define TIMER_NOINLINE __attribute__ ((noinline))
2  class Timer
3  {
4  public:
5      TIMER_NOINLINE void start ()
6      {
7          gettimeofday (&begin, nullptr);
8      }
```

When stopping the `Timer`, we use `gettimeofday` again and then calculate the result:

```
1      TIMER_NOINLINE void stop ()
2      {
3          gettimeofday (&end, nullptr);
4
5          timer_t result = end.tv_sec - begin.tv_sec;
6          result *= usec_factor;
7          result += end.tv_usec - begin.tv_usec;
8          results.push_back (result);
9      }
```

For the `Timer`, we use the following data types:

```
1 private:
2     struct timeval begin;
3     struct timeval end;
4     typedef long long timer_t;
5     typedef std::vector<timer_t> results_t;
6     results_t results;
7     static const timer_t usec_factor = 1000000LL;
8 };
```

We globally instantiated a `Timer` for every source code to benchmark. We called `start` and `stop` for every measurement. We repeated every measurement 11 times and report median values. We chose the number 11 because then the median is a measured value and not an average of two values.

Threats to Validity

It is well-known that experimental analysis requires high standards [140]. Measuring with `gettimeofday` has several problems: It fails under untypical load, when the clock adjusts itself, etc. To mitigate these problems, we repeated every measurement 11 times. Outliers are likely due to problems in the measurement. We define *outliers* to be data points not within 1.5∗interquartile range. We report medians to exclude these outliers.

The experiment conduction can be flawed. Thus we conducted most experiments from scratch many times.

Source code of the benchmarks is found in ELEKTRA's repository:

```
https://git.libelektra.org
```

7.1.2   RQ 8.1.1: Context-aware APIs

Context-oriented programming typically yields a major drawback: Overhead of 75 %[1] to 99 % [17] is a criterion for exclusion for many types of real-world applications. Improving performance is one of the major claims of our chosen contextual values' design. We answer **RQ 8.1.1** [235]:

---

[1]cj and ContextL performed better in specific cases.

RQ 8.1.1. How much can we improve the performance of configuration access using context-oriented programming?

Method

We evaluate the impact of the number of active layers at run-time by activation of zero to nine layers. We use the same setup as used for the comparison of the different implementation techniques described in Section 4.2.3. As already explained in Section 4.2.3, we use a loop with 100 billion (100,000,000,000) iterations. Different from before, we use a `with` statement outside the loop.

Example 7.1. Using two layers the source code looks as follows [235]:

```
1 s.context ().with<Layer1> ().with<Layer2> ()([&]
2 {
3     s.bm = value;
4     Integer::type x = 0;
5     for (long long i=0; i<iterations; ++i)
6     {
7         x ^= add_contextual (s.bm, s.bm);
8     }
9     dump << x << endl;
10 });
```

The variable `value` is the predefined constant 55 and `s.bm` is a contextual value. To make sure that the calculation takes place, we dump the calculated value to a file (line 9).▲

Result

Figure 7.1 shows the measurement of our implementation ("context cmp noif", as presented in Section 4.2.3) and the measurement with native non-contextual variables ("native cmp noif"). In our benchmark, the implementation has no run-time overhead compared to native non-contextual variables [235].

As shown in Figure 7.2, increasing the number of active layers does not measurably affect the performance. All differences are within 20 milliseconds. Because of the huge number of loop iterations (100 billion), accessing contextual values is the dominant factor, and activating layers is negligible [235].

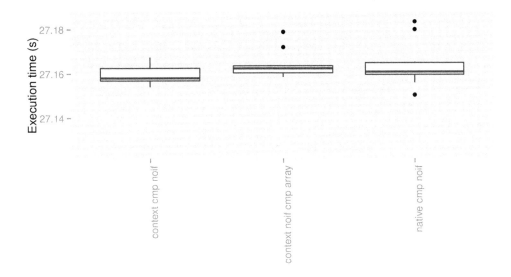

Figure 7.1: Comparison of contextual values to native performance of variables [235]. The figure shows a boxplot with linear scale. Black dots are outliers, i.e., measurements not within 1.5*interquartile range [226].

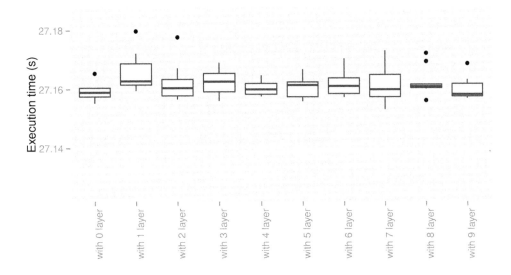

Figure 7.2: Access with active layers [235].

Discussion

The reason for the absence of performance overhead is simple: Compilers perform aggressive optimizations—such as inlining the method that accesses the cache of the contextual value—completely eliminating the performance overhead. There is, however, no guarantee that the compiler actually does such optimizations.

We answer **RQ 8.1.1**:

RQ 8.1.1. How much can we improve the performance of configuration access using context-oriented programming?

Finding. *In our model accessing contextual values can be without overhead—regardless of the number of active layers. Only constant memory overhead occurs for each contextual value.*

API users do not have to restrict the use of contextual values directly in loops and performance-critical code, fulfilling the requirement:

Requirement 10. *Developers must have guarantees that read-only configuration access is fast and updates only happen if wanted.*

Avoiding non-context-aware copies of contextual value makes sure that context and updates are always considered, helping in the requirement:

Requirement 6. *Configuration libraries must provide ways to keep transient and persistent views consistent.*

7.1.3   RQ 8.1.2: Web Server: Multi-thread Overhead

Here we benchmark the first version of the Web server introduced in Section 6.3.2. We exclusively use the multi-threaded contextual values of ELEKTRA's frontend.

Method 1

We conducted the first benchmark on the EliteBook (see Section 7.1.1). We measured replies per seconds by executing `httperf` using the arguments [226]:

```
httperf --hog --num-conn=600000 --rate=6000 --server localhost
```

We determined num-conn and rate by optimizing for highest throughput with close-to-zero errors. To make the setup better reproducible we did not manually tamper the device. Instead we implemented a loop simulating a tampering event every N nanoseconds [226]:

```
1 while (!shutdown)
2 {
3     tc.activate<Tamper> ();
4     std::this_thread::sleep_for (N);
5     tc.deactivate<Tamper> ();
6     std::this_thread::sleep_for (N);
7 }
```

Result 1

The loop produced a high number of layer activations and deactivations but even with only a nanosecond delay ($N = 1$) we could not measure any decay of replies per seconds. Only by removing the delay altogether we experienced slowdown [226].

Method 2: Realistic Long-held Locks

We suspected that the slowdown is caused by internal synchronization barriers of the Coordinator. To explore this effect, we started with a realistic setup: The source code, responsible for serializing configuration settings, needs to hold a lock. We wrote an endless loop executed in the background to continuously require and release a lock while serializing configuration settings.

Result 2

In this scenario, again we could not measure any performance decay [226].

Method 3: Enforced Long-held Locks

Due to lack of realistic setups, we enforced locking of the internal synchronization barriers for a fixed time of 10 milliseconds. Then we vary the time variable L, during which the internal synchronization barriers are not locked [226]:

```
1 while (!shutdown)
2 {
3     std::this_thread::sleep_for (milliseconds (L));
4     t.syncLayers ();
5     std::unique_lock<std::mutex> l = c.requireLock ();
6     std::this_thread::sleep_for (milliseconds (10));
7 }
```

The method `requireLock` returns a lock for the internal synchronization barriers. With `unique_lock` we keep this lock until the end of the block implementing the loop, i.e., until the next loop iteration starts. In this loop we always lock internal synchronization barriers for 10 milliseconds, while the unlocked time is controlled by L.

Result 3

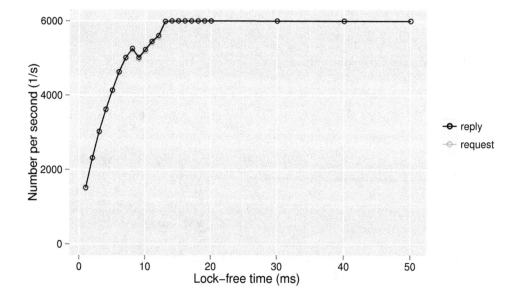

Figure 7.3: HTTP replies and requests per second measured using the EliteBook. Requests nearly perfectly overlap with the replies, and are thus hardly visible in the graph. We increase the lock-free time L in milliseconds. The time $L = 10$ corresponds to 50 % lock-free time. We measure both reply and requests to indicate the occurred errors [226].

As we see in Figure 7.3, with 14 milliseconds, i.e. 58.3% unlocked time, we achieve the full throughput time of 6000 replies per second. With shorter lock-free periods requests and replies per seconds descent. A difference between requests and replies is an unwanted error rate.

Method 4: Embedded Single-processor System

On a single-processor system the picture looks differently. We again use the loop of Method 1. In the next benchmark we started the Web server on the Raspberry Pi. The benchmark tool `httperf` was running on the EliteBook. The two devices were connected via an 100MB/s switch. When optimizing the throughput rate with minimal error rate, we found 150 replies per second to be the maximum. Therefore, we used the following arguments [226]:

```
httperf --hog --num-conn=15000 --rate=150 --server pi
```

Result 4

As we see in Figure 7.4, in this single-core embedded setup a performance decay is clearly visible. The decay starts at a sleep time of around 7 milliseconds [226].

Discussion

We do not expect enforced long-held locks to be a problem because it is a programmer's error to lock the `Coordinator` for such a long time [226]. If we use expensive serialization techniques[2], we easily avoid long locks with the following source code:

---

[2]In the benchmarks, we did not find a serialization technique expensive enough to create a problem. But, for example, network delays of 10 milliseconds would be equivalent to forced locks of 10 milliseconds.

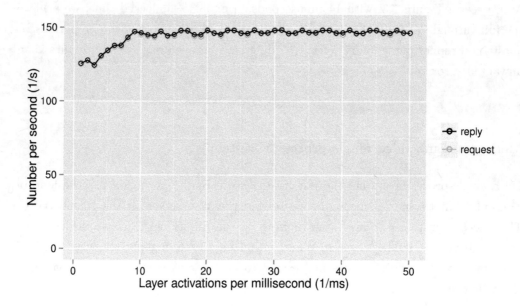

Figure 7.4: HTTP requests and replies per seconds using Raspberry Pi. We decrease layer switches per milliseconds (N). We show both requests and replies to make visible that the error rate is low [226].

```
1 KeySet duplicate;
2 {
3     std::unique_lock<std::mutex> l = c.requireLock ();
4     duplicate = deepDup (ks);
5 }
6 // serialize without holding the lock
7 kdb.set (duplicate);
```

Duplicating a key set is, compared to the serialization, an efficient operation. Nevertheless, we did not come in a situation, which would require the additional two lines of code (lines 1 and 4), answering **RQ 8.1.2**:

RQ 8.1.2. What is the overhead of context changes in an embedded, multi-threaded use case?

Finding. *We found* ELEKTRA *to be suitable for an embedded Web server setup, even with a high number of layer switches. The current implementation of* ELEKTRA *is sensitive to long-held locks.*

We found multi-thread layer switches to be more efficient in multi-core setups. In multi-core setups, the task of switching layers is done in another thread as background task.

7.1.4   RQ 8.1.3: Performance Comparison

We address **RQ 8.1.3**:

RQ 8.1.3. What is the cost of ELEKTRA's individual operations?

Method

For the following benchmarks, we again use `gettimeofday` with `Timer`. Each benchmark invokes specific operations 100,000 times. We reduced the number of invocations because the following operations are more expensive. We measured overhead of `ksLookup` using a small key set searching for a non-present key. The operation `context.evaluate` (see Definition 3.48 on page 111) is used to replace 3 *context placeholders* in a 43 characters long string. The operation `switch` means that we use `activate` followed by `deactivate`. For `with`N and `switch`N benchmarks 50,000 loop iterations are enough to perform 100,000 invocations. We started each benchmark eleven times. We report the results of benchmarks executed on the EliteBook [226].

Result

As shown in Figure 7.5, the C++11 hash map lookup is the fastest operation (0.016 seconds). The lookup in ELEKTRA's KeySet (`ksLookup`) is about twice as slow (0.03 seconds). The operation `syncLayer` takes about 0.08 seconds. The operation `context.evaluate` (named `evaluate` in Figure 7.5) needs 0.11 seconds [226].

As demonstrated in Figure 7.6, the number of connected contextual values influences the execution time [226].

Discussion

We expect `ksLookup` to be slower than a hash map lookup due to its additional features. For example, cascading lookups have extra treatment to handle specifications and

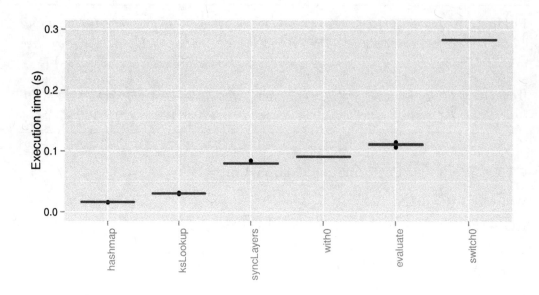

Figure 7.5: Comparison of the duration of operations executed on the EliteBook [226].

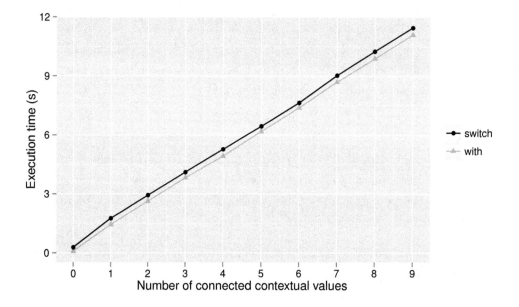

Figure 7.6: Comparison of layer switches (i. e., the methods `activate` and `deactivate`) and the method `with`. We vary the number of connected contextual values [226].

namespaces. From Figure 7.6, we conclude that costs increase linearly in time with a larger number of connected contextual values. The difference between `switch` and `with` is a small constant offset [226], answering **RQ 8.1.3**:

RQ 8.1.3. What is the cost of ELEKTRA's individual operations?

Finding. *All of* ELEKTRA*'s operations have little overhead if only a few values are connected. The operations* `activate` *and* `with` *have linearly more execution time depending on the number of connected contextual values.*

Implication. *Developers need to take care to only connect contextual values with layers as needed.*

7.1.5   RQ 8.1.4: Resource Utilization

We deal with **RQ 8.1.4**:

RQ 8.1.4. How is ELEKTRA's resource utilization of hard disk storage?

Method

We measured the binary sizes of executables using the command `ls`.

Result

The binary of the stripped library `libelektra.so.0.8.10`, i.e. LIBELEKTRA's core, has a size of 109,912 bytes on `amd64`, and 98,456 bytes on `armhf`. The over 50 plugins range from 8 kilobytes for an iteration plugin to 100 kilobytes for a type-checker plugin. To parse INI files, we need an additional plugin that occupies 22,760 bytes (libelektra-ini). To resolve file names in a multi-process-safe and multi-thread-safe way, 47,560 extra bytes are needed (libelektra-resolver) [226]. As comparison, the library `libxml2.so.2.8.0` (that is used by others for the same purpose, i.e., configuration file validation and parsing) requires 1,436,984 bytes on `amd64` and 1,196,108 bytes on `armhf`.

Discussion

Because of the high degree of modularity within our implementation, users can choose which plugins to install. This way, only space for needed functionality is occupied—leading us to the answer of **RQ 8.1.4**:

RQ 8.1.4. How is ELEKTRA's resource utilization of hard disk storage?

Finding. ELEKTRA *has a smaller binary size than XML libraries, about* $\frac{1}{10}$ *if including typical functionality.*

Implication. ELEKTRA *is well suited for embedded systems and otherwise resource-constrained systems.*

7.1.6   RQ 8.1.5: Activation of Contextual Values

We want to respond to **RQ 8.1.5**:

RQ 8.1.5. What are the performance trade-offs towards high-level abstractions for context changes?

Method

We benchmarked ELEKTRA on the EliteBook as described in Section 7.1.1. Because a long time passed during these experiments, we upgraded the operating system to Debian GNU/Linux Jessy 8.4 amd64, which has the compiler GCC 4.9.2-10 as default. We again did not alter the systems for performance improvements but on our system the maximum number of file descriptors was increased to $65,536$ [231].

We created four microbenchmarks. Each of them measures the cost of activating layers 1,000 times. Every shown number is the median value from 11 executions. The main design criteria for the microbenchmarks are their merits for helping in deciding which activation strategy to use. The results and discussions of all four microbenchmarks follow afterwards. For all benchmarks, we use the following variables [231]:

```
1 Timer t;          // see  Section 7.1.1
2 ThreadContext c;  // see  Section 4.3.4
3 Value<long> tcv;  // contextual value for benchmark
```

Our first benchmark (**activate**) measures layer activations using layer classes Layer0 to Layer8 [231]. In this benchmark, we do not activate contextual values, but we pass n contextual values using the parameter cv. The contextual values cv and tcv are connected with the context c. The parameter n ranges from 0 to 9, activating no layer for $n = 0$, activating Layer0 for $n = 1$, activating Layer0 and Layer1 for $n = 2$, etc.

```
1  void benchmarkActivate (std::vector<Value<long>> & cv, long n)
2  {
3      t.start ();
4      for (long i = 0; i < 1000; ++i)
5      {
6          if (n>0) c.activate<Layer0> ();
7          // ..
8          if (n>8) c.activate<Layer8> ();
9          x ^= tcv + tcv;
10     }
11     t.stop ();
12 }
```

We take the measurement between line 3 and line 11. Lines 6–8 contain the relevant parts to be measured. We added line 9 to disable aggressive compiler optimizations that would eliminate the loop. This line does not affect the measurement because it only reads contextual values. We know this operation is as fast as reading native variables [231].

In the second microbenchmark (**activate cv**), we avoided context-unaware activation and used the contextual-value-activation feature introduced in Section 4.4. In the lines 6–8, we activated 0 to 9 contextual values (the 9 contextual values are called cv[0] to cv[8]), which activated 0 to 9 layers [231]:

```
1  void benchmarkActivateCV (vector<Value<long>> & cv, long n)
2  {
3      t.start ();
4      for (long i = 0; i < 1000; ++i)
5      {
6          if (n>0) c.activate (cv[0]);
7          // .. <continues on the next page>
```

```
 8          if (n>8) c.activate (cv[8]);
 9          x ^= tcv + tcv;
10      }
11
12      t.stop ();
13 }
```

In the third benchmark (**sync**), we facilitate the sync feature as described in Section 4.4. Line 7 synchronizes all n contextual values passed as argument. For every activation every contextual value must be recalculated. Here we do not reload contextual values from the execution environment [231]:

```
 1 void benchmarkSync (std::vector<Value<long>> & cv)
 2 {
 3      // cv.values () contains 0 to n contextual values
 4      t.start ();
 5      for (long i = 0; i < 1000; ++i)
 6      {
 7          c.sync ();
 8          x ^= tcv + tcv;
 9      }
10      t.stop ();
11 }
```

In the forth microbenchmark (**reload**), we additionally synchronized the execution environment. In this benchmark, we parsed configuration files from hard disk before every sync. As described in Section 3.2.2, due to an optimization repeated invocations of kdb.get would not repeatedly parse unchanged configuration files. Therefore, we used a new KDB instance for every kdb.get (lines 3–4, and line 8) [231], which forced kdb to parse the configuration file:

```
1  void benchmarkReload (std::vector<Value<long>> & cv)
2  {
3      std::vector<KDB> kdb;
4      kdb.resize (1000);
5      t.start ();
6      for (long i = 0; i < 1000; ++i)
7      {
8          kdb[i].get (cv.values ());
9          c.sync ();
10         x ^= tcv + tcv;
11     }
12     t.stop ();
13 }
```

Result

The results of all four microbenchmarks are displayed in Figure 7.7. Again the number of activations is dependent on the contextual values to be updated. More flexible activation strategies have additional costs (**activate cv** and **sync**). Round trips to persistent, textual configuration files add a constant overhead (**reload**) [231].

Discussion

Figure 7.7 indicates that we have a linear increase of execution time if more contextual values or layers are involved. The offset in the **reload** benchmark is large but constant, only measuring the time to parse the configuration file [231]. We answer **RQ 8.1.5**:

RQ 8.1.5. What are the performance trade-offs towards high-level abstractions for context changes?

Finding. *The run-time overhead of activating contextual values is comparable to activations of layer classes. Higher-level abstractions such as synchronizing all layers are more expensive.*

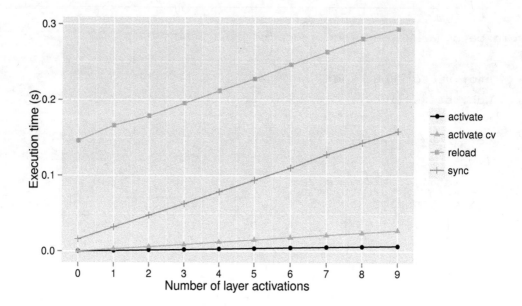

Figure 7.7: Comparison of 1,000 iterations with four microbenchmarks: **activate:** directly activate layers; **activate cv:** activation of contextual values; **reload:** sync with reloading from persistent storage; and **sync:** sync all contextual values in memory. We increase the number of activations of layers or contextual values [231].

7.1.7   RQ 8.1.6: Web Server: Inter-process Layers

Here we benchmark the second version of the Web server, which has been introduced in Section 6.3.2. We already benchmarked the first version of the Web server in Section 7.1.3. Here we benchmark inter-process layers, answering **RQ 8.1.6**:

RQ 8.1.6. What is the overhead of high-level abstractions for context changes in embedded scenarios?

Method

We extend the Web server benchmark to use reloading from configuration settings in the way as benchmarkReload does. Although in our setup we use a thread for context changes, by design several processes can be used instead. In this benchmark we found 2,200 requests per seconds as highest throughput without errors. Again we use httperf on the EliteBook via localhost [231]:

```
httperf --hog --timeout=1 --rate=2200 --num-conn=50000 \
        --num-call=1 --server=localhost
```

Result

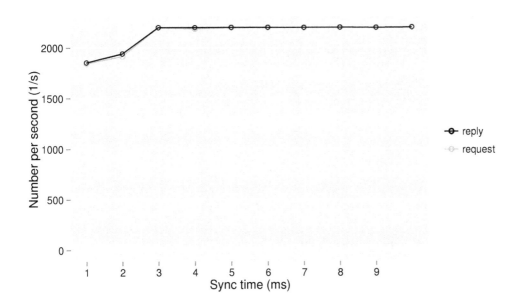

Figure 7.8: Request and reply rate of a Web server. The **sync time** is the wait interval given in milliseconds. The interval is used to sleep until the next activation of inter-process layers [231].

In Figure 7.8 there is an effect for **sync times** below 3 milliseconds. We see a small error rate (difference between requests and replies) in the sync times of 2 and 4 milliseconds.

Discussion

We expect that with frequent synchronizations the internal barriers in `Coordinator` are locked too long, reducing the throughput [231]. We answer **RQ 8.1.6**:

RQ 8.1.6. What is the overhead of high-level abstractions for context changes in embedded scenarios?

Finding. *Different from multi-thread layer switches, inter-process layer switches have measurable overhead in a Web server setup but only for switch rates every few milliseconds.*

Implication. ELEKTRA *is efficient enough to be used in embedded applications. The number of context changes has a small effect, even with inter-process layer switches [231].*

7.2   Comparison: Frontends Versus Backends

For some features it is unclear if an implementation is better done in the frontend or in the backend. In this section we investigate **RQ 8.2**:

RQ 8.2. What are the considerations to implement a feature in the frontends versus in the backends?

Arguments in favor of implementing features in the backends are:

- that the features are immediately available consistently for all frontends,

- that tools with different frontends have the same behavior, and

- system administrators can manipulate the specification without recompilation.

The main argument for implementations in the frontend is performance: The code generator is not restrained by a common data structure and can introspect the specification at compile-time. Nevertheless, we recommend conducting a benchmark before features are woven into the frontends. Unfortunately, such benchmarking is time-consuming and it is unrealistic that every decision is backed up by a benchmark. Thus we demonstrate in a benchmark a more complicated algorithm that features several aspects relevant for such decisions. We guide through a benchmark for cascading lookup with links and namespaces, as defined in Section 3.3.2. We took this algorithm because of its high number of property lookups.

7.2.1   Method

We conducted the benchmarks again on the EliteBook as described in Section 7.1.1. The operating system at that time was Debian GNU/Linux Wheezy 7.5, with GCC compiler version 4.7.2-5. We ran every benchmark eleven times for the boxplots [227].

We implemented two variants of the cascading lookup algorithm: for the backend and for the frontend [227]. Here we summarize important differences:

In the backend variant properties needed for decisions are available via metadata. We cannot know in advance which properties are present. Instead in this variant, we always need to exhaustively introspect every relevant property.

As precondition, applications need to be able to successfully read the configuration specification. To avoid this precondition to fail, we recommend having a built-in copy of the specification. Then the application starts up without a working key database as demonstrated in Section 3.4.6 [227].

In the frontend variant the source code implementing the properties is woven into the application's source code. In this variant, the code generator only adds source code for specified properties. If no link is specified, we get the same source code as if the feature did not exist at all. This variant avoids any overhead if no properties are present.

We implemented and measured both the frontend and the backend variant. We measure `ksLookup` with N override links. We make 200,000 lookups with a contextual value. To make sure that we call `ksLookup`, we synchronize the contextual value's cache for every access. We always use a `KeySet` with five keys. The key to look up has $N = 0$ to 9 `override` properties [227].

Example 7.2. The key with 2 properties `override` is [227]:

```
1 [benchmark/#2]
2   default:=33
3   type:=unsigned_long
4   override/#0:=/benchmark/override/#0
5   override/#1:=/benchmark/override/#1
```

As next step, we benchmark a word counting tool that reimplements the standard UNIX tool `wc`. We intensively used the property `override` (algorithm given in Section 3.3.2) in SPECELEKTRA for the elektrified tool `wc`. We utilized the technique as described in Example 6.2 to implement the check if different features are combined [227]:

```
 1 [sw/wc/show/max_line_length]
 2   type:=boolean
 3   default:=false
 4   opt:=L
 5   opt/long:=max_line_length
 6 [sw/wc/show/no_default_args]
 7   type:=boolean
 8   default:=false
 9   override/#0:=/sw/wc/show/lines
10   override/#1:=/sw/wc/show/words
11   override/#2:=/sw/wc/show/chars
12   override/#3:=/sw/wc/show/bytes
13   override/#4:=/sw/wc/show/max_line_length
```

As input of the wc tool, we used a LaTeX file of 32 kilobyte size. We facilitated Callgrind 3.7.0 to profile the whole application [227].

7.2.2 Result

Figure 7.9 shows the growth in execution time depending on the number of override properties. In the figure already for 0 properties override, the overhead for the backend is 1.8 times higher, and then it grows 22 % faster [227].

For Figure 7.10, we grouped the counted instructions of the wc application into [227]:

process: the main functionality of the application. The processing of the characters in the LaTeX file dominates with 64 % of the counted instructions.

kdb.open: the bootstrapping as explained in Section 3.2.2. It takes about 17 %, mainly due to configuration file parsing. The configuration file parser in use is about 12 times slower than the word counter.

kdb.get: the parsing of the application's configuration file. It costs about 11 % of overall cycles, also mainly due to configuration file parsing.

lookup: the base costs of the lookup without property override.

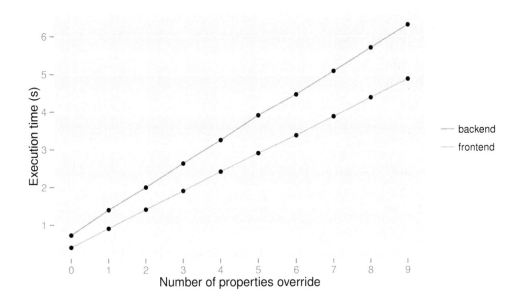

Figure 7.9: Lookup time in backend and frontend implementation variant. We use a linear scale [227].

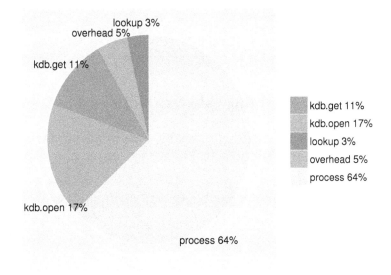

Figure 7.10: Overhead of an *elektrified* application [227].

overhead: the additional costs of the lookup if links are present in the specification. Without any links, only 9 instead of 27 cascading lookups are needed. In total, the overhead due to links of the application is 5 % in this application.

7.2.3   Discussion

In microbenchmarks resolving links the frontend variant is clearly faster. In whole applications, however, the difference is minimal. The overhead might be caused by other factors, such as the parsing time of the additional configuration specification, and not only by the lookup itself. We answer **RQ 8.2**:

RQ 8.2. What are the considerations to implement a feature in the frontends versus in the backends?

Finding.

1. *For the benchmark we needed to turn off frontend caches to measure differences. Without caches, the overhead for the backend is 1.8 times higher and grows 22 % faster [227].*

2. *Even in an application that excessively uses links, the overhead of having the link properties present, is only 5 %.*

Implication. *Differences in overhead are little, at least for the* `ksLookup` *algorithm. Thus features, such as links, shall be implemented in the backend.*

7.3   Overhead of Modular Abstractions

It is well-known that modular abstractions usually come with a price tag: overhead. In this section we benchmark the vertical and horizontal modular abstraction as introduced in Section 5.3, answering **RQ 8.3**:

RQ 8.3. What is the overhead of ELEKTRA's modular abstractions?

7.3.1   Method

We benchmarked SPECELEKTRA on the EliteBook as described on Section 7.1.1 with the operating system Debian GNU/Linux Wheezy 8.2 `amd64`. We employed the compiler GCC 4.9.2 with the compiler option `-O2` [230]. The benchmark setups are described in the individual sub-sections.

7.3.2 Vertical Modularity

Method

To evaluate the overhead of vertical modularity, we increase the number of present mountpoints for an application. With zero mountpoints, ELEKTRA serializes the key set into the *default mountpoint*. For more mountpoints, we use the property `mountpoint`.

Example 7.3. With three mountpoints, we have the following specification [230]:

```
1 [benchmark/0]
2   mountpoint:=/tmp/file0
3 [benchmark/1]
4   mountpoint:=/tmp/file1
5 [benchmark/2]
6   mountpoint:=/tmp/file2
```

Result

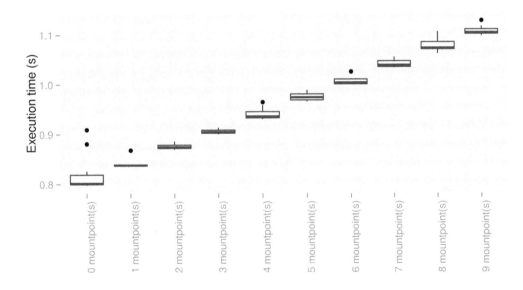

Figure 7.11: Access time using 1,000 keys with 100,000 iterations. On the *x*-axis we increase the number of mountpoints [230].

Figure 7.11 shows that the execution time for nine mountpoints is about 28 % higher compared to the execution time with zero mountpoints.

7.3.3   Horizontal Modularity

Method

To measure the overhead of horizontal modularity, we implemented a plugin called `iterate`. It searches all keys for the property `iterate`. The plugin `iterate` simulates an action required by most plugins in ELEKTRA: It investigates which action is required by which key. In the benchmark, we increase the number of plugins present in one mountpoint. Then we use `gettimeofday` to measure how long it takes to parse and serialize the configuration files, with the plugins present.

Example 7.4. In the benchmark with three plugins, we have the following configuration specification [230]:[3]

```
1  [benchmark]
2    mountpoint:=/tmp/file
3    infos/needs:=iterate#0 iterate#1 iterate#2
```

Result

We were not able to measure any overhead by adding more plugins. When increasing the number of keys, we only increased the parsing time. The time spent in the plugin `iterate` was too little using our measurement method [230].

7.3.4   Discussion

From Figure 7.11 we conclude the answer to **RQ 8.3**:

RQ 8.3. What is the overhead of ELEKTRA's modular abstractions?

Finding.

1. *Vertical modularity, i. e., applications accessing the configuration files of each other, has run-time overhead correlating linearly with the number of used mountpoints.*

---

[3]The array index at the end of the plugin name enables multiple instantiations of the same plugin.

2. *The run-time overhead of horizontal modularity, i. e., plugins executed during configuration access, is negligible.*

Implication. *The overhead of SPECELEKTRA does not give reasons to avoid modularity. Concerning performance, every feature shall be implemented as separate plugin and every application shall use its own configuration file [230].*

7.4 Context Awareness without Source-code Modification

We practically apply our tool in large real-world applications and a systematic software-engineering process described in Section 5.4.4 to answer **RQ 8.4**:

RQ 8.4. What are the characteristics of a system in which context-unaware software was made more context aware without any modifications in the source code?

To answer the overall question, in each of the sub-sections, we respond to one of the sub-questions:

RQ 8.4.1. How many `getenv` invocations can be exploited to improve context awareness without any modifications in the source code?

RQ 8.4.2. How can we practically make applications more context aware without any modifications in the source code?

RQ 8.4.3. What overhead occurs in applications intercepted by ELEKTRA?

RQ 8.4.4. What is the performance implication that occurs on context changes?

7.4.1 Method

For this evaluation, we chose the same 16 popular systems in the same versions as selected in Table 2.1. We investigated all of these applications but here we mainly report on browsers. Reports of other applications are described in earlier work [232, 234], with similar results.

We used Debian GNU/Linux Jessie 8.1 for our evaluation. To enable the interception of ELEKTRA globally, we used `/etc/ld.so.preload`. This way, ELEKTRA's `getenv` is preferred to the system's `getenv` implementation. The benchmarks were executed on the EliteBook, as described in Section 7.1.1. Overhead is measured using Valgrind by executing applications with and without ELEKTRA [232]. Individual methods are described in the respective sub-sections.

Threats to Validity

To mitigate measurement problems we cross-checked with two profiling tools: We used Valgrind Callgrind and Linux Perf.

The benchmarks are conducted comparatively with the system's libc. We compared with getenv of the Eglibc 2.19 implementation. Results may vary with other libc implementations [234].

The benchmarks yield different results depending on the used configuration file formats and even depending on the size of the used configuration files. To mitigate this problem, we took special care that our setup is realistic. We mounted 8 different configuration files and especially chose slow storage plugins. It should be straightforward to repeat our benchmarks measuring even less overhead than reported by us [232].

Many alternative configuration access APIs exist, but none of them is standardized and ubiquitous. We are positive that the results are not specific to getenv but can be reproduced for other configuration access APIs as well. Other configuration access APIs have the same purpose and only differ in how to use them [232].

We added logging to count the number of getenv occurrences. Extensive logging can influence a system adversely. To mitigate this problem, we reran all tests with deactivated logging [232].

We did not consider applications that already were implemented with context awareness in mind. Thus we need to exclude such applications from our claims and cannot draw general conclusions for context-aware applications. Nevertheless, our study unveils important insights about context-aware configuration, particularly for FLOSS [232].

7.4.2   RQ 8.4.1: Unanticipated Context Awareness

In Section 2.3, we already demonstrated that the use of getenv is pervasive, even after startup. Here we validate how many getenv invocations are intercepted and controlled at run-time by ELEKTRA. We show that changes in the context—and hence in the variables returned by getenv—have an influence on the behavior of the application [232], answering **RQ 8.4.1**:

RQ 8.4.1. How many getenv invocations can be exploited to improve context awareness without any modifications in the source code?

Method

First we launched the applications, used the menus, and clicked on buttons of the user interface. While doing so, we traced every `getenv` invocation with its parameters. To check if `getenv` invocations are context aware, we changed the return values of `getenv` while the application was still executing. After repeating the user-interaction, we checked for visual differences to know if the `getenv` invocation influenced behavior [234].

The run-time analysis considers calls to `getenv` throughout the stack by all participating libraries, complementing our earlier source code analysis in Section 2.3. We aim to find how often changed return values of `getenv` invocations in the whole stack actually modify the behavior of 5 different browsers [234].

For some of the settings ($\geq$ in Table 7.1), we lacked the resources to investigate them in detail, even though further settings are likely context aware. The effort to determine context awareness of a single setting sometimes is immense. For example, some configuration settings need installations of servers which use out-dated certificates. Others require buying CPUs implementing different accelerations for cryptographic algorithms.

Result

Application	getenv all	all uniq	later uniq	later config	context aware
Chromium	2,723	1,056	73	≥ 24	≥ 1
Curl	87	14	9	6	6
Firefox	8,185	273	210	118	≥ 15
Lynx	1,428	45	23	19	16
Wget	13	7	1	1	1

Table 7.1: Achieved context awareness in software without source code modifications [234].

Table 7.1 has the following columns: In the first column **getenv all**, we show how often the browsers called `getenv` (in total). The next column **all uniq** considers the number of `getenv` invocations with unique parameters. The column **later uniq** exclusively displays `getenv` invocations with unique parameters and only after startup. The next column **later config** shows good candidates for context awareness: They are not related to debugging, testing, and similar. The last column **context aware** presents candidates that are able to successfully modify behavior at run-time without reloading [234].

Table 7.1 presents the number of `getenv` invocations from applications started on a freshly installed Debian GNU/Linux system. The number of invocations varies not only between applications but it depends heavily on the system it runs on, for example, the installed software. On other machines, we detected several times more unique `getenv` invocations for Firefox [234]. The upper bound is not necessarily the number of `getenv` invocations found in the source code analysis because libraries call `getenv`, too.

To give an example, let us walk through the behavior of all browsers for the environment variable `http_proxy`. Lynx requests `http_proxy` via `getenv` before trying to fetch content. We can return proxies suitable for the network to seamlessly display every page without proxy errors. Wget also requests `http_proxy` for every recursive download. Curl adds even more fine-grained control: 7 additional environment variables allow us to distinguish protocols. Firefox rereads `http_proxy` for every page, except when they are already in cache. Chromium is the only browser that does not query `http_proxy` [232]. Instead it rereads many other environment variables such as `GOOGLE_API_KEY` after start-up. In Chromium, we only found `PRINTER_LIST` to be exploitable for flawless context awareness.

In rare situations, context awareness leads to wrong behavior. In these situations, developers required `getenv` invocations to keep returning the same values. For example, the environment variable `CC` determines which C compiler is used. With ELEKTRA, the environment variable `CC` can be changed during the compilation of software [230]. Because not all compilers and linkers are completely compatible, unexpected switching in the middle of the process can lead to compilation and linker errors.

Discussion

We answer **RQ 8.4.1**:

RQ 8.4.1. How many `getenv` invocations can be exploited to improve context awareness without any modifications in the source code?

Finding.

1. *In each of the 16 applications, user interactions caused `getenv` invocations. They were often useful to influence behavior at run-time. For Lynx even 42 % of the `getenv` invocations improve context awareness. Thus the interception is suitable to improve context awareness without changes in the source code.*

2. *In 4 out of 5 browsers,* ELEKTRA *enables seamless context-aware proxy settings with* getenv *[234].*

3. *Limitations include that some* getenv *invocations do not allow us to produce visible impact. Context changes can lead to incorrect behavior in rare cases [232].*

Implication. ELEKTRA *increases the context awareness for our evaluated applications. Specific configuration settings were even flawlessly adapted to the context.*

7.4.3   RQ 8.4.2: Case Study

Here we show that intercepting applications without source code modifications is not only feasible but practical, answering the research question:

RQ 8.4.2. How can we practically make applications more context aware without any modifications in the source code?

Method

First, we conducted the entire context-oriented software engineering process as described in Section 5.4.4. As software without source code modifications we chose Firefox. When changing workplaces, Firefox shall always pick [234]

1. the correct proxy, and

2. a nearby printer.

Second, we looked at the open interception using Firefox, investigating if all configuration settings can be made context aware.

For both steps we measured the time.

Result

Within a day we conducted the process that Firefox fully-automatically selected nearby printers and proxies. Updates in the user interface happened immediately on network changes, for example, available printers are even modified while the printer dialog is open.

We utilized one-line hooks in the /etc/NetworkManager scripts to implement the context sensor [234]. Then we specified http_proxy and PRINTER_LIST as environment variables of interest (as already depicted in Section 5.4.4) with configuration settings like:

```
1 http_proxy/wlan/home=proxy.example.org
2 printer/wlan/home=laserprinter
```

ELEKTRA allows us to intercept open to return handles to dynamically serialized configuration files. To enable Firefox to reparse its configuration files, we needed 9 hours to understand the complex, historically grown AutoConfig. Afterwards, we enabled AutoConfig with small changes exclusively in configuration files. Future users only need to run a script to do the complete setup. The setup does not involve source code changes but only changes Firefox's configuration settings.

In 2 more hours, we implemented a storage plugin for Firefox's configuration files. Jin et al. [139] found 1,957 configuration settings to be available in Firefox. With open interception, we have a mechanism to make all of them context aware.

Discussion

Our approach is by no means limited to Firefox. Instead it permits any configuration setting from any application to be adapted to context as long:

- ELEKTRA has a binding for the respective configuration access API or has support for the respective configuration file format (for open interception).

- The application reiterates configuration access or has support to reload its configuration settings.

Applications always repeat all relevant configuration accesses during initialization. It is implied that every configuration access is context aware by restarting the application. Thus when invoking external applications, all configuration accesses are by design always fully context aware.

Different interception techniques sometimes complete each other: While open provides more settings, the printer integration in Firefox is smoother via getenv interception.

ELEKTRA supports any context, not only mobile workplaces. Other examples include: user-specific privacy, security, and performance (for example, turning on hardware support).

Furthermore, context can be derived from user data such as calendars, contacts, and activities. We did not need to validate the research questions for individual contexts: Every context sensor collaborates with every application as implied by our complete separation of context sensors and applications.

We addressed the research question:

RQ 8.4.2. How can we practically make applications more context aware without any modifications in the source code?

Finding. *It is practical to utilize Firefox without source code modifications along with* ELEKTRA *in a case study. For retrofitting context awareness in the context of flexible workplaces, we required only three actions completed within a day:*

1. *we specified contextual values,*

2. *we created configuration settings for each workplace, and*

3. *we implemented context sensors to switch layers.*

In case of Firefox, run-time serialization of configuration files is more powerful than `getenv` *interception although the combination of both is even more capable.*

Implication. ELEKTRA *can be practically applied to large-scale, real-world software for non-trivial use cases.*

7.4.4 RQ 8.4.3: Overhead

In this experiment we want to investigate the overhead of context changes using ELEKTRA by answering **RQ 8.4.3**:

RQ 8.4.3. What overhead occurs in applications intercepted by ELEKTRA?

Method

We activated ELEKTRA's interception technique throughout the whole experiment. To measure the overhead of context changes, we change the key database during program execution. This causes ELEKTRA to reparse its configuration file [232].

The setup is as follows: We locally installed the Web server Lighttpd reachable as `localhost`. We used Curl to download ten files from this Web server: `curl -o`

`"#1 http://localhost/test/[1-10]"`. The files have sizes of 1 megabyte to 10 megabytes, respectively [232]. The file sizes were chosen to be substantially larger than any involved configuration file. Otherwise, the overhead caused by parsing of the configuration files dominates.

We needed to take care that our experiment did not influence the control flow of the application. For example, if we modify the `no_proxy` variable, searching for proxy is skipped and the performance improves unwantedly. Thus instead, we changed `COLUMNS`, which is requested during every download but is unrelated to the download itself [232].

We ran three experiments and let Valgrind count the instructions for each experiment [232]:

1. The downloading of the ten files with ELEKTRA's interception active.

2. The downloading of the ten files with ELEKTRA's polling of changes in the configuration files (see Section 5.4.3 for different techniques of how to handle context changes). In this case, ELEKTRA tries to detect changes in the key database, although they do not happen in the second experiment.

3. The downloading of the ten files with an actual change in the key database. Here we modified the key `COLUMNS` in the key database in the middle of the downloads. This causes ELEKTRA to reparse configuration files and return a new value for the next `getenv("COLUMNS")`.

Result

The results of the three experiments is as follows [232]:

1. Without any polling or reloading of the key database, Curl needed 83,786,947 instructions.

2. With polling of configuration files in a rate of not more than every millisecond, the configuration was retrieved 91 times instead of 4 times. This caused Valgrind to count 91,569,790 instructions, i. e., an overhead of 9.3 %.

3. When changing `COLUMNS` in the middle of the downloads, Curl executed 95,248,722 instructions. This is again an overhead of $\sim 4\%$ [232].

Discussion

We described a small part of all experiments measuring performance and overhead [232, 234]. The experiment above confirms those other experiments. For example, we fully recompiled the source code of ELEKTRA while interception was activated. Although the compilation spawned 6847 processes[4] only 14 % overhead occurred [232].

We answer the question:

RQ 8.4.3. What overhead occurs in applications intercepted by ELEKTRA?

Finding.

1. *In applications that work with files smaller than the involved configuration files, overhead dominates. In intense but realistic scenarios, ELEKTRA adds run-time overhead up to 14 % [232].*

2. *Interception with polling of configuration files adds about 10 % overhead.*

3. *With changes in the key database the run-time overhead increases again by $\sim 4\,\%$ in a realistic HTTP-proxy transition.*

7.4.5   RQ 8.4.4: Performance: Layer Switches

In this section we answer **RQ 8.4.4**:

RQ 8.4.4. What is the performance implication that occurs on context changes?

Method

To evaluate the performance, we benchmarked different browsers during a proxy transition on the EliteBook as already introduced in Section 7.1.1 [234]. We measured the number of simulated CPU instructions with Valgrind's tool Callgrind and cross-checked with Linux Perf. We summarize the inclusive costs, i. e., costs of the `getenv` invocation including every callee. Because Valgrind simulates a CPU, we get deterministic results [234].

We conducted three experiments with Lynx and one experiment with Firefox. We profiled Lynx because it is implemented leanly and thus has negligible startup-times. Such a minimalist implementation enables more precise exploration of the ramifications the context changes have [234].

---

[4]Each of which parsed configuration settings and specifications.

1. First we launched Lynx without ELEKTRA and visited two links by typing them in the address bar.

2. Then we turned on ELEKTRA interception and directly modified the proxy before opening the second link.

3. In the next experiment, again with ELEKTRA, we first opened a Web page, then changed the context via layers, and finally opened another Web page. We used a contextual value with two layers: `network` and `interface`.

4. The comparison with Firefox turned out to be more difficult because it consumes resources even without any user interaction. The startup-times of Firefox using Valgrind are nearly two minutes, which made it implausible to measure the relevant time precisely enough. Therefore, we could not do a comparative analysis by the total count of instructions with and without ELEKTRA. Instead we estimated the overhead by analyzing the profile data.

Result

The results of the four benchmarks are [234]:

1. Without context-aware interception, Valgrind counted 92,888,073 instructions (median of three Valgrind invocations). The `getenv` invocations used 0.33 % of these instructions.

2. If we modified `env/override/http_proxy` directly (not changing layers as it normally should be done), we counted 114,049,336 instructions (this is about 18.5 % more instructions than from Benchmark 1) of which `getenv` uses 24.51 %.

3. If we changed a layer value before opening a second link, the `getenv` invocations used 25.27 % of all instructions.

4. Firefox required 20,362,848,539 instructions to start up and to display two Web pages. Summing up all costs from the ELEKTRA library results in 68,750,481, i. e., 0.39 % (maximum value of two measurements). The function `g_getenv` (a wrapper of `getenv` in Firefox) needed 16,614,089 instructions (i. e., 0.08 %) rather than 22,703 instructions (i. e., 0.00 %) without ELEKTRA.

Discussion

We respond to **RQ 8.4.4**:

RQ 8.4.4. What is the performance implication that occurs on context changes?

Finding. *In minimalist applications, such as Lynx, ELEKTRA caused* 18.5 % *to* 25.27 % *overhead. For feature-rich applications the overhead was below* 1 %.

The performance difference between directly modifying the configuration values and changing layer values is minimal: It is less than one percentage point more overhead in getenv*'s instructions.*

Implication. *Developers shall prefer to facilitate contextual values and shall change configuration values indirectly via layers.*

7.4.6 Discussion

We answer **RQ 8.4** about intercepting applications without source code modifications:

RQ 8.4. What are the characteristics of a system in which context-unaware software was made more context aware without any modifications in the source code?

Finding. *It is practical and feasible to intercept configuration access API invocations from applications without source code modifications.*

Even for large-scale legacy applications, where rewriting the application for more context awareness would be an immense effort, adding context awareness with ELEKTRA *has little time effort (hours to days) and overhead (∼ 1 % for feature-rich applications).*

CHAPTER 8

Related Work

begin virus
I am a book virus! Copy me into your book to help me spread!
end.

In this chapter we compare our work with others. In Section 8.1 we look into other systems providing configuration access. In this book, we introduced context awareness and related new programming techniques, related work of which we discuss in Section 8.2 and Section 8.3. In Section 8.4 we focus on methodology in other work. We aim to answer the question:

RQ 9. Why does related work not solve the configuration integration problem?

8.1 Configuration

Systems that provide access to configuration are naturally related to ELEKTRA. We found, however, that only in rare exceptions the abstractions are similar to the abstractions in ELEKTRA. Thus most systems providing configuration access are not as similar to ELEKTRA as one might think. In this section we discuss different approaches to various systems and describe the differences in their abstractions.

8.1.1   Configuration Libraries

In general, other configuration libraries differ from ELEKTRA by having no or little external specifications. They require applications to hard code their configuration access, which prevents introspection, external validation, adapted tooling, and other wanted properties.

Apache Commons Configuration [95, 199] abstracts over different configuration sources using the factory pattern [71, 98]. Different from ELEKTRA, developers need to hard code which sources and validations they want to use. Thus it does not enable introspection. Furthermore, it is tightly integrated in Java technology. In the Version 2.1 (released on 20th August, 2016), Apache Commons Configuration

- requires applications to completely specify which configuration files in which syntax shall be used, causing the configuration integration problem,

- does not support any form of external specifications except for those that are tied to specific configuration file formats such as XML,

- does not provide any context awareness, and

- introduces a complex multi-threading model.

Nosál and Porubän [199, 200] extended the ideas of Apache Commons Configuration. Their work enables users to integrate source code annotations into a coherent system abstracting configuration sources. Their meta-configuration is similar to bootstrapping in ELEKTRA. Different from ELEKTRA, the solution is tightly coupled to Java technology and neither has support for validation nor for context awareness.

Roll [250] introduced a way to generate CORBA initialization code from XML specifications. Her idea was to avoid hard-coded initialization code. She had goals similar to our high-level API but she focused on CORBA and did not support context awareness.

Denisov [72] summarized different requirements for configuration libraries. Unfortunately, the outlined configuration library was not fully implemented. No empirical evidence was given for these requirements. Nevertheless, our empirical results confirm most of these requirements. From our data, however, we cannot find argumentation for two of his requirements:

- *"support for complex data structures"*: We did not find any case of complex data structures in the configuration settings of the software we analyzed. Complex data structures that refer to other elements can easily be avoided by improved lookup that resolve links in data structures. We argue that objects shall not be directly serialized into configuration files, but instead configuration settings shall be designed from a system administrator's perspective. We agree that collections shall be supported but we would not say that they are "complex data structures".

- We did not see why *"support of cloud services"* requires more than *"support for different configuration sources/persistent backing stores"* for a configuration library. Non-file-based storage is needed for many systems and its need is not limited to cloud services. ELEKTRA works with network file systems, and can directly request configuration files from URLs via Curl resolvers. From the survey we cannot confirm that there are additional requirements for cloud-based systems: Only a single person of the survey mentioned "cloud-init based configuration" (without giving new requirements) although several OpenStack developers participated in the questionnaire. We agree that cloud-based setups can be different in aspects related to configuration management.

8.1.2 Configuration File Parsing

One of the main difficulties in ELEKTRA is the support of the many configuration file formats. A significant portion of the development time went into the many parsers and serializers. We considered different ways of how to implement configuration file parsers efficiently. Here we mention some techniques of parsing configuration files, which got attention from the research community.

Lenses promise to solve the problem of having separate implementations of parsers and serializers [41, 160, 177]: A single specification, i.e., a lens, is used to parse and serialize configuration files, leading to trouble-free *round-tripping* properties. We found that most of the development time is invested in better abstracting the configuration settings from the concrete syntax; and not in having separate source code for parsers and serializers. Augeas [177] is an implementation of these ideas focusing on configuration file manipulation. We already discussed its properties in Section 1.1.1. We found Augeas useful because of its preservation of all white spaces and comments. It is well suited to access legacy formats such as `sshd` or `ntp` that do not provide parsing libraries. Thus we integrated Augeas in ELEKTRA.

The PADS language [91–93] tackles the more general problem of processing ad hoc data sources. From a type specification of ad hoc data, parsers and serializers are generated.

Different from ELEKTRA, PADS has fewer assumptions on how the data looks like. The data might even contain errors, and PADS can still work with them. We find the (error) model of PADS elegant, but a potential adaptation to ELEKTRA is future work.

8.1.3 Validation

Validation languages are a wide topic we cannot fully cover here. Hartmann [122] evaluated requirements of different stakeholders for data applications and published 81 types of constraints. We interpret the many types of constraints as confirmation that ELEKTRA needs to be extensible to capture any types of constraints.

Murata et al. [193] created a taxonomy of XML schema languages using formal language theory. XML schemas excel most of ELEKTRA's validation strategies in terms of expressibility. ELEKTRA, however, allows users to combine many strategies, which is difficult using XML schemas. It would require to solve the problem of fully-automatic schema matching, which is impossible in general [28, 76, 240]. For example, if we need to check integrity constraints, we use Schematron, and miss the features of XDuce [135]. Changing from one schema to the other often means rewriting the whole schema.[1] One of the rare exceptions within XML is RELAX NG [56], which allows users at least to combine different data types. In ELEKTRA we easily combine validation strategies. If a feature is missing, we extend the configuration specification language with new plugins.

XML technology is not known to be ideally suitable for describing key-value pairs nor configuration settings [43]. Furthermore, it is easily too verbose to be written by hand [42]. Thus often syntactic alternatives are proposed, which are less verbose and can be transformed with a single specification [42]. As another example, RELAX NG supports an XML syntax and a compact syntax [56].

8.1.4 Links

XML technologies have a variety of ways to express links. They are not specified to be used outside of XML technologies. Configuration files, however, are often not in XML syntax. XPointer [109] permits identifying XML fragments. XInclude [181] provides an element "fallback" similar to the property `default` as described in this book. For the other link properties we described no similar concepts are provided [227].

---

[1]Only for the most popular XML schemas conversion tools exist, for example, Trang or the Multi-Schema Validator.

Configuration links were proposed and formally developed by Reiser [243, 245]. They differ from our fallback and override links because they [227]

- exclusively refer within specifications, while ELEKTRA's links refer to configuration settings and specifications,

- are interpreted when serializing configuration settings, while ELEKTRA's links are evaluated at run-time,

- adopt propositional logic to identify selections, and

- seem to lack support for transformation rules.

8.1.5 Misconfiguration

There is a large body of research for fixing misconfigurations that already became manifest [21, 302, 307, 309, 310]. On contrary, ELEKTRA wants to avoid that misconfigurations occur in the first place. Taking more context into account avoids some kinds of misconfigurations.

Nagaraja et al. [195] tried to avoid having a completely duplicated production environment and wanted to nevertheless catch misconfigurations degrading performance. In an extensive user study with system administrators they observed 42 misconfigurations. They distinguished between local and global misconfigurations. Both kinds of misconfigurations involve context at different levels. While some misconfigurations would be caught by trivial SPECELEKTRA validations, other operation errors are out of scope for ELEKTRA (for example restarting services). We are positive, however, that the combination of modern configuration management tools together with ELEKTRA catches all errors described in the paper [195].[2]

ConfErr [154] is able to localize misconfiguration by trying to inject possibly invalid configuration settings. ConfErr does not use a configuration specification nor does it analyze the source code, which puts severe limitations on its effectiveness. ConfErr could benefit from guidance of SPECELEKTRA to explore border cases in a more targeted way.

AutoBash [272] and ConfAid [21] have similar goals as ELEKTRA. Unlike ELEKTRA, predicates that test the application must be available on the productive system. In

---

[2] Assuming that the workflows are adapted to a more modern style coherent with how the configuration management tools work. For example, you would not manually migrate database servers in modern, redundant, infrastructure-as-a-code systems.

ELEKTRA, problems are ruled out by the specification, so that they cannot occur in the productive system.

Spex [304] infers parts of the configuration specification by analyzing the source code of applications. Spex's approach is complementing ELEKTRA in the sense that it can be used for initial construction of the specification for large existing applications. Spex is not suitable to be used for development and generation of end-user documentation.

Xu et al. [305] questioned which of the many configuration settings are used in practice. They argue that users are confused by too many settings. We fully agree and are positive that SPECELEKTRA helps by automatically deducing many settings from context. These augmented settings can be removed from user guides. Advanced users still have the possibility to override such configuration settings, addressing our findings in the survey [234].

Jin et al. [139] portrayed obstacles in configuring real-world systems. The authors calculated that Firefox has 1,957 settings and guessed that they overlooked only a small part of settings. In our study we show, however, that the configuration access API `getenv` drastically increases the total amount of available configuration settings [234].

Nadi et al. [194], Rabkin and Katz [238] extracted program configuration specifications from source code. They confirm that, even though many specifications are extracted, we need additional external knowledge. We show in our work how context awareness contributes as external knowledge [232].

PCheck [306] aims at validating configuration settings early. The tool searches for validation checks within the source code and moves them into start-up code. Different from ELEKTRA, it requires validation code to be present in the application. But as unveiled in our study, the present validation specifications are often incomplete because of missing context information.

Another idea is to detect inadequate error messages for misconfiguration [311]. ELEKTRA systematically avoids some problems in error messages by automatically adding important information, such as the affected configuration file, the mountpoint, etc.

Other related work assumes that only a single programming language is applied. Rabkin and Katz [238] describe how configuration settings are extracted statically. Zhang and Ernst [309] present a tool that finds wrongly configured settings in a fully automated way. Rabkin and Katz [237] precompute possible misconfigurations diagnosis. In contrast, ELEKTRA has no assumption on the choice of programming languages.

Xu and Zhou [303] surveyed different ways of how to improve on misconfiguration. At that time, the idea of context-aware configuration was in an early stage [235]. Thus context-aware configuration was not part of this survey.

8.1.6 Configuration Management

Configuration management is related to the topic of the book, but configuration management is situated one level higher. While configuration management is concerned about the content of configuration settings, ELEKTRA is concerned about how applications access these configuration settings. In ELEKTRA both configuration settings and specifications are well suited to be managed via configuration management tools. This gives an important advantage because configuration management tools struggle to work with the many ways to access configuration settings [45].

Configuration management includes managing configuration settings for all nodes in a network [68]. In this context, directly changing configuration files is regarded as anti-pattern. For smart phones and other customizable devices users often desire to directly reconfigure their personal devices. SpecElektra allows personal customization, while still enforcing the configuration specification managed by system administrators [230]. Configuration management tools do not support to locally validate configuration. Misconfiguration easily reaches the systems, in particular if the consistency problems are related to context. ELEKTRA mitigates these problems by local, context-aware validation.

Zdun [308] argues that the concern *"behavioral composition and configuration"* shall be treated as a first-class entity. This approach goes a different direction than ELEKTRA. It values composition, reusability and modularity of source code more than the resulting system administrators' interfaces [227].

Gruber [110] used ontologies for sharing data. He aimed at minimal ontological commitment, i. e., to tolerate different forms of representation. For example, different date formats such as "1993" or "March 1993" shall be accepted. In ELEKTRA plugins make sure that different formats are canonicalized so that frontends receive expected values. Gruber [110] facilitated references similar to ELEKTRA's key names [227].

Syrjänen [273] formalized the dependences of the Debian Package management system using the stable model semantics. The goal was to get better diagnostic information for error messages.

8.2   Context Awareness

In this section we discuss related work on context awareness.

8.2.1   Context-oriented Programming

Context-oriented programming plays a role within software engineering [24, 141, 255]. It aims at comprehensible programs being more context aware. As extension, ELEKTRA adds context awareness without source code modification [232].

Plaice and Mancilla [216] applied a Cartesian approach to context. One of the differences is the use of an n-dimensional table with lazy computation instead of our one-dimensional key set with eagerly computed values. While the Cartesian approach is theoretically more powerful, it has the disadvantage that its contents cannot easily be serialized. However, efficient serialization is a requirement for working with execution environments [235].

Watanabe and Takeno [295] introduced an actor-based model for cross-context messages. They improved the receiving of messages in the correct context. Different from them ELEKTRA works with threads and processes instead of actors [226].

Costanza et al. [61] provided ContextL as an extension to Common Lisp Object System (CLOS) and relied on its features: dynamic class generation, multiple inheritance, dynamically scoped variables, and multiple dispatch. In most programming languages these features are not available. For example, C++ only supports multiple inheritance from this set of features [235].

Dynamic aspect weaving, for example, in the Steamloom virtual machine [39], provides language constructs for the activation of partial program definitions. Different from ELEKTRA, it requires virtual machines [235].

Kamina et al. [146] proposed a generalized activation mechanism using contexts and subscribers. ELEKTRA only provides a subset of these generalized activation mechanism. Their implicit activation, however, can have serious impact on the performance, conflicting with our performance requirements [231].

Pape et al. [208] used a meta-tracing just-in-time compiler to better cope with non-standard lookups. This line of research promises to get implicit activation with acceptable costs. Their work needs just-in-time compilation to work, not available in some of ELEKTRA's supported languages.

Bainomugisha et al. [23] suggested that even currently running code shall be interrupted and restarted to better fit the viewpoint time of context awareness. This idea nicely fits into our concept of synchronization points: ELEKTRA's frontends can be extended to jump back to the last synchronization point on context changes. Cardozo et al. [51], Taing et al. [274] instead focused on consistency of unanticipated adaptation of context.

Chiba et al. [54] demonstrated that modularity does not necessarily need syntactic extensions. Instead they introduced a database and browser for cross-cutting concerns. The database contains the information which code snippets shall be kept synchronous. The ideas of the approach can be applied to SPECELEKTRA.

8.2.2 Contextual Values

Asirelli et al. [18], Montangero et al. [191] pioneered contextual values already in 1975. Similar to the key set in ELEKTRA, they use context-value pairs where all values in all contexts are stored.

Löwis et al. [290] proposed an updated form of contextual values[3] extending on context-oriented programming. Their layer activation[4] forces the developer to explicitly declare layers. Thus their approach would benefit from having contextual values as layers [290]. Their proposal for implicit layer activations avoids explicit synchronization points at a high price: They check context on every use of every contextual value [290].

Tanter [275] analyzed the semantics of contextual values in-depth. Different from ELEKTRA, these contextual values need modifications in the Scheme interpreter.

8.2.3 Context-aware Applications

Schilit et al. [258] proposed context-aware computing. They already envisioned automatic contextual reconfiguration. Since the work of Dey and Abowd [74], the research topic received more attention.

Most approaches—to make applications more context aware—require modifications in the source code. To mitigate efforts, context-oriented middleware [13, 103, 111, 125] and frameworks [239, 299] were introduced. ELEKTRA can be seen a light-weight context-aware middleware or framework for local configuration settings [232].

---

[3]Named context variables in their work.
[4]They call it binding of contextual values.

Riva et al. [248] extracted design patterns from context-aware applications. They found that a hybrid mediator-observer is used in almost all of their surveyed context-oriented programming systems. ELEKTRA is no exception and uses the observer pattern for thread synchronization [226].

Alegre et al. [5], Baldauf et al. [24], Jong-yi et al. [141] surveyed the field of context-aware applications in depth. Mens et al. [186] introduced a taxonomy of approaches to context-aware applications. As in our work, they found the execution environment as source for context information. Based on their taxonomy, ELEKTRA shall be classified as follows:

- ELEKTRA does not support behavior missing in the source code. It enables, however, to switch between existing behavior at run-time as needed by the context.

- ELEKTRA supports both contextual and context features: The decision is up to the application.

- ELEKTRA uses a one-branch context tree: Without context placeholders contextual values are non-context-aware configuration settings.

- ELEKTRA supports programmer-declared dependences [231].

Alexandrov et al. [7] uses intercepting of library calls to promote user experience but with a different goal than ELEKTRA.

Lee et al. [166] proposes a context-aware, deployment-oriented development process similar to our context-oriented software engineering process. Different from ELEKTRA, context needs to be known at design time.

Parra et al. [210] argued that context-aware specifications need integration into context-aware applications using compiler technologies. While this might be a good idea for some specifications, in general we propose the opposite: Even if many context specifications are interpreted at run-time, the overhead is little. Additionally, only if context specifications are evaluated at run-time flexible adaptations for new viewpoints of contexts are possible.

Kamina et al. [145] defined layers as binary information: They are either activated or deactivated. For location information, for example, we could use `inAustria` and `inArgentinia` as layers. With a high number of locations, however, the number of layers gets unmanageable. To avoid such high numbers of layers we prefer key-value pairs for layer information [151]. Then even contextual specifications with few layer names describe a large set of possible values.

8.2.4 Context-aware Web Services

Niu et al. [198] reported on a framework, called WIF4InL, for indoor localization. Similar to ELEKTRA, it provides an application-neutral API. Niu et al. [198] used layering of Web-based APIs: Their composite API *"allows high-level queries by internally combing some fundamental API."* [198]. Different from ELEKTRA, only queries regarding locations are provided. ELEKTRA's design is different: We would expect the application to not care about localization details and directly query the configuration settings. For example, suppose a screen shall automatically change its brightness according to the indoor location. In WIF4InL, the developer would directly query the API and encode the rules about the brightness as part of the program. In ELEKTRA, the developer would ask for the current brightness. Internally, ELEKTRA could use WIF4InL as context sensor to calculate the correct brightness. While ELEKTRA provides more portability for its applications, using WIF4InL directly opens more possibilities for behavior where several real-world objects interact. Furthermore, WIF4InL provides topological and navigational features, for which ELEKTRA is not the appropriate tool.

Kapitsaki et al. [148] argued that context awareness is an *"essential aspect—almost a requirement—of mobile services"*. They propose a context-oriented Web service architecture using the SOAP protocol and build upon work of Keidl and Kemper [153]. They share with ELEKTRA that their architecture is plugin based and that it supports manipulation of responses the user gets.

8.3 Programming Techniques

In this section we elaborate on programming techniques similar to programming techniques used in ELEKTRA.

8.3.1 Product Lines

Software product lines [35, 190, 217, 257] investigate configuration settings at design time using feature models [167]. They aim at manufacturing software products by combining features. While they share some goals with ELEKTRA, other goals are completely different. Whereas product lines focus on creating customized products, ELEKTRA targets on customizing software at run-time and on-demand. ELEKTRA's specifications can be seen as variability model, but ELEKTRA has its focus on run-time configuration access for FLOSS applications. Thus ELEKTRA's goals are more in line with goals of FLOSS software, where distributions avoid variants of the same software packages.

Linux, by using the Kconfig language, can be considered as highly-configurable product [211]. Compilation variants of plugins in ELEKTRA work similarly. Berger et al. [33] compare two variability modeling languages: Kconfig and CDL.

Leite and Penciuc [169] suggested to facilitate ideas from software product line for configuration management. They also propose to replace imperative scripts with descriptions of desired features.

Recent advances in software product lines switched from compile-time to load-time variability [291]. Mauro et al. [183] built on these dynamic software product lines and extended them with context awareness. Similar to ELEKTRA, they proposed a single specification that includes context information. Mauro et al. [183] relied on constraint solving, an approach that could also be applied as validation plugin within ELEKTRA.

8.3.2   Database Management Systems

Stored procedures [82] are used to validate or transform data but cannot tamper with some semantics of the database. For example, there are limitations in which way a stored procedure can reconfigure the database. Furthermore, automatic program modifications of the stored procedures are challenging.

Elmongui et al. [84] introduced context-aware data management systems. Such query languages can be on top of ELEKTRA [231].

Grier et al. [107] argued that security of plugins can be enforced if direct access to the system is restricted. Plugin architectures were also proposed on operating system level [67].

8.3.3   Meta-level Programming

Umuhoza et al. [284] studied different code generation techniques for mobile development. Loques et al. [175] discussed the correspondence between concepts of configuration and meta-level programming. Aktemur and Kamin [4] compared different techniques to implement customizable libraries. They did not consider context [231].

Jung et al. [143] facilitated code generation. They target embedded systems with focus on resource utilization as discussed in Section 7.1.5. Using partial evaluation they removed Libxml2 dependences to make the resulting binaries fit on their target platform. Different from ELEKTRA, they assume configuration settings to be static, i.e., neither context aware nor customizable.

Österlund and Löwe [204]—using the ideas of Ericsson [86]—presented a way of how programs, that use conservative locking, can be accelerated. They used run-time knowledge in order to choose the optimal locking scheme [205]. The frontends of ELEKTRA can profit from this technique.

8.4 Methodology

Here we describe work that used similar methods or elaborated on methodology we used.

8.4.1 Type systems

Type systems [49, 113, 172, 215, 221–224, 261, 296] allow developers to specify constraints on data. Configuration values are data, thus configuration specifications can be supported by type systems.

Gannon [99] conducted the first user research on type systems. The first experiment was quantitative, with nearly no qualitative aspect. Their work has a subjective tone, for example, the paper states that these *"results come as no surprise"*. The next paper conducting a user study was written ten years later [219]. Again it follows a quantitative approach, but it puts as goal to not take personal anecdotes as granted. It was still not mentioned that results might not be universally valid. The work of Daly et al. [65] is one of the early qualitative papers. Their results focused on the usefulness of error messages.

Hanenberg [116] finally established user research for type systems at a greater scale. The major contribution was that he doubted some previously well-established opinions about the positive impact of static type systems. The effort of his study was huge: He developed two computer languages that were identical with the only exception that one had static types and the other had not. Even with 49 subjects, of whom each worked over 27 hours, he could not demonstrate a statistical significant difference. In his experimental setup, he combined a small application with a larger one. While in the smaller application the static-typed language yielded disadvantages, this was not the case for the larger application.

The main methodology for type systems is to prove soundness and completeness [215]. SPECELEKTRA currently does not have sound and complete checking of the configuration specification nor settings. Candidate type systems for ELEKTRA are:

1. More powerful data types, for example, supporting units of measurement [75, 215].

2. Ways to define subtyping between configuration settings and subtrees thereof [215].

3. Sum types are both self-describing and their tag is one of the simplest form of metadata. Sum types are the opposite of the subtypes: They allow us to loosen the strictness of a type. For example, to allow a string to be empty or to contain a number, we use sum types.

4. Constraint programming [97], for example with Gecode, COIN-OR LP, and Z3.

5. Data schemas, for example, Relax NG schema [56], and XSD [264].

6. Check relations and infer types from relations (type reconstruction) [118, 215].

7. Any combination of the techniques above.

8.4.2 Surveys

Berger et al. [34] and Villela et al. [288] conducted a questionnaire asking about variability modeling. Their survey targets a different group.

Several studies focused on FLOSS developers. Michlmayr et al. [189] explored quality problems using interviews. We affirm that documentation often is missing. Barcomb et al. [25] explored how developers acquire FLOSS skills. Crowston et al. [63] surveyed other FLOSS development studies.

8.4.3 Human Computer Interaction

Human computer interaction has a broad spectrum of user research methodology, including "research through design" [102]. Its goal is to produce knowledge by studying the process of designing and the interaction of design with users [270]. So design is merely the means to extend the ability to investigate and acquire new knowledge. Nevertheless, the main interest of this research is how things can be improved and not how things are. We agree with Tichy [280], who argued that computer scientists should experiment more.

The similarly called "design science" is a rigorous method used to design and evaluate information systems in case studies [298]. For software engineering "theory of cases" was developed [80, 83].

8.4.4 Application Integration

Integration via middleware is a well-established research topic. For example, Paul et al. [212] introduced the tool interconnection language. It improves the integration of components by specifying operational and event interfaces. The tool interconnection language compiler generates adapter code, which influences the run-time environment. In the case study, they used CORBA.

Integration of software engineering tooling is well-researched, too. For example, DesignSpace [70] integrates development artifacts and their relations. Monto [152] allows users to integrate different programming language environments into integrated development environments.

Enterprise application integration [57] has a completely different focus: It tries to better integrate support of business processes.

Application integration via configuration settings is a novelty of this book. We could not find literature that tried to integrate software configuration settings and specifications by context-aware configuration.

CHAPTER 9

Conclusion and Future Work

We are what we think. All that we are arises with our thoughts. With our thoughts we make the world.

— Siddhartha Gautama, rendering of Thomas Byrom

Humans are involved in an endless struggle to express themselves. In this book we described some contributions that help users, system administrators, and developers to reveal their thoughts related to context-aware configuration. In particular, the framework ELEKTRA and the modular specification language SPECELEKTRA are a promising way to specify configuration access for FLOSS systems. We are ready to answer our main research question for the different *stakeholders*:

RQ 1. Why is current FLOSS configuration access rarely context aware and how can we improve on the situation?

Developers had obstacles that they were missing decent frontends with a high level of abstraction. Thus they hard-coded inflexible and mostly context-unaware configuration accesses. ELEKTRA improves on the problem by the concept of contextual values as configuration settings. These better frontends enable developers to directly work with variables that contain context-aware configuration.

System administrators were not empowered to connect configuration settings and context information. ELEKTRA improves on the configuration integration problem by globally sharing configuration settings and context information in a key database.

To not lose any modularity, we mount backends and put needed functionality in plugins. SPECELEKTRA empowers system administrators to improve on configuration validation and context awareness with requirements and context information encoded as configuration settings.

End users rarely had context awareness in their applications. Instead, they had to manually change settings of every application. With ELEKTRA, they benefit from increased context awareness of the configuration settings. We showed that this even works for applications in which no source code is modified. Furthermore, ELEKTRA provides user interfaces so that end users can avoid any contact with configuration files.

We conclude the answer of **RQ 1** by walking through the four initial goals. We revisit contributions to each goal and describe future work. As structure, we use the steps needed to create and evaluate the modular, system-level, context-oriented configuration specification language SPECELEKTRA:

- Before we created SPECELEKTRA, we had to understand the requirements and challenges. We conclude on our challenges in Section 9.1.

- SPECELEKTRA alone would be an incomplete solution if applications misinterpret configuration settings internally. In Section 9.2, we conclude our efforts to provide better and safer frontends that avoid missing considerations of context.

- In Section 9.3 we give final remarks about the modularity and efficiency of SPEC-ELEKTRA.

- In Section 9.4 we summarize how we achieve context-aware configuration for both elektrified applications and applications without source code modifications.

9.1 Challenges

In the beginning of our work we found that state-of-the-art literature only reported the phenomenon misconfiguration but hardly elaborated on its causes. Thus we had to unveil these causes ourselves. From the causes, we derived requirements aiming at Goal Requirement:

Goal (Requirement). *A goal of this book is to unveil requirements by empirically analyzing how applications access configuration settings and why developers programmed it that way.*

To accomplish the goal, we addressed the following research question:

RQ 3. Why do FLOSS applications lack *context awareness* and *configuration validation* for configuration settings and what are the challenges in providing them?

The answer is that validations and context information is encoded in the applications in a way so that they are [233]

- not reusable, requiring error-prone duplication,

- not introspectable by external tools, and

- incapable of using knowledge of the system and its context.

We supported our claims by an experience report, a questionnaire, and a large-scale source code analysis [233]. We framed the disclosed challenges as *configuration integration problem*: Applications are currently unable to access configuration settings and specifications present in the system.

In this book, we collected the first empirically-founded requirements for configuration access. Some requirements fundamentally differ from all current implementations. In particular, LIBELEKTRA is the first implementation with external configuration specifications and consistent introspection. These properties are, however, essential to mitigate the configuration integration problem that was found important by 96 % of 173 survey participants.

Furthermore, we learned that current frontends are already used as if they were context aware, although they are not. Based on that, we split our efforts into two paths for possible improvements on context-aware configuration:

- By providing novel frontends, we mitigate problems for newly-written software.

- By reimplementing current frontends, we mitigate problems for legacy software.

Future Work: We plan to conduct studies on misconfiguration with systems that use ELEKTRA. In particular, similar studies as discussed in Chapter 2 and Section 6.4.4 should be repeated. This way, new ways of misconfiguration can be unveiled and the effectiveness of ELEKTRA can be improved.

9.2   Context-oriented Programming

We would not achieve much if developers continue to access configuration settings in error-prone, non-unifiable ways. Thus we first looked at Goal Frontend:

Goal (Frontend). *We aim at a context-aware, type-safe frontend that mitigates problems unveiled before. The effort to let applications participate with this run-time system shall be kept at a minimum.*

We demonstrated the possibility of supporting contextual values without overhead on reading them—unconcerned of the number of active layers. A declarative specification of contextual values diminishes the burden of implementing type-safe contextual classes implementing contextual values and layers. Additionally, we avoid superfluous cache updates on context changes by specifying dependences between values and contexts [235].

Specifications in combination with active layers yield unique names for all contextual values in each context. These names allow introspection and improve debugging support of contextual values [235].

Ubiquitous Computing: In this book, we improved context awareness and customizations without compromise on efficiency in multi-threaded applications. Developers can choose whether context changes are across all threads or target specific thread(s) [226].

We demonstrated that our approach improves on multi-core-processor support for context-aware ubiquitous computing. ELEKTRA facilitates algorithms to read contextual values concurrently with full control with respect to performance [226].

In benchmarks we demonstrated that even frequent context changes do not slow down the page replies of a Web server application. Only on a single-core processor we noticed decay if using a high number of context changes. On a multi-core processor we needed an unrealistic-long global lock to reduce the number of replies per seconds [226].

Our contributions for ubiquitous computing are summarized as follows [226]:

- ELEKTRA enables developers to facilitate contextual values in embedded, multi-threaded applications.

- In a case study, we reported on our experience on developing a Web server running on embedded hardware.

- We analyzed the performance in single-core and multi-core setups.

These contributions are significant because in other implementations, context awareness had a much larger performance impact unsuitable for embedded systems [226].

Another important aspect of our tool is the build-in persistence of the execution environment. In our approach, command-line options and configuration files initialize all contextual values for every known context. ELEKTRA enables serializing users' customizations to configuration files.

Mobile Computing: In this book we demonstrated how contextual values are used for layer activation. We considered several limitations and benefits [231]:

- Layer activations automatically consider context.

- Applications are enabled to synchronize layers activations.

- Applications share context information across programming languages.

The approach is practical and relevant to mobile development. It simplifies accounting for the current context. Furthermore, it supports individual customization and sharing context between applications. Even end users can redefine configuration settings in a specific context [231].

In benchmarks, we demonstrated that activating contextual values does not add much cost to layer activations. ELEKTRA also supports synchronization with the key database to enable sharing of contextual values between applications. A real-world Web server benchmark illustrates that only high synchronization rates with the key database, such as every few milliseconds, influence the number of served requests on a multi-core computer [231].

Our contributions in mobile computing are summarized as follows [231]:

- With ELEKTRA, we introduced a tool with a unique combination of performance, context awareness, and customization.

- ELEKTRA empowers developers to facilitate contextual values in multi-threaded and multi-process applications.

- Contextual values are shareable across applications.

- ELEKTRA currently supports development, also for embedded systems, in C++, Python, Haskell, Lua, Shell, Ruby, and Java.

- In a case study we reported our experience in embedded development. We analyzed the performance in microbenchmarks and using a Web server.

Future Work: Many further optimization techniques are open to be explored. For example, layer switching can be accelerated by using an array per contextual value. It might require compression techniques to keep the size of arrays acceptable.

9.3 Modular Specification Language SpecElektra

We conclude on Goal Abstraction:

Goal (Abstraction). *We create an abstraction by designing the configuration specification language* SPECELEKTRA. *This abstraction shall enable users to reduce effects of the configuration integration problem by unifying configuration access, simplifying configuration validation, and enabling context awareness.*

SPECELEKTRA is in a sweet spot of configuration specification languages that enables modularity: In SPECELEKTRA, modularity supports developers to reach system-oriented and context-oriented requirements. The modularization in the specification language supports applications to include their specific validation strategies. This way we reach an improvement of the validation precision without introducing a complex configuration specification language. SPECELEKTRA enables us to externalize many cross-cutting concerns related to configuration access [230].

We implemented most parts of SPECELEKTRA in backends so that specifications are automatically enforced for all applications. Bugs are easily fixed for all applications at a single place. We took care to keep the backends extensible by implementing all features as plugins. We presented an algorithm that automatically assembles plugins using the configuration specifications and the plugins' contracts.

In benchmarks we showed that overhead introduced by modular abstraction is negligible. All current features, except of the cache for contextual values, can be implemented within plugins in the backends. Even better, the impact of a higher number of plugins is irrelevant compared to overall costs [230].

The benefits of SPECELEKTRA are thus that it [230]

- opens up a unified way to access configuration settings,

- enables documentation, validation, and even calculations of configuration settings,

- avoids restrictions for plugins,

- introduces plugins with run-time and compile-time variability, and

- enables us to introduce high-level configuration settings from which ELEKTRA derives suitable context-aware configurations.

Future Work: There is some doubt that POSIX abstractions cover the needs of applications [20]. We agree and think that configuration access is an important need of applications. In further work, ELEKTRA's API, KDB, and its abstractions should be reimplemented in different programming languages. For implementations of ELEKTRA's API, compliance levels should be defined.

Further research is needed to decide which type systems fit best for such a configuration specification language. Several type systems, as described in Section 8.4.1, can be implemented and compared. We also leave type-safe upgrading of configuration specifications as further work.

9.4 Context awareness

We contributed to Goal Context:

Goal (Context). *We aim at a run-time system that automatically chooses the best suitable configuration settings with regard to the context. We want to enable users to consistently manipulate and introspect which configuration settings an application receives. Making changes in configuration settings shall be futz-free.*

In this book, we claimed that applications can be enriched to be more context aware without any source code modifications. We showed that such a run-time system exists and, furthermore, is practical. We evaluated ELEKTRA on 16 large, real-world FLOSS applications and presented more detailed case studies on some of the applications. Only by changing configuration settings and writing simple specifications, we improved context awareness in several case studies, often even flawlessly. We applied a context-oriented software engineering process that supports systematic applicability [234].

We facilitated a context-aware key database using configuration files. Calls to frontends, such as `getenv` and `open`, are forwarded to ELEKTRA's implementation of context-aware configuration access. Furthermore, the same context information, configuration settings, and specifications are reused between applications to improve on the configuration integration problem. A unique property of our approach is that it enables context awareness without any modifications in source code [232].

Our results related to unanticipated context awareness are [232]:

- With our approach applications are more aware of their context. This context awareness leverages application integration.

- Our work demonstrates that deducing configuration settings from context is realistic.

- We provide experimental validation in a case study of significant complexity.

- The evaluation offers some clues on the potential of context awareness.

Avoiding manual considerations of context and validation in configuration access addresses a source of misconfiguration [234].

Our approach demonstrates that it is not required to foresee every possible context during development. Instead we introduce layers and configuration settings during deployment. ELEKTRA is modular due to the separation of context sensors and applications. The source code and run-time analysis shows that dependence injection, i. e., 'hijacking' existing `getenv` and `open` invocations, enables more context awareness [234].

We showed how we systematically integrated all 1,957 configuration settings of Firefox to provide seamless adaptation to workplaces. We never needed to modify Firefox's source code [234].

Future Work: We plan to integrate more context awareness and to conduct larger case studies [230]. Ideally, whole desktop environments are elektrified with a single implementation of an API. The `open` interception can be reimplemented as file system in user space (FUSE), which is a less intruding solution. We take advantage of the fact that ELEKTRA is by no means limited to intercepting `getenv` and `open`. For example, we started implementing the API GSettings used within the desktop environment GNOME. It has the potential to make all GNOME settings context aware. Extensions to make even more forms of configuration context aware (configuration for plugins, modules, mobile APIs etc.) remain as future work [234].

List of Figures

List of Tables

Index

access specification, 37

active layer, **111**

application programming interface (API), 8, **27**, 145, 197

array index, **96**

backend, **21**, **100**, **114**, **179**

basename, **85**

below, **95**

bootstrap, 67, **101**

bootstrapping, 201, 210

cascading key, **88**

cascading lookup, **32**, **91**, 117, 185, 222

character set, **84**

clause, **122**

clean string, **85**

compilation variant, **201**

compile-time, 30

configurable application, **28**

configuration access, 1, **29**

configuration access API, 8, **29**

configuration access point, **29**, 206

configuration data, *see* configuration setting

configuration file, **28**

configuration file format, **35**

configuration file manipulation, **37**

configuration integration problem, **6**, 179, 195, 307

configuration item, *see* configuration setting

configuration library, 8, **31**

configuration management, 12, **37**, 224

configuration management tool, **37**

configuration option, *see* configuration setting

configuration parameter, *see* configuration setting

configuration property, *see* property

configuration setting, 1, **28**, 92

configuration source, **32**, 86

configuration sources, 1

configuration specification, **4**, **35**, **92**

configuration specification language, 8, 11, **41**, **98**

configuration validation, **3**, 19, 36, 53, 307

configuration value, **28**

consume, **13**, 28

context, **1**, **39**

context awareness, 1, 19, **50**, 53, 307

context change, 24

context changes, **41**

context placeholder, 261

context sensor, **40**, **189**, 211

317

Bibliography

[1] *getenv(3) Linux User's Manual*, March 2017.

[2] *open(2) Linux User's Manual*, March 2017.

[3] Serge Abiteboul. Querying semi-structured data. In *International Conference on Database Theory*, pages 1–18. Springer, 1997.

[4] Baris Aktemur and Sam Kamin. A comparative study of techniques to write customizable libraries. In *Proceedings of the 2009 ACM Symposium on Applied Computing*, SAC '09, pages 522–529, New York, NY, USA, 2009. ACM. ISBN 978-1-60558-166-8. doi: 10.1145/1529282.1529391. URL http://dx.doi.org/10.1145/1529282.1529391.

[5] Unai Alegre, Juan Carlos Augusto, and Tony Clark. Engineering context-aware systems and applications: A survey. *Journal of Systems and Software*, 117:55–83, 2016. ISSN 0164-1212. doi: 10.1016/j.jss.2016.02.010. URL http://www.sciencedirect.com/science/article/pii/S0164121216000467.

[6] Andrei Alexandrescu. *Modern C++ design: generic programming and design patterns applied*. Addison-Wesley, 2001.

[7] Albert D. Alexandrov, Maximilian Ibel, Klaus E. Schauser, and Chris J. Scheiman. UFO: A personal global file system based on user-level extensions to the operating system. *ACM Trans. Comput. Syst.*, 16(3):207–233, August 1998. ISSN 0734-2071. doi: 10.1145/290409.290410. URL http://dx.doi.org/10.1145/290409.290410.

[8] Eric Arnold Anderson. *Researching system administration*. PhD thesis, University of California at Berkeley, 2002.

[9]   Paul Anderson. Local system configuration for syssies. Technical report, CS-TN-38, Department of Computer Science, University of Edinburgh, Edinburgh, 1991.

[10] Paul Anderson. Towards a high-level machine configuration system. In *LISA*, volume 94, pages 19–26, 1994.

[11] Paul Anderson, Alastair Scobie, et al. Lcfg: The next generation. In *UKUUG Winter conference*, pages 4–7, 2002.

[12] Chris Andreae, James Noble, Shane Markstrum, and Todd Millstein. A framework for implementing pluggable type systems. In *Proceedings of the 21st Annual ACM SIGPLAN Conference on Object-oriented Programming Systems, Languages, and Applications*, OOPSLA '06, pages 57–74, New York, NY, USA, 2006. ACM. ISBN 1-59593-348-4. doi: 10.1145/1167473.1167479. URL http://dx.doi.org/10.1145/1167473.1167479.

[13] Richard Anthony, DeJiu Chen, Mariusz Pelc, Magnus Persson, and Martin Törngren. Context-aware adaptation in DySCAS. *Electronic Communications of the EASST*, 19, 2009. URL http://gala.gre.ac.uk/5533/.

[14] Tomoyuki Aotani, Tetsuo Kamina, and Hidehiko Masuhara. Unifying multiple layer activation mechanisms using one event sequence. In *Proceedings of 6th International Workshop on Context-Oriented Programming*, COP'14, pages 2:1–2:6, New York, NY, USA, 2014. ACM. ISBN 978-1-4503-2861-6. doi: 10.1145/2637066.2637068. URL http://dx.doi.org/10.1145/2637066.2637068.

[15] Sven Apel, Thomas Leich, Marko Rosenmüller, and Gunter Saake. *FeatureC++: On the Symbiosis of Feature-Oriented and Aspect-Oriented Programming*, pages 125–140. Springer Berlin Heidelberg, Berlin, Heidelberg, 2005. ISBN 978-3-540-31977-1. doi: 10.1007/11561347_10. URL http://dx.doi.org/10.1007/11561347_10.

[16] Malte Appeltauer, Robert Hirschfeld, and Tobias Rho. Dedicated programming support for context-aware ubiquitous applications. In *Mobile Ubiquitous Computing, Systems, Services and Technologies, Second UBICOMM.*, pages 38–43. IEEE, 2008.

[17] Malte Appeltauer, Robert Hirschfeld, Michael Haupt, Jens Lincke, and Michael Perscheid. A comparison of context-oriented programming languages. In *International Workshop on Context-Oriented Programming*, COP '09, New York, NY,

USA, 2009. ACM. ISBN 978-1-60558-538-3. doi: 10.1145/1562112.1562118. URL `http://dx.doi.org/10.1145/1562112.1562118`.

[18] Patrizia Asirelli, Pierpaolo Degano, Giorgio Levi, Alberto Martelli, Ugo Montanari, Giuliano Pacini, Franco Sirovich, and Franco Turini. A flexible environment for program development based on a symbolic interpreter. In *Proceedings of the 4th International Conference on Software Engineering*, ICSE '79, pages 251–263, Piscataway, NJ, USA, 1979. IEEE Press. URL `http://dl.acm.org/citation.cfm?id=800091.802946`.

[19] Uwe Aßmann. *Invasive Software Composition*, pages 107–145. Springer Berlin Heidelberg, Berlin, Heidelberg, 2003. ISBN 978-3-662-05082-8. doi: 10.1007/978-3-662-05082-8_4. URL `https://dx.doi.org/10.1007/978-3-662-05082-8_4`.

[20] Vaggelis Atlidakis, Jeremy Andrus, Roxana Geambasu, Dimitris Mitropoulos, and Jason Nieh. POSIX abstractions in modern operating systems: The old, the new, and the missing. In *Proceedings of the Eleventh European Conference on Computer Systems*, EuroSys '16, pages 19:1–19:17, New York, NY, USA, 2016. ACM. ISBN 978-1-4503-4240-7. doi: 10.1145/2901318.2901350. URL `http://dx.doi.org/10.1145/2901318.2901350`.

[21] Mona Attariyan and Jason Flinn. Automating configuration troubleshooting with dynamic information flow analysis. In *Proceedings of the 9th USENIX Conference on Operating Systems Design and Implementation*, OSDI'10, pages 1–11, Berkeley, CA, USA, 2010. USENIX Association.

[22] David F. Bacon and Peter F. Sweeney. Fast static analysis of C++ virtual function calls. In *Proceedings of the 11th ACM SIGPLAN Conference on Object-oriented Programming, Systems, Languages, and Applications*, OOPSLA '96, pages 324–341, New York, NY, USA, 1996. ACM. ISBN 0-89791-788-X. doi: 10.1145/236337.236371. URL `http://dx.doi.org/10.1145/236337.236371`.

[23] Engineer Bainomugisha, Jorge Vallejos, Coen De Roover, Andoni Lombide Carreton, and Wolfgang De Meuter. Interruptible context-dependent executions: A fresh look at programming context-aware applications. In *Proceedings of the ACM International Symposium on New Ideas, New Paradigms, and Reflections on Programming and Software*, Onward! 2012, pages 67–84, New York, NY, USA,

2012. ACM. ISBN 978-1-4503-1562-3. doi: 10.1145/2384592.2384600. URL
http://dx.doi.org/10.1145/2384592.2384600.

[24] Matthias Baldauf, Schahram Dustdar, and Florian Rosenberg. A survey on context-
aware systems. *International Journal of Ad Hoc and Ubiquitous Computing*, 2(4):
263–277, 2007.

[25] Ann Barcomb, Michael Grottke, Jan-Philipp Stauffert, Dirk Riehle, and Sabrina
Jahn. How developers acquire FLOSS skills. In *IFIP International Conference on
Open Source Systems*, pages 23–32. Springer, 2015.

[26] Rob Barrett, Yen-Yang Michael Chen, and Paul P. Maglio. System administrators
are users, too: Designing workspaces for managing internet-scale systems. In *CHI
'03 Extended Abstracts on Human Factors in Computing Systems*, CHI EA '03,
pages 1068–1069, New York, NY, USA, 2003. ACM. ISBN 1-58113-637-4. doi: 10.
1145/765891.766152. URL http://dx.doi.org/10.1145/765891.766152.

[27] Rob Barrett, Eser Kandogan, Paul P. Maglio, Eben M. Haber, Leila A. Takayama,
and Madhu Prabaker. Field studies of computer system administrators: analysis of
system management tools and practices. In *Proceedings of the 2004 ACM conference
on Computer supported cooperative work*, pages 388–395. ACM, 2004.

[28] Carlo Batini, Maurizio Lenzerini, and Shamkant B. Navathe. A comparative analysis of methodologies for database schema integration. *ACM Comput. Surv.*, 18
(4):323–364, December 1986. ISSN 0360-0300. doi: 10.1145/27633.27634. URL
http://dx.doi.org/10.1145/27633.27634.

[29] Don Batory. A tutorial on feature oriented programming and product-lines. In
Proceedings of the 25th International Conference on Software Engineering, ICSE '03,
pages 753–754, Washington, DC, USA, 2003. IEEE Computer Society. ISBN 0-7695-
1877-X. URL http://dl.acm.org/citation.cfm?id=776816.776935.

[30] Farnaz Behrang, Myra B. Cohen, and Alessandro Orso. Users beware: Preference
inconsistencies ahead. In *Proceedings of the 2015 10th Joint Meeting on Foundations
of Software Engineering*, ESEC/FSE 2015, pages 295–306, New York, NY, USA,
2015. ACM. ISBN 978-1-4503-3675-8. doi: 10.1145/2786805.2786869. URL http:
//dx.doi.org/10.1145/2786805.2786869.

[31] Artyom Beilis. http://cppcms.com. Accessed January 2015.

[32] Oren Ben-Kiki, Clark Evans, and Brian Ingerson. YAML ain't markup language (YAML™) version 1.1. *yaml.org, Tech. Rep*, 2005.

[33] Thorsten Berger, Steven She, Rafael Lotufo, Andrzej Wąsowski, and Krzysztof Czarnecki. Variability modeling in the real: A perspective from the operating systems domain. In *Proceedings of the IEEE/ACM International Conference on Automated Software Engineering*, ASE '10, pages 73–82, New York, NY, USA, 2010. ACM. ISBN 978-1-4503-0116-9. doi: 10.1145/1858996.1859010. URL http://dx. doi.org/10.1145/1858996.1859010.

[34] Thorsten Berger, Ralf Rublack, Divya Nair, Joanne M. Atlee, Martin Becker, Krzysztof Czarnecki, and Andrzej Wąsowski. A survey of variability modeling in industrial practice. In *Proceedings of the Seventh International Workshop on Variability Modelling of Software-intensive Systems*, VaMoS '13, pages 7:1–7:8, New York, NY, USA, 2013. ACM. ISBN 978-1-4503-1541-8. doi: 10.1145/2430502.2430513. URL http://dx.doi.org/10.1145/2430502.2430513.

[35] Thorsten Berger, Daniela Lettner, Julia Rubin, Paul Grünbacher, Adeline Silva, Martin Becker, Marsha Chechik, and Krzysztof Czarnecki. What is a feature? A qualitative study of features in industrial software product lines. In *Proceedings of the 19th International Conference on Software Product Line*, pages 16–25. ACM, 2015.

[36] Felix Berlakovich. A universal storage plugin for Elektra. https://www. libelektra.org/ftp/elektra/berlakovich2016universal.pdf, 2016. Accessed January 2017.

[37] Stephen M. Blackburn, Amer Diwan, Matthias Hauswirth, Peter F. Sweeney, José Nelson Amaral, Tim Brecht, Lubomír Bulej, Cliff Click, Lieven Eeckhout, Sebastian Fischmeister, Daniel Frampton, Laurie J. Hendren, Michael Hind, Antony L. Hosking, Richard E. Jones, Tomas Kalibera, Nathan Keynes, Nathaniel Nystrom, and Andreas Zeller. The truth, the whole truth, and nothing but the truth: A pragmatic guide to assessing empirical evaluations. *ACM Trans. Program. Lang. Syst.*, 38(4):15:1–15:20, October 2016. ISSN 0164-0925. doi: 10.1145/2983574. URL http://dx.doi.org/10.1145/2983574.

[38] Joshua Bloch. How to design a good API and why it matters. In *Companion to the 21st ACM SIGPLAN symposium on Object-oriented programming systems, languages, and applications*, page 507. ACM, 2006. Invited Talk.

[39] Christoph Bockisch, Michael Haupt, Mira Mezini, and Klaus Ostermann. Virtual
      machine support for dynamic join points. In *Proceedings of the 3rd International
      Conference on Aspect-oriented Software Development*, AOSD '04, pages 83–92, New
      York, NY, USA, 2004. ACM. ISBN 1-58113-842-3. doi: 10.1145/976270.976282.
      URL http://dx.doi.org/10.1145/976270.976282.

[40] Christoph Bockisch, Sebastian Kanthak, Michael Haupt, Matthew Arnold, and
      Mira Mezini. Efficient control flow quantification. In *ACM SIGPLAN Notices*,
      volume 41, pages 125–138. ACM, 2006.

[41] Aaron Bohannon, J. Nathan Foster, Benjamin C. Pierce, Alexandre Pilkiewicz,
      and Alan Schmitt. Boomerang: resourceful lenses for string data. In *POPL '08:
      Proceedings of the 35th annual ACM SIGPLAN-SIGACT symposium on Principles
      of programming languages*, pages 407–419, New York, NY, USA, 2008. ACM. ISBN
      978-1-59593-689-9. doi: http://dx.doi.org/10.1145/1328438.1328487.

[42] Claus Brabrand, Anders Møller, and Michael I. Schwartzbach. Dual syntax for
      XML languages. *Information Systems*, 33(4):385–406, 2008.

[43] Tim Bray, Jean Paoli, C. Michael Sperberg-McQueen, Eve Maler, and François
      Yergeau. Extensible markup language (XML). *W3C Recommendation*, 2(4):27–66,
      1997.

[44] Hendrik Brummermann, Markus Keunecke, and Klaus Schmid. Formalizing dis-
      tributed evolution of variability in information system ecosystems. In *Proceedings
      of the Sixth International Workshop on Variability Modeling of Software-Intensive
      Systems*, VaMoS '12, pages 11–19, New York, NY, USA, 2012. ACM. ISBN 978-
      1-4503-1058-1. doi: 10.1145/2110147.2110149. URL http://dx.doi.org/10.
      1145/2110147.2110149.

[45] Mark Burgess. A site configuration engine. In *USENIX Computing systems*,
      volume 8, pages 309–337, 1995.

[46] Mark Burgess. On the theory of system administration. *Science of Computer Pro-
      gramming*, 49(1):1–46, 2003. ISSN 0167-6423. doi: http://dx.doi.org/10.1016/j.scico.
      2003.08.001. URL http://www.sciencedirect.com/science/article/
      pii/S0167642303000315.

[47] Brendan Burns, Brian Grant, David Oppenheimer, Eric Brewer, and John Wilkes. Borg, Omega, and Kubernetes. *Commun. ACM*, 59(5):50–57, April 2016. ISSN 0001-0782. doi: 10.1145/2890784. URL http://dx.doi.org/10.1145/2890784.

[48] Brad Calder and Dirk Grunwald. Reducing indirect function call overhead in C++ programs. In *Proceedings of the 21st ACM SIGPLAN-SIGACT Symposium on Principles of Programming Languages*, POPL '94, pages 397–408, New York, NY, USA, 1994. ACM. ISBN 0-89791-636-0. doi: 10.1145/174675.177973. URL http://dx.doi.org/10.1145/174675.177973.

[49] Luca Cardelli and Peter Wegner. On understanding types, data abstraction, and polymorphism. *ACM Comput. Surv.*, 17(4):471–523, December 1985. ISSN 0360-0300. doi: 10.1145/6041.6042. URL http://dx.doi.org/10.1145/6041.6042.

[50] Nicolás Cardozo. Emergent software services. In *Proceedings of the 2016 ACM International Symposium on New Ideas, New Paradigms, and Reflections on Programming and Software*, Onward! 2016, pages 15–28, New York, NY, USA, 2016. ACM. ISBN 978-1-4503-4076-2. doi: 10.1145/2986012.2986016. URL http://dx.doi.org/10.1145/2986012.2986016.

[51] Nicolás Cardozo, Laurent Christophe, Coen De Roover, and Wolfgang De Meuter. Run-time validation of behavioral adaptations. In *Proceedings of 6th International Workshop on Context-Oriented Programming*, COP'14, pages 5:1–5:6, New York, NY, USA, 2014. ACM. ISBN 978-1-4503-2861-6. doi: 10.1145/2637066.2637071. URL http://dx.doi.org/10.1145/2637066.2637071.

[52] Sang Kil Cha, Maverick Woo, and David Brumley. Program-adaptive mutational fuzzing. In *2015 IEEE Symposium on Security and Privacy*, pages 725–741, May 2015. doi: 10.1109/SP.2015.50.

[53] Daniel Chalmers. *Contextual mediation to support ubiquitous computing*. PhD thesis, University of London, 2002.

[54] Shigeru Chiba, Michihiro Horie, Kei Kanazawa, Fuminobu Takeyama, and Yuuki Teramoto. Do we really need to extend syntax for advanced modularity? In *Proceedings of the 11th annual international conference on Aspect-oriented Software Development*, pages 95–106. ACM, 2012.

[55] Tsun Chow and Dac-Buu Cao. A survey study of critical success factors in agile
      software projects. *Journal of Systems and Software*, 81(6):961–971, 2008.

[56] James Clark. Relax NG compact syntax. `http://www.oasis-open.org/`
      `committees/relax-ng/compact-20021121.html`, 2002. Accessed August
      2014.

[57] Stefan Conrad, Wilhelm Hasselbring, Arne Koschel, and Roland Tritsch. *Enterprise
      Application Integration*. Spektrum Akademischer Verlag, Heildelberg, 2005. URL
      `http://eprints.uni-kiel.de/14569/`.

[58] Lionel Cons and Piotr Poznanski. Pan: A high-level configuration language.
      In *LISA*, volume 2, pages 83–98, 2002. URL `http://static.usenix.org/`
      `events/lisa02/tech/full_papers/cons/cons_html/`.

[59] Fernando J. Corbató, Fernando H. Saltzer, and C. T. Clingen. Multics: The
      first seven years. In *Proceedings of the May 16-18, 1972, Spring Joint Computer
      Conference*, AFIPS '72 (Spring), pages 571–583, New York, NY, USA, 1972. ACM.
      doi: 10.1145/1478873.1478950. URL `http://dx.doi.org/10.1145/1478873.`
      `1478950`.

[60] Software Productivity Consortium Services Corporation. *Reuse-driven Software
      Processes Guidebook: SPC-92019-CMC, Version 02.00. 03*. Software Productivity
      Consortium Services Corporation, 1993.

[61] Pascal Costanza, Robert Hirschfeld, and Wolfgang De Meuter. Efficient layer activa-
      tion for switching context-dependent behavior. In DavidE. Lightfoot and Clemens
      Szyperski, editors, *Modular Programming Languages*, volume 4228 of *Lecture Notes
      in Computer Science*, pages 84–103. Springer, 2006. ISBN 978-3-540-40927-4. URL
      `http://dx.doi.org/10.1007/11860990_7`.

[62] Douglas Crockford. JSON: The fat-free alternative to XML. In *Proceedings of
      XML*, volume 2006, 2006.

[63] Kevin Crowston, Kangning Wei, James Howison, and Andrea Wiggins. Free/libre
      open-source software development: What we know and what we do not know. *ACM
      Comput. Surv.*, 44(2):7:1–7:35, March 2008. ISSN 0360-0300. doi: 10.1145/2089125.
      2089127. URL `http://dx.doi.org/10.1145/2089125.2089127`.

[64] Krzysztof Czarnecki, Paul Grünbacher, Rick Rabiser, Klaus Schmid, and Andrzej Wąsowski. Cool features and tough decisions: A comparison of variability modeling approaches. In *Proceedings of the Sixth International Workshop on Variability Modeling of Software-Intensive Systems*, VaMoS '12, pages 173–182, New York, NY, USA, 2012. ACM. ISBN 978-1-4503-1058-1. doi: 10.1145/2110147.2110167. URL `http://dx.doi.org/10.1145/2110147.2110167`.

[65] Mark T. Daly, Vibha Sazawal, and Jeffrey S. Foster. Work in progress: an empirical study of static typing in ruby. In *Evaluation and Usability of Programming Languages and Tools (PLATEAU) at the ACM Onward! Conference*, 2009.

[66] Al Danial. Cloc–count lines of code. `https://github.com/AlDanial/cloc`, 2017. Accessed Februar 2017.

[67] Dan Decasper, Zubin Dittia, Guru M. Parulkar, and Bernhard Plattner. Router plugins: a software architecture for next-generation routers. *IEEE/ACM Transactions on Networking*, 8(1):2–15, February 2000. ISSN 1063-6692. doi: 10.1109/90.836474.

[68] Thomas Delaet, Wouter Joosen, and Bart Vanbrabant. A survey of system configuration tools. LISA'10, pages 1–8. USENIX, 2010. URL `http://dl.acm.org/citation.cfm?id=1924976.1924977`.

[69] TINA-C Deliverable. Tina object definition language manual. 1996. URL `http://tinac.com/specifications/documents/odl96_public.pdf`.

[70] Andreas Demuth, Markus Riedl-Ehrenleitner, Alexander Nöhrer, Peter Hehenberger, Klaus Zeman, and Alexander Egyed. Designspace: An infrastructure for multi-user/multi-tool engineering. In *Proceedings of the 30th Annual ACM Symposium on Applied Computing*, SAC '15, pages 1486–1491, New York, NY, USA, 2015. ACM. ISBN 978-1-4503-3196-8. doi: 10.1145/2695664.2695697. URL `http://dx.doi.org/10.1145/2695664.2695697`.

[71] Victor Denisov. Overview of java application configuration frameworks. *International Journal of Open Information Technologies*, 1(6):5–9, 2013.

[72] Victor S. Denisov. Functional requirements for a modern application configuration framework. *International Journal of Open Information Technologies*, 10:6–10, 2015.

[73] PostgreSQL Developers. `http://doxygen.postgresql.org/guc_8c_source.html`. Accessed February 2017.

[74] Anind K. Dey and Gregory D. Abowd. The what, who, where, when, why and how of context-awareness. In *CHI '00 Extended Abstracts on Human Factors in Computing Systems*, CHI EA '00, NY, 2000. ACM. ISBN 1-58113-248-4. URL ftp://ftp.cc.gatech.edu/pub/gvu/tr/1999/99-22.pdf.

[75] Deepak Dhungana, Andreas Falkner, and Alois Haselböck. Generation of conjoint domain models for system-of-systems. In *Proceedings of the 12th International Conference on Generative Programming: Concepts & Experiences*, GPCE '13, pages 159–168, New York, NY, USA, 2013. ACM. ISBN 978-1-4503-2373-4. doi: 10.1145/2517208.2517224. URL http://dx.doi.org/10.1145/2517208.2517224.

[76] Hong-Hai Do, Sergey Melnik, and Erhard Rahm. *Comparison of Schema Matching Evaluations*, pages 221–237. Springer Berlin Heidelberg, Berlin, Heidelberg, 2003. ISBN 978-3-540-36560-0. doi: 10.1007/3-540-36560-5_17. URL http://dx.doi.org/10.1007/3-540-36560-5_17.

[77] Eelco Dolstra and Armijn Hemel. Purely functional system configuration management. In *HotOS*, 2007.

[78] Karel Driesen and Urs Hölzle. The direct cost of virtual function calls in C++. In *Proceedings of the 11th ACM SIGPLAN Conference on Object-oriented Programming, Systems, Languages, and Applications*, OOPSLA '96, pages 306–323, New York, NY, USA, 1996. ACM. ISBN 0-89791-788-X. doi: 10.1145/236337.236369. URL http://dx.doi.org/10.1145/236337.236369.

[79] Bob DuCharme. Documents vs. data, schemas vs. schemas. In *XML 2004*, Washington D.C., USA, 2004.

[80] Steve Easterbrook, Janice Singer, Margaret-Anne Storey, and Daniela Damian. Selecting empirical methods for software engineering research. In Forrest Shull, Janice Singer, and Dag I. K. Sjøberg, editors, *Guide to Advanced Empirical Software Engineering*, pages 285–311. Springer, 2008. ISBN 978-1-84800-043-8. URL http://dx.doi.org/10.1007/978-1-84800-044-5_11.

[81] Holger Eichelberger and Klaus Schmid. A systematic analysis of textual variability modeling languages. In *Proceedings of the 17th International Software Product Line Conference*, SPLC '13, pages 12–21, New York, NY, USA, 2013. ACM. ISBN 978-1-4503-1968-3. doi: 10.1145/2491627.2491652. URL http://dx.doi.org/10.1145/2491627.2491652.

[82] Andrew Eisenberg. New standard for stored procedures in SQL. *SIGMOD Rec.*, 25(4):81–88, December 1996. ISSN 0163-5808. doi: 10.1145/245882.245907. URL http://dx.doi.org/10.1145/245882.245907.

[83] Kathleen M. Eisenhardt and Melissa E. Graebner. Theory building from cases: Opportunities and challenges. *Academy of management journal*, 50(1):25–32, 2007.

[84] Hicham G. Elmongui, Walid G. Aref, and Mohamed F. Mokbel. Chameleon: Context-awareness inside DBMSs. In *2009 IEEE 25th International Conference on Data Engineering*, pages 1335–1338, March 2009. doi: 10.1109/ICDE.2009.234.

[85] S. Endrikat and S. Hanenberg. Is aspect-oriented programming a rewarding investment into future code changes? a socio-technical study on development and maintenance time. In *Program Comprehension (ICPC), 2011 IEEE 19th International Conference on*, pages 51–60, June 2011. doi: 10.1109/ICPC.2011.46.

[86] Morgan Ericsson. *Composition and Optimization*. PhD thesis, Växjö University, 2008.

[87] Rémy Evard. An analysis of UNIX system configuration. In *LISA*, volume 97, pages 179–194, 1997.

[88] Alexander Felfernig, Gerhard Friedrich, and Dietmar Jannach. Knowledge acquisition for configuration systems: Uml as a link between ai and software engineering. In *PuK*, 1999.

[89] Alexander Felfernig, Gerhard E Friedrich, and Dietmar Jannach. Uml as domain specific language for the construction of knowledge-based configuration systems. *International Journal of Software Engineering and Knowledge Engineering*, 10(04): 449–469, 2000.

[90] Alexander Felfernig, Gerhard Friedrich, Dietmar Jannach, Markus Stumptner, and M Zanker. A joint foundation for configuration in the semantic web. In *Proc. of the Configuration Workshop on 15th European Conference on Artificial Intelligence (ECAI-2002)*, pages 89–94, 2002.

[91] Kathleen Fisher and Robert Gruber. Pads: A domain-specific language for processing ad hoc data. In *Proceedings of the 2005 ACM SIGPLAN Conference on Programming Language Design and Implementation*, PLDI '05, pages 295–304, New York, NY, USA, 2005. ACM. ISBN 1-59593-056-6. doi: 10.1145/1065010.1065046. URL http://dx.doi.org/10.1145/1065010.1065046.

[92] Kathleen Fisher and David Walker. The pads project: An overview. In *Proceedings of the 14th International Conference on Database Theory*, ICDT '11, pages 11–17, New York, NY, USA, 2011. ACM. ISBN 978-1-4503-0529-7. doi: 10.1145/1938551. 1938556. URL http://dx.doi.org/10.1145/1938551.1938556.

[93] Kathleen Fisher, Yitzhak Mandelbaum, and David Walker. The next 700 data description languages. *J. ACM*, 57(2):10:1–10:51, February 2010. ISSN 0004-5411. doi: 10.1145/1667053.1667059. URL http://dx.doi.org/10.1145/1667053. 1667059.

[94] John Nathan Foster. *Bidirectional programming languages*. PhD thesis, University of Pennsylvania, 2010. URL http://repository.upenn.edu/cis_reports/921/.

[95] Apache Software Foundation. https://commons.apache.org/configuration/. Accessed February 2017.

[96] Gerhard Friedrich and Markus Stumptner. Consistency-based configuration. In *In AAAI-99, Workshop on Configuration*, pages 35–40. AAAI Press, 1999.

[97] Thom Frühwirth and Slim Abdennadher. *Essentials of constraint programming*. Springer, 2003.

[98] Erich Gamma, Richard Helm, Ralph Johnson, and John Vlissides. *Design patterns: elements of reusable object-oriented software*. Pearson Education, 1994.

[99] J. D. Gannon. An experimental evaluation of data type conventions. *Commun. ACM*, 20(8):584–595, August 1977. ISSN 0001-0782. doi: 10.1145/359763.359800. URL http://dx.doi.org/10.1145/359763.359800.

[100] Michael L. Gassanenko. Context-oriented programming: Evolution of vocabularies. In *9th euroFORTH conference on the Forth Programming Language and Forth Processors*, EuroForth '93, October 1993.

[101] Michael L. Gassanenko. Context-oriented programming. In *14th euroFORTH conference on the FORTH Programming Language*, EuroForth '98, September 1998.

[102] William Gaver. What should we expect from research through design? In *Proceedings of the SIGCHI Conference on Human Factors in Computing Systems*, CHI '12, pages 937–946, New York, NY, USA, 2012. ACM. ISBN 978-1-4503-1015-4.

doi: 10.1145/2207676.2208538. URL http://dx.doi.org/10.1145/2207676.
2208538.

[103] Kurt Geihs, Paolo Barone, Frank Eliassen, Jacqueline Floch, Rolf Fricke, Eli Gjørven, Svein O. Hallsteinsen, Geir Horn, Mohammad Ullah Khan, Alessandro Mamelli, George A. Papadopoulos, Nearchos Paspallis, Roland Reichle, and Erlend Stav. A comprehensive solution for application-level adaptation. *Software: Practice and Experience*, 39(4):385–422, 2009. ISSN 1097-024X. URL http://dx.doi.org/
10.1002/spe.900.

[104] Holger Giese, Stephan Hildebrandt, Stefan Neumann, and Sebastian Wätzold. *Industrial case study on the integration of SysML and AUTOSAR with triple graph grammars*. Number 57. Universitätsverlag Potsdam, 2012.

[105] Ian Goldberg, David Wagner, Randi Thomas, and Eric A. Brewer. A secure environment for untrusted helper applications: Confining the wily hacker. In *Proceedings of the 6th conference on USENIX Security Symposium, Focusing on Applications of Cryptography*, volume 6, pages 1–1, 1996.

[106] Sebastián González, Nicolás Cardozo, Kim Mens, Alfredo Cádiz, Jean-Christophe Libbrecht, and Julien Goffaux. *Subjective-C*, pages 246–265. Springer Berlin Heidelberg, Berlin, Heidelberg, 2011. ISBN 978-3-642-19440-5. doi: 10.1007/978-3-642-19440-5_15. URL http://dx.doi.org/10.1007/978-3-642-19440-5_15.

[107] Chris Grier, Samuel T. King, and Dan S. Wallach. How i learned to stop worrying and love plugins. In *In Web 2.0 Security and Privacy*, 2009.

[108] Thomas Grill, Ondrej Polacek, and Manfred Tscheligi. *Methods towards API Usability: A Structural Analysis of Usability Problem Categories*, pages 164–180. Springer Berlin Heidelberg, Berlin, Heidelberg, 2012. ISBN 978-3-642-34347-6. doi: 10.1007/978-3-642-34347-6_10. URL http://dx.doi.org/10.1007/978-3-642-34347-6_10.

[109] Paul Grosso, Eve Maler, Jonathan Marsh, and Norman Walsh. Xpointer framework. *W3C Recommendation*, 25, 2003.

[110] Thomas R. Gruber. Toward principles for the design of ontologies used for knowledge sharing. *International Journal of Human-Computer Studies*, 43(5–6):907–

928, 1995. ISSN 1071-5819. doi: 10.1006/ijhc.1995.1081. URL http://www.sciencedirect.com/science/article/pii/S1071581985710816.

[111] Tao Gu, Hung Keng Pung, and Da Qing Zhang. A middleware for building context-aware mobile services. In *Vehicular Technology Conference, 2004. VTC 2004-Spring. 2004 IEEE 59th*, volume 5, pages 2656–2660. IEEE, 2004.

[112] Sebastian Günther, Thomas Cleenewerck, and Viviane Jonckers. Software variability: the design space of configuration languages. In *Proceedings of the Sixth International Workshop on Variability Modeling of Software-Intensive Systems*, pages 157–164. ACM, 2012. URL http://dl.acm.org/citation.cfm?id=2110165.

[113] John Guttag. Abstract data types and the development of data structures. *Communications of the ACM*, 20(6):396–404, June 1977. ISSN 0001-0782. doi: 10.1145/359605.359618. URL http://dx.doi.org/10.1145/359605.359618.

[114] Eben M. Haber and John Bailey. Design guidelines for system administration tools developed through ethnographic field studies. In *Proceedings of the 2007 Symposium on Computer Human Interaction for the Management of Information Technology*, CHIMIT '07, New York, NY, USA, 2007. ACM. ISBN 978-1-59593-635-6. doi: 10.1145/1234772.1234774. URL http://dx.doi.org/10.1145/1234772.1234774.

[115] Niklaus Haldiman, Marcus Denker, and Oscar Nierstrasz. Practical, pluggable types for a dynamic language. *Computer Languages, Systems & Structures*, 35(1):48–62, 2009. ISSN 1477-8424. doi: http://dx.doi.org/10.1016/j.cl.2008.06.003. URL //www.sciencedirect.com/science/article/pii/S1477842408000262. {ESUG} 2007 International Conference on Dynamic Languages (ESUG/ICDL 2007).

[116] Stefan Hanenberg. An experiment about static and dynamic type systems: Doubts about the positive impact of static type systems on development time. *SIGPLAN Not.*, 45(10):22–35, October 2010. ISSN 0362-1340. doi: 10.1145/1932682.1869462. URL http://dx.doi.org/10.1145/1932682.1869462.

[117] Stefan Hanenberg, Sebastian Kleinschmager, and Manuel Josupeit-Walter. Does aspect-oriented programming increase the development speed for crosscutting code? an empirical study. In *Proceedings of the 2009 3rd International Symposium on Empirical Software Engineering and Measurement*, ESEM '09, pages 156–167,

Washington, DC, USA, 2009. IEEE Computer Society. ISBN 978-1-4244-4842-5. doi: 10.1109/ESEM.2009.5316028. URL `http://dx.doi.org/10.1109/ESEM.2009.5316028`.

[118] Daco C. Harkes, Danny M. Groenewegen, and Eelco Visser. IceDust: Incremental and eventual computation of derived values in persistent object graphs. In Shriram Krishnamurthi and Benjamin S. Lerner, editors, *30th European Conference on Object-Oriented Programming (ECOOP 2016)*, volume 56 of *Leibniz International Proceedings in Informatics (LIPIcs)*, pages 11:1–11:26, Dagstuhl, Germany, 2016. Schloss Dagstuhl–Leibniz-Zentrum fuer Informatik. ISBN 978-3-95977-014-9. doi: http://dx.doi.org/10.4230/LIPIcs.ECOOP.2016.11. URL `http://drops.dagstuhl.de/opus/volltexte/2016/6105`.

[119] Magnus Harlander. Central system administration in a heterogeneous Unix environment: GeNUAdmin. In *LISA VIII Proceedings*, 1994.

[120] Neil B Harrison, Paris Avgeriou, and Uwe Zdun. Using patterns to capture architectural decisions. *Software, IEEE*, 24(4):38–45, 2007. ISSN 0740-7459. doi: 10.1109/MS.2007.124.

[121] William Harrison and Harold Ossher. Subject-oriented programming: A critique of pure objects. In *Proceedings of the Eighth Annual Conference on Object-oriented Programming Systems, Languages, and Applications*, OOPSLA '93, pages 411–428, New York, NY, USA, 1993. ACM. ISBN 0-89791-587-9. doi: 10.1145/165854.165932. URL `http://dx.doi.org/10.1145/165854.165932`.

[122] Thomas Hartmann. *Validation Framework for RDF-based Constraint Languages*. PhD thesis, Dissertation, Karlsruhe, Karlsruher Institut für Technologie (KIT), 2016, 2016.

[123] Lynn Hasher, David Goldstein, and Thomas Toppino. Frequency and the conference of referential validity. *Journal of verbal learning and verbal behavior*, 16(1):107–112, 1977. ISSN 0022-5371. doi: http://dx.doi.org/10.1016/S0022-5371(77)80012-1.

[124] Les Hatton. Reexamining the fault density component size connection. *IEEE Software*, 14(2):89–97, Mar 1997. ISSN 0740-7459. doi: 10.1109/52.582978.

[125] Karen Henricksen, Jadwiga Indulska, Ted McFadden, and Sasitharan Balasubramaniam. Middleware for distributed context-aware systems. In *OTM Confederated*

International Conferences "On the Move to Meaningful Internet Systems", pages 846–863. Springer, 2005.

[126] Marjan Hericko, Matjaz B. Juric, Ivan Rozman, Simon Beloglavec, and Ales Zivkovic. Object serialization analysis and comparison in java and .net. *SIGPLAN Not.*, 38(8):44–54, August 2003. ISSN 0362-1340. doi: 10.1145/944579.944589. URL `http://dx.doi.org/10.1145/944579.944589`.

[127] John A. Hewson and Paul Anderson. Modelling system administration problems with CSPs. In *Proceedings of the 10th International Workshop on Constraint Modelling and Reformulation (Mod-Ref'11)*, pages 73–82, 2011. URL `http://homepages.inf.ed.ac.uk/dcspaul/homepage/live/pdf/ConfSolve-ModRef2011.pdf`.

[128] John A. Hewson, Paul Anderson, and Andrew D. Gordon. A declarative approach to automated configuration. In *LISA*, volume 12, pages 51–66. USENIX Association, 2012.

[129] Imazu Hideyo. OMNICONF–making os upgrades and disk crash recovery easier. In *LISA VIII Proceedings*, 1994.

[130] James H Hill. Modeling interface definition language extensions (idl3+) using domain-specific modeling languages. In *Object/Component/Service-Oriented Real-Time Distributed Computing (ISORC), 2011 14th IEEE International Symposium on*, pages 75–82. IEEE, 2011. URL `http://ieeexplore.ieee.org/xpls/abs_all.jsp?arnumber=5753594`.

[131] Johannes Hintsch, Carsten Görling, and Klaus Turowski. A review of the literature on configuration management tools. 2016.

[132] Robert Hirschfeld, Pascal Costanza, and Oscar Nierstrasz. Context-oriented programming. *Journal of Object Technology*, 7(3), 2008.

[133] Robert Hirschfeld, Hidehiko Masuhara, Atsushi Igarashi, and Tim Felgentreff. Visibility of context-oriented behavior and state in l. In *Proceedings of the 31th JSSST Annual Conference*, pages 2–1, 2014.

[134] David A. Holland, William Josephson, Kostas Magoutis, Margo I. Seltzer, Christopher A. Stein, and Ada Lim. Research issues in no-futz computing. In *Hot Topics in Operating Systems, 2001. Proceedings of the Eighth Workshop on*, pages 106–110. IEEE, May 2001. doi: 10.1109/HOTOS.2001.990069.

[135] Haruo Hosoya and Benjamin C. Pierce. XDuce: A statically typed XML processing language. *ACM Trans. Internet Technol.*, 3(2):117–148, May 2003. ISSN 1533-5399. doi: 10.1145/767193.767195. URL http://dx.doi.org/10.1145/767193.767195.

[136] Edward Huang, Randeep Ramamurthy, and Leon F. McGinnis. System and simulation modeling using sysml. In *Proceedings of the 39th Conference on Winter Simulation: 40 Years! The Best is Yet to Come*, WSC '07, pages 796–803, Piscataway, NJ, USA, 2007. IEEE Press. ISBN 1-4244-1306-0. URL http://dl.acm.org/citation.cfm?id=1351542.1351687.

[137] Peng Huang, William J. Bolosky, Abhishek Singh, and Yuanyuan Zhou. ConfValley: a systematic configuration validation framework for cloud services. In *EuroSys*, page 19, 2015.

[138] Eeva-Mari Ihantola and Lili-Anne Kihn. Threats to validity and reliability in mixed methods accounting research. *Qualitative Research in Accounting & Management*, 8(1):39–58, 2011. doi: 10.1108/11766091111124694. URL http://dx.doi.org/10.1108/11766091111124694.

[139] Dongpu Jin, Xiao Qu, Myra B. Cohen, and Brian Robinson. Configurations everywhere: Implications for testing and debugging in practice. In *Companion Proceedings of the 36th International Conference on Software Engineering*, ICSE Companion 2014, pages 215–224, New York, NY, USA, 2014. ACM. ISBN 978-1-4503-2768-8. doi: 10.1145/2591062.2591191. URL http://dx.doi.org/10.1145/2591062.2591191.

[140] David S. Johnson. A theoretician's guide to the experimental analysis of algorithms. In *Proceedings of the 5th and 6th DIMACS Implementation Challenges*, 2002. URL http://davidsjohnson.net/papers/experguide.pdf.

[141] Hong Jong-yi, Suh Eui-ho, and Kim Sung-Jin. Context-aware systems: A literature review and classification. *Expert Systems with Applications*, 36(4):8509–8522, 2009. ISSN 0957-4174. URL http://dx.doi.org/10.1016/j.eswa.2008.10.071.

[142] Nicolai M. Josuttis. *C++ Templates: The Complete Guide*. Addison-Wesley Professional, 2003.

[143] Michael Jung, Ralf Laue, and Sorin Alexander Huss. A case study on partial evaluation in embedded software design. In *Software Technologies for Future Embedded and Ubiquitous Systems, 2005. SEUS 2005. Third IEEE Workshop on*, pages 16–21, May 2005. doi: 10.1109/SEUS.2005.1.

[144] Arthur B. Kahn. Topological sorting of large networks. *Commun. ACM*, 5(11): 558–562, November 1962. ISSN 0001-0782. doi: 10.1145/368996.369025. URL http://dx.doi.org/10.1145/368996.369025.

[145] Tetsuo Kamina, Tomoyuki Aotani, Hidehiko Masuhara, and Tetsuo Tamai. Context-oriented software engineering: A modularity vision. In *Proceedings of the 13th International Conference on Modularity*, MODULARITY '14, pages 85–98, New York, NY, USA, 2014. ACM. ISBN 978-1-4503-2772-5.

[146] Tetsuo Kamina, Tomoyuki Aotani, and Hidehiko Masuhara. Generalized layer activation mechanism through contexts and subscribers. In *Proceedings of the 14th International Conference on Modularity*, MODULARITY 2015, pages 14–28, New York, NY, USA, 2015. ACM. ISBN 978-1-4503-3249-1. doi: 10.1145/2724525. 2724570. URL http://dx.doi.org/10.1145/2724525.2724570.

[147] Kyo C. Kang, Sholom G. Cohen, James A. Hess, William E. Novak, and A. Spencer Peterson. Feature-oriented domain analysis (FODA) feasibility study. Technical report, Carnegie Mellon University, 1990.

[148] Georgia M. Kapitsaki, Dimitrios A. Kateros, and Iakovos S. Venieris. Architecture for provision of context-aware web applications based on web services. In *2008 IEEE 19th International Symposium on Personal, Indoor and Mobile Radio Communications*, pages 1–5, September 2008. doi: 10.1109/PIMRC.2008.4699629.

[149] Andrzej Kapolka, Don McGregor, and Michael Capps. A unified component framework for dynamically extensible virtual environments. In *Proceedings of the 4th International Conference on Collaborative Virtual Environments*, CVE '02, pages 64–71, New York, NY, USA, 2002. ACM. ISBN 1-58113-489-4. doi: 10.1145/571878. 571889. URL http://dx.doi.org/10.1145/571878.571889.

[150] Gautam Kar, Alexander Keller, and Seraphin B. Calo. Managing application services over service provider networks: architecture and dependency analysis. In *Network Operations and Management Symposium, 2000. NOMS 2000. 2000 IEEE/I-FIP*, pages 61–74, 2000. doi: 10.1109/NOMS.2000.830375.

[151] Roger Keays and Andry Rakotonirainy. Context-oriented programming. In *Proceedings of the 3rd ACM International Workshop on Data Engineering for Wireless and Mobile Access*, MobiDe '03, pages 9–16, New York, NY, USA, 2003. ACM. ISBN 1-58113-767-2. doi: 10.1145/940923.940926. URL http://dx.doi.org/ 10.1145/940923.940926.

[152] Sven Keidel, Wulf Pfeiffer, and Sebastian Erdweg. The ide portability problem and its solution in monto. In *Proceedings of the 2016 ACM SIGPLAN International Conference on Software Language Engineering*, SLE 2016, pages 152–162, New York, NY, USA, 2016. ACM. ISBN 978-1-4503-4447-0. doi: 10.1145/2997364.2997368. URL http://dx.doi.org/10.1145/2997364.2997368.

[153] Markus Keidl and Alfons Kemper. Towards context-aware adaptable web services. In *Proceedings of the 13th International World Wide Web Conference on Alternate Track Papers &Amp; Posters*, WWW Alt. '04, pages 55–65, New York, NY, USA, 2004. ACM. ISBN 1-58113-912-8. doi: 10.1145/1013367.1013378. URL http://dx.doi.org/10.1145/1013367.1013378.

[154] Lorenzo Keller, Prasang Upadhyaya, and George Candea. Conferr: A tool for assessing resilience to human configuration errors. In *Dependable Systems and Networks With FTCS and DCC, 2008.*, pages 157–166. IEEE, 2008.

[155] Ashraf Khalil and Kay Connelly. *Context-Aware Configuration: A Study on Improving Cell Phone Awareness*, pages 197–209. Springer Berlin Heidelberg, Berlin, Heidelberg, 2005. ISBN 978-3-540-31890-3. doi: 10.1007/11508373_15. URL http://dx.doi.org/10.1007/11508373_15.

[156] Ashraf Khalil and Kay Connelly. *Improving Cell Phone Awareness by Using Calendar Information*, pages 588–600. Springer Berlin Heidelberg, Berlin, Heidelberg, 2005. ISBN 978-3-540-31722-7. doi: 10.1007/11555261_48. URL http://dx.doi.org/10.1007/11555261_48.

[157] Emre Kiciman and Yi-Min Wang. Discovering correctness constraints for self-management of system configuration. In *International Conference on Autonomic Computing, 2004. Proceedings.*, pages 28–35. IEEE, May 2004. doi: 10.1109/ICAC. 2004.1301344.

[158] Gregor Kiczales, John Lamping, Anurag Mendhekar, Chris Maeda, Cristina Lopes, Jean-Marc Loingtier, and John Irwin. *Aspect-oriented programming*, pages 220–242.

Springer Berlin Heidelberg, Berlin, Heidelberg, 1997. ISBN 978-3-540-69127-3. doi: 10.1007/BFb0053381. URL http://dx.doi.org/10.1007/BFb0053381.

[159] Manuele Kirsch-Pinheiro, Raúl Mazo, Carine Souveyet, and Danillo Sprovieri. Requirements analysis for context-oriented systems. *Procedia Computer Science*, 83:253–261, 2016. ISSN 1877-0509. doi: http://dx.doi.org/10.1016/j.procs.2016.04.123. URL http://www.sciencedirect.com/science/article/pii/S1877050916301466. The 7th International Conference on Ambient Systems, Networks and Technologies (ANT 2016) / The 6th International Conference on Sustainable Energy Information Technology (SEIT-2016) / Affiliated Workshops.

[160] Hsiang-Shang Ko, Tao Zan, and Zhenjiang Hu. Bigul: A formally verified core language for putback-based bidirectional programming. In *Proceedings of the 2016 ACM SIGPLAN Workshop on Partial Evaluation and Program Manipulation*, PEPM '16, pages 61–72, New York, NY, USA, 2016. ACM. ISBN 978-1-4503-4097-7. doi: 10.1145/2847538.2847544. URL http://dx.doi.org/10.1145/2847538.2847544.

[161] Daniel Kroening and Michael Tautschnig. *CBMC – C Bounded Model Checker*, pages 389–391. Springer Berlin Heidelberg, Berlin, Heidelberg, 2014. ISBN 978-3-642-54862-8. doi: 10.1007/978-3-642-54862-8_26. URL http://dx.doi.org/10.1007/978-3-642-54862-8_26.

[162] Ralf Lämmel, Ekaterina Pek, and Jürgen Starek. Large-scale, AST-based API-usage analysis of open-source java projects. In *Proceedings of the 2011 ACM Symposium on Applied Computing*, SAC '11, pages 1317–1324, New York, NY, USA, 2011. ACM. ISBN 978-1-4503-0113-8. doi: 10.1145/1982185.1982471. URL http://dx.doi.org/10.1145/1982185.1982471.

[163] Leslie Lamport and Lawrence C. Paulson. Should your specification language be typed. *ACM Transactions on Programming Languages and Systems (TOPLAS)*, 21(3):502–526, 1999.

[164] Peter J. Landin. The next 700 programming languages. *Commun. ACM*, 9(3): 157–166, March 1966. ISSN 0001-0782. doi: 10.1145/365230.365257. URL http://dx.doi.org/10.1145/365230.365257.

[165] Neal Lathia, Kiran Rachuri, Cecilia Mascolo, and George Roussos. Open source smartphone libraries for computational social science. In *Proceedings of the 2013*

ACM Conference on Pervasive and Ubiquitous Computing Adjunct Publication, UbiComp '13 Adjunct, pages 911–920, New York, NY, USA, 2013. ACM. ISBN 978-1-4503-2215-7. doi: 10.1145/2494091.2497345. URL http://dx.doi.org/ 10.1145/2494091.2497345.

[166] Ka Chun Anthony Lee, Maria-Teresa Segarra, and Stephane Guelec. A deployment-oriented development process based on context variability modeling. In *Model-Driven Engineering and Software Development (MODELSWARD), 2014 2nd International Conference on,* pages 454–459. IEEE, 2014. URL http://ieeexplore. ieee.org/xpls/abs_all.jsp?arnumber=7018496.

[167] Kwanwoo Lee, Kyo C. Kang, and Jaejoon Lee. Concepts and guidelines of feature modeling for product line software engineering. In *Software Reuse: Methods, Techniques, and Tools,* pages 62–77. Springer, 2002.

[168] Michael J. Lee and Andrew J. Ko. Personifying programming tool feedback improves novice programmers' learning. In *Proceedings of the Seventh International Workshop on Computing Education Research,* ICER '11, pages 109–116, New York, NY, USA, 2011. ACM. ISBN 978-1-4503-0829-8. doi: 10.1145/2016911.2016934. URL http://dx.doi.org/10.1145/2016911.2016934.

[169] Alessandro Ferreira Leite and Diana Penciuc. A computing environment configuration management pattern based on a software product line engineering method. *SugarLoafPLoP'16,* 2016.

[170] Zhenkai Liang, V. N. Venkatakrishnan, and R. Sekar. Isolated program execution: an application transparent approach for executing untrusted programs. In *19th Annual Computer Security Applications Conference, 2003. Proceedings.,* pages 182–191, December 2003. doi: 10.1109/CSAC.2003.1254323.

[171] Hubert W. Lilliefors. On the Kolmogorov-Smirnov test for normality with mean and variance unknown. *Journal of the American Statistical Association,* 62(318): 399–402, 1967. doi: 10.1080/01621459.1967.10482916. URL http://amstat. tandfonline.com/doi/abs/10.1080/01621459.1967.10482916.

[172] Barbara H. Liskov and Jeannette M. Wing. A behavioral notion of subtyping. *ACM Trans. Program. Lang. Syst.,* 16(6):1811–1841, November 1994. ISSN 0164-0925. doi: 10.1145/197320.197383. URL http://dx.doi.org/10.1145/197320. 197383.

[173] Simon Lock. Strider: configuration modelling and analysis of complex systems. In *Software Maintenance, 2005. ICSM'05. Proceedings of the 21st IEEE International Conference on*, pages 495–504, Sept 2005. doi: 10.1109/ICSM.2005.86.

[174] Calvin Loncaric, Satish Chandra, Cole Schlesinger, and Manu Sridharan. A practical framework for type inference error explanation. In *Proceedings of the 2016 ACM SIGPLAN International Conference on Object-Oriented Programming, Systems, Languages, and Applications*, OOPSLA 2016, pages 781–799, New York, NY, USA, 2016. ACM. ISBN 978-1-4503-4444-9. doi: 10.1145/2983990.2983994. URL http://dx.doi.org/10.1145/2983990.2983994.

[175] Orlando Loques, Alexandre Sztajnberg, Julius Leite, and Marcelo Lobosco. On the integration of configuration and meta-level programming approaches. In *Reflection and Software Engineering*, pages 189–208. Springer, 2000.

[176] Marin Lujak and Alberto Fernández. Orcas: Optimized robots configuration and scheduling system. 2015. URL http://www.ia.urjc.es/~lujak/ORCAS.pdf.

[177] David Lutterkort. Augeas–a configuration API. In *Linux Symposium, Ottawa, ON*, pages 47–56, 2008.

[178] Basel Magableh and Stephen Barrett. Primitive component architecture description language. In *Informatics and Systems (INFOS), 2010 The 7th International Conference on*, pages 1–7, March 2010.

[179] Ratul Mahajan, David Wetherall, and Tom Anderson. Understanding BGP misconfiguration. In *Proceedings of the 2002 Conference on Applications, Technologies, Architectures, and Protocols for Computer Communications*, SIGCOMM '02, pages 3–16, New York, NY, USA, 2002. ACM. ISBN 1-58113-570-X.

[180] Donna Malayeri and Jonathan Aldrich. *Integrating Nominal and Structural Subtyping*, pages 260–284. Springer Berlin Heidelberg, Berlin, Heidelberg, 2008. ISBN 978-3-540-70592-5. doi: 10.1007/978-3-540-70592-5_12. URL http://dx.doi.org/10.1007/978-3-540-70592-5_12.

[181] Jonathan Marsh, David Orchard, and Daniel Veillard. XML inclusions (XInclude) version 1.0. *W3C Working Draft*, 10, 2006.

[182] Nicholas D. Matsakis and Felix S. Klock, II. The rust language. In *Proceedings of the 2014 ACM SIGAda Annual Conference on High Integrity Language Technology*, HILT '14, pages 103–104, New York, NY, USA, 2014. ACM. ISBN 978-1-4503-3217-0. doi: 10.1145/2663171.2663188. URL http://dx.doi.org/10.1145/2663171.2663188.

[183] Jacopo Mauro, Michael Nieke, Christoph Seidl, and Ingrid Chieh Yu. Context aware reconfiguration in software product lines. In *Proceedings of the Tenth International Workshop on Variability Modelling of Software-intensive Systems*, VaMoS '16, pages 41–48, New York, NY, USA, 2016. ACM. ISBN 978-1-4503-4019-9. doi: 10.1145/2866614.2866620. URL http://dx.doi.org/10.1145/2866614.2866620.

[184] John McCarthy. Recursive functions of symbolic expressions and their computation by machine, part i. *Commun. ACM*, 3(4):184–195, April 1960. ISSN 0001-0782. doi: 10.1145/367177.367199. URL http://dx.doi.org/10.1145/367177.367199.

[185] Malcolm D. McIlroy, E. N. Pinson, and B. A. Tague. UNIX time-sharing system: Foreword. *Bell System Technical Journal*, 57(6):1899–1904, 1978.

[186] Kim Mens, Rafael Capilla, Nicolas Cardozo, Bruno Dumas, et al. A taxonomy of context-aware software variability approaches. In *Workshop on Live Adaptation of Software Systems, collocated with Modularity 2016 conference*, 2016.

[187] Tom Mens, Michel Wermelinger, Stéphane Ducasse, Serge Demeyer, Robert Hirschfeld, and Mehdi Jazayeri. Challenges in software evolution. In *8th International Workshop on Principles of Software Evolution*, pages 13–22, Lisabon, Portugal, September 2005. IEEE.

[188] Mira Mezini and Klaus Ostermann. Variability management with feature-oriented programming and aspects. In *Proceedings of the 12th ACM SIGSOFT Twelfth International Symposium on Foundations of Software Engineering*, SIGSOFT '04/FSE-12, pages 127–136, New York, NY, USA, 2004. ACM. ISBN 1-58113-855-5. doi: 10.1145/1029894.1029915. URL http://dx.doi.org/10.1145/1029894.1029915.

[189] Martin Michlmayr, Francis Hunt, and David Probert. Quality practices and problems in free software projects. In *Proceedings of the First International Conference on Open Source Systems*, pages 24–28, 2005.

[190] Jan Midtgaard, Claus Brabrand, and Andrzej Wasowski. Systematic derivation of static analyses for software product lines. In *Proceedings of the 13th International Conference on Modularity*, MODULARITY '14, pages 181–192, New York, NY, USA, 2014. ACM. ISBN 978-1-4503-2772-5. doi: 10.1145/2577080.2577091. URL http://dx.doi.org/10.1145/2577080.2577091.

[191] Carlo Montangero, Giuliano Pacini, and Franco Turini. MAGMA-Lisp: A "machine language" for artificial intelligence. In *Proceedings of the 4th International Joint Conference on Artificial Intelligence - Volume 1*, IJCAI'75, pages 556–561, San Francisco, CA, USA, 1975. Morgan Kaufmann Publishers Inc. URL http://dl.acm.org/citation.cfm?id=1624626.1624713.

[192] Carroll Morgan and Bernard Sufrin. Specification of the UNIX filing system. *IEEE Transactions on Software Engineering*, SE-10(2):128–142, 1984.

[193] Makoto Murata, Dongwon Lee, Murali Mani, and Kohsuke Kawaguchi. Taxonomy of XML schema languages using formal language theory. *ACM Trans. Internet Technol.*, 5(4):660–704, November 2005. ISSN 1533-5399. doi: 10.1145/1111627.1111631. URL http://dx.doi.org/10.1145/1111627.1111631.

[194] Sarah Nadi, Thorsten Berger, Christian Kästner, and Krzysztof Czarnecki. Mining configuration constraints: static analyses and empirical results. In *ICSE*, pages 140–151, 2014.

[195] Kiran Nagaraja, Fábio Oliveira, Ricardo Bianchini, Richard P. Martin, and Thu D. Nguyen. Understanding and dealing with operator mistakes in internet services. In *In Proceedings of the USENIX Symposium on Operating Systems Design and Implementation (OSDI'04*, volume 4, pages 61–76, 2004.

[196] Nicholas Nethercote and Julian Seward. Valgrind: A framework for heavyweight dynamic binary instrumentation. In *Proceedings of the 28th ACM SIGPLAN Conference on Programming Language Design and Implementation*, PLDI '07, pages 89–100, New York, NY, USA, 2007. ACM. ISBN 978-1-59593-633-2. doi: 10.1145/1250734.1250746. URL http://dx.doi.org/10.1145/1250734.1250746.

[197] Oscar Nierstrasz. What is the "object" in object-oriented programming. In *Proceedings of the CERN School of Computing*, pages 43–53, 1987.

[198] Long Niu, Sachio Saiki, Shinsuke Matsumoto, and Masahide Nakamura. WIF4InL: Web-based integration framework for indoor location. *International Journal of Pervasive Computing and Communications*, 2016.

[199] Milan Nosál and Jaroslav Porubän. Supporting multiple configuration sources using abstraction. *Open Computer Science*, 2(3):283–299, 2012.

[200] Milan Nosál and Jaroslav Porubän. XML to annotations mapping definition with patterns. *Computer Science and Information Systems*, 11(4):1455–1477, 2014.

[201] Judit Novák. *Automatic Installation and Configuration for Large Scale Farms.* PhD thesis, CERN, 2005.

[202] David Oppenheimer, Archana Ganapathi, and David A. Patterson. Why do Internet services fail, and what can be done about it? In *USENIX Symposium on Internet Technologies and Systems*, volume 67. Seattle, WA, 2003.

[203] Harold Ossher and Peri Tarr. Using subject-oriented programming to overcome common problems in object-oriented software development/evolution. In *Proceedings of the 21st International Conference on Software Engineering*, ICSE '99, pages 687–688, New York, NY, USA, 1999. ACM. ISBN 1-58113-074-0. doi: 10.1145/302405.302958. URL http://dx.doi.org/10.1145/302405.302958.

[204] Erik Österlund and Welf Löwe. Concurrent transformation components using contention context sensors. In *Proceedings of the 29th ACM/IEEE International Conference on Automated Software Engineering*, ASE '14, pages 223–234, New York, NY, USA, 2014. ACM. ISBN 978-1-4503-3013-8. doi: 10.1145/2642937.2642995. URL http://dx.doi.org/10.1145/2642937.2642995.

[205] Erik Österlund and Welf Löwe. Self-adaptive concurrent components. *Automated Software Engineering*, Aug 2017. ISSN 1573-7535. doi: 10.1007/s10515-017-0219-0. URL https://doi.org/10.1007/s10515-017-0219-0.

[206] Sudhir Pandey. Investigating community, reliability and usability of cfengine, chef and puppet, 2012. URL http://scholar.google.com/https://www.duo.uio.no/handle/10852/9083.

[207] Ioannis Papagiannopoulos. JSON application programming interface for discrete event simulation data exchange. *Master's thesis, University of Limerick*, 2015.

[208] Tobias Pape, Tim Felgentreff, and Robert Hirschfeld. Optimizing sideways composition: Fast context-oriented programming in contextpypy. In *Proceedings of the 8th International Workshop on Context-Oriented Programming*, COP'16, pages 13–20, New York, NY, USA, 2016. ACM. ISBN 978-1-4503-4440-1. doi: 10.1145/2951965.2951967. URL http://dx.doi.org/10.1145/2951965.2951967.

[209] Matthew M. Papi, Mahmood Ali, Telmo Luis Correa, Jr., Jeff H. Perkins, and Michael D. Ernst. Practical pluggable types for java. In *Proceedings of the 2008 International Symposium on Software Testing and Analysis*, ISSTA '08, pages 201–212, New York, NY, USA, 2008. ACM. ISBN 978-1-60558-050-0. doi: 10.1145/1390630.1390656. URL http://dx.doi.org/10.1145/1390630.1390656.

[210] Carlos Andrés Parra, Maja D'Hondt, Carlos Noguera, and Ellen Van Paesschen. Introducing context-awareness in applications by transforming high-level rules. In *3rd Workshop on Object Technology for Ambient Intelligence and Pervasive Systems (OT4AmI) at ECOOP'07*, Berlin, Germany, July 2007. URL https://hal.inria.fr/inria-00180432.

[211] Leonardo Passos, Jesús Padilla, Thorsten Berger, Sven Apel, Krzysztof Czarnecki, and Marco Tulio Valente. Feature scattering in the large: A longitudinal study of linux kernel device drivers. In *Proceedings of the 14th International Conference on Modularity*, MODULARITY 2015, pages 81–92, New York, NY, USA, 2015. ACM. ISBN 978-1-4503-3249-1. doi: 10.1145/2724525.2724575. URL http://dx.doi.org/10.1145/2724525.2724575.

[212] Georg Paul, Kai-Uwe Sattler, and Martin Endig. An integration framework for open tool environments. In *DAIS*. Citeseer, 1997. URL http://citeseerx.ist.psu.edu/viewdoc/download?doi=10.1.1.52.8384&rep=rep1&type=pdf.

[213] Jeff H. Perkins, Sunghun Kim, Sam Larsen, Saman Amarasinghe, Jonathan Bachrach, Michael Carbin, Carlos Pacheco, Frank Sherwood, Stelios Sidiroglou, Greg Sullivan, Weng-Fai Wong, Yoav Zibin, Michael D. Ernst, and Martin Rinard. Automatically patching errors in deployed software. In *Proceedings of the ACM SIGOPS 22Nd Symposium on Operating Systems Principles*, SOSP '09, pages 87–102, New York, NY, USA, 2009. ACM. ISBN 978-1-60558-752-3. doi: 10.1145/1629575.1629585. URL http://dx.doi.org/10.1145/1629575.1629585.

[214] Soila Pertet and Priya Narasimhan. Causes of failure in web applications (cmu-pdl-05-109). *Parallel Data Laboratory*, page 48, 2005.

[215] Benjamin C. Pierce. *Types and programming languages*. MIT press, 2002.

[216] John Plaice and Blanca Mancilla. The cartesian approach to context. In *Proceedings of the 2nd International Workshop on Context-Oriented Programming*, COP '10, New York, NY, USA, 2010. ACM. ISBN 978-1-4503-0531-0. doi: 10.1145/1930021. 1930024. URL http://dx.doi.org/10.1145/1930021.1930024.

[217] Klaus Pohl, Günter Böckle, and Frank J van Der Linden. *Software product line engineering: foundations, principles and techniques*. Springer, 2005. ISBN 3642063640, 9783642063640.

[218] Jaroslav Porubän and Milan Nosál. Common abstraction of configuration from multiple sources. *Acta Electrotechnica et Informatica*, 11(4):25, 2011.

[219] Lutz Prechelt and Walter F. Tichy. A controlled experiment to assess the benefits of procedure argument type checking. *Software Engineering, IEEE Transactions on*, 24(4):302–312, April 1998. ISSN 0098-5589. doi: 10.1109/32.677186.

[220] Christian Prehofer. *Feature-oriented programming: A fresh look at objects*, pages 419–443. Springer Berlin Heidelberg, Berlin, Heidelberg, 1997. ISBN 978-3-540-69127-3. doi: 10.1007/BFb0053389. URL http://dx.doi.org/10.1007/BFb0053389.

[221] Franz Puntigam. Type specifications with processes. In *Proceedings FORTE'95*, pages 143–158. IFIP WG 6.1, October 1995.

[222] Franz Puntigam. *Coordination requirements expressed in types for active objects*, pages 367–388. Springer Berlin Heidelberg, Berlin, Heidelberg, 1997. ISBN 978-3-540-69127-3. doi: 10.1007/BFb0053387. URL https://doi.org/10.1007/BFb0053387.

[223] Franz Puntigam. Black & white, never grey: On interfaces, synchronization, pragmatics, and responsibilities. In *Twelfth International Workshop on Component-Oriented Programming (WCOP 2007)*, Berlin, Germany, July 2007. URL http://www.complang.tuwien.ac.at/franz/papers/Punt07a.pdf.

[224] Franz Puntigam. See the pet in the beast: How to limit effects of aliasing. In *International Workshop on Aliasing, Confinment and Ownership in object-oriented programming (IWACO 2007)*, Berlin, Germany, July 2007. URL http://www.complang.tuwien.ac.at/franz/papers/Punt07b.pdf.

[225] Markus Raab. A modular approach to configuration storage. *Master's thesis, Vienna University of Technology*, 2010.

[226] Markus Raab. Global and thread-local activation of contextual program execution environments. In *Proceedings of the IEEE 18th International Symposium on Real-Time Distributed Computing Workshops (ISORCW/SEUS)*, pages 34–41, April 2015. doi: 10.1109/ISORCW.2015.52.

[227] Markus Raab. Sharing software configuration via specified links and transformation rules. In *Technical Report from KPS 2015*, volume 18. Vienna University of Technology, Complang Group, 2015.

[228] Markus Raab. Safe management of software configuration. In *Proceedings of the CAiSE'2015 Doctoral Consortium*, pages 74–82, urn:nbn:de:0074-1415-4, 2015. http://ceur-ws.org/Vol-1415/. URL http://ceur-ws.org/Vol-1415/CAISE2015DC09.pdf.

[229] Markus Raab. Elektra: universal framework to access configuration parameters. *The Journal of Open Source Software*, 1(8):1–2, December 2016. doi: 10.21105/joss.00044. URL http://dx.doi.org/10.21105/joss.00044.

[230] Markus Raab. Improving system integration using a modular configuration specification language. In *Companion Proceedings of the 15th International Conference on Modularity*, MODULARITY Companion 2016, pages 152–157, New York, NY, USA, 2016. ACM. ISBN 978-1-4503-4033-5. doi: 10.1145/2892664.2892691. URL http://dx.doi.org/10.1145/2892664.2892691.

[231] Markus Raab. Persistent contextual values as inter-process layers. In *Proceedings of the 1st International Workshop on Mobile Development*, Mobile! 2016, pages 9–16, New York, NY, USA, 2016. ACM. ISBN 978-1-4503-4643-6. doi: 10.1145/3001854.3001855. URL http://dx.doi.org/10.1145/3001854.3001855.

[232] Markus Raab. Unanticipated context awareness for software configuration access using the getenv API. In *Computer and Information Science*, pages 41–57. Springer International Publishing, Cham, 2016. ISBN 978-3-319-40171-3. doi: 10.1007/978-3-319-40171-3_4. URL http://dx.doi.org/10.1007/978-3-319-40171-3_4.

[233] Markus Raab and Gergö Barany. *Challenges in Validating FLOSS Configuration*, pages 101–114. Springer International Publishing, Cham, 2017. ISBN 978-3-319-

57735-7. doi: 10.1007/978-3-319-57735-7_11. URL http://dx.doi.org/10.1007/978-3-319-57735-7_11.

[234] Markus Raab and Gergö Barany. Introducing context awareness in unmodified, context-unaware software. In *Proceedings of the 12th International Conference on Evaluation of Novel Approaches to Software Engineering - Volume 1: ENASE,,* pages 218–225. INSTICC, ScitePress, 2017. ISBN 978-989-758-250-9. doi: 10.5220/0006326602180225.

[235] Markus Raab and Franz Puntigam. Program execution environments as contextual values. In *Proceedings of 6th International Workshop on Context-Oriented Programming*, pages 8:1–8:6, New York, NY, USA, 2014. ACM. ISBN 978-1-4503-2861-6. URL http://dx.doi.org/10.1145/2637066.2637074.

[236] Markus Raab and Patrick Sabin. Implementation of Multiple Key Databases for Shared Configuration. ftp://www.markus-raab.org/elektra.pdf, March 2008. Accessed February 2014.

[237] Ariel Rabkin and Randy Katz. Precomputing possible configuration error diagnoses. In *Proceedings of the 2011 26th IEEE/ACM International Conference on Automated Software Engineering*, ASE '11, pages 193–202, Washington, DC, USA, 2011. IEEE Computer Society. ISBN 978-1-4577-1638-6. doi: 10.1109/ASE.2011.6100053. URL http://dx.doi.org/10.1109/ASE.2011.6100053.

[238] Ariel Rabkin and Randy Katz. Static extraction of program configuration options. In *Software Engineering (ICSE), 2011 33rd International Conference on*, pages 131–140. IEEE, 2011.

[239] Mika Raento, Antti Oulasvirta, Renaud Petit, and Hannu Toivonen. ContextPhone: a prototyping platform for context-aware mobile applications. *IEEE Pervasive Computing*, 4(2):51–59, January 2005. ISSN 1536-1268. doi: 10.1109/MPRV.2005.29.

[240] Erhard Rahm and Philip A. Bernstein. A survey of approaches to automatic schema matching. *The VLDB Journal*, 10(4):334–350, 2001. ISSN 0949-877X. doi: 10.1007/s007780100057. URL http://dx.doi.org/10.1007/s007780100057.

[241] Balasubramaniam Ramesh and Matthias Jarke. Toward reference models for requirements traceability. *IEEE Transactions on Software Engineering*, 27(1):58–93, 2001.

[242] Eric S. Raymond. *The art of Unix programming*. Addison-Wesley Professional, 2003.

[243] Mark-Oliver Reiser. *Core Concepts of the Compositional Variability Management Framework (CVM): A Practitioner's Guide*. TU, Professoren der Fak. IV, 2009.

[244] Mark-Oliver Reiser. *Core Concepts of the Compositional Variability Management Framework (CVM): A Practitioner's Guide*. TU, Professoren der Fak. IV, 2009.

[245] Mark-Oliver Reiser. *Managing complex variability in automotive software product lines: subscoping and configuration links*. Südwestdt. Verlag für Hochschulschriften, 2009.

[246] Tim Rentsch. Object oriented programming. *SIGPLAN Not.*, 17(9):51–57, September 1982. ISSN 0362-1340. doi: 10.1145/947955.947961. URL http://dx.doi.org/10.1145/947955.947961.

[247] Linda Rising and N. S. Janoff. The scrum software development process for small teams. *Software, IEEE*, 17(4):26–32, 2000. ISSN 0740-7459. doi: 10.1109/52.854065.

[248] Oriana Riva, Cristiano di Flora, Stefano Russo, and Kimmo E. E. Raatikainen. Unearthing design patterns to support context-awareness. In *Pervasive Computing and Communications Workshops, 2006. PerCom Workshops 2006. Fourth Annual IEEE International Conference on*, pages 5 pp.–387, March 2006. URL http://dx.doi.org/10.1109/PERCOMW.2006.138.

[249] James Roche. Adopting devops practices in quality assurance. *Commun. ACM*, 56 (11):38–43, November 2013. ISSN 0001-0782. doi: 10.1145/2524713.2524721. URL http://dx.doi.org/10.1145/2524713.2524721.

[250] Wendy Roll. Towards model-based and CCM-based applications for real-time systems. In *Object-Oriented Real-Time Distributed Computing, 2003. Sixth IEEE International Symposium on*, pages 75–82, May 2003. doi: 10.1109/ISORC.2003.1199238.

[251] John P. Rouillard and Richard B. Martin. Config: A mechanism for installing and tracking system configurations. In *LISA*, 1994.

[252] Cindy Rubio-González and Ben Liblit. Expect the unexpected: Error code mismatches between documentation and the real world. In *Proceedings of the 9th ACM SIGPLAN-SIGSOFT Workshop on Program Analysis for Software Tools and*

Engineering, PASTE '10, pages 73–80, New York, NY, USA, 2010. ACM. ISBN 978-1-4503-0082-7. doi: 10.1145/1806672.1806687. URL http://dx.doi.org/10.1145/1806672.1806687.

[253] Rusty Russell. Virtio: Towards a de-facto standard for virtual i/o devices. *SIGOPS Oper. Syst. Rev.*, 42(5):95–103, July 2008. ISSN 0163-5980. doi: 10.1145/1400097.1400108. URL http://dx.doi.org/10.1145/1400097.1400108.

[254] Daniel Sabin and Rainer Weigel. Product configuration frameworks - a survey. *IEEE Intelligent Systems*, pages 42–49, 1988.

[255] Guido Salvaneschi, Carlo Ghezzi, and Matteo Pradella. Context-oriented programming: A software engineering perspective. *Journal of Systems and Software*, 85 (8):1801–1817, 2012. ISSN 0164-1212. URL http://dx.doi.org/10.1016/j.jss.2012.03.024.

[256] Russel Sandberg, David Goldberg, Steve Kleiman, Dan Walsh, and Bob Lyon. Design and implementation of the Sun network filesystem. In *Proceedings of the Summer USENIX conference*, pages 119–130, 1985.

[257] Ina Schaefer and Reiner Hähnle. Formal methods in software product line engineering. *IEEE Computer*, 44(2):82–85, 2011.

[258] Bill N. Schilit, Norman Adams, and Roy Want. Context-aware computing applications. In *1994 First Workshop on Mobile Computing Systems and Applications*, pages 85–90, Dec 1994. doi: 10.1109/WMCSA.1994.16.

[259] Hans Schippers, Tim Molderez, and Dirk Janssens. A graph-based operational semantics for context-oriented programming. In *Proceedings of the 2nd International Workshop on Context-Oriented Programming*, COP '10, New York, NY, USA, 2010. ACM. ISBN 978-1-4503-0531-0. doi: 10.1145/1930021.1930027. URL http://dx.doi.org/10.1145/1930021.1930027.

[260] Z. Cliffe Schreuders, Tanya Jane McGill, and Christian Payne. Towards usable application-oriented access controls: qualitative results from a usability study of SELinux, AppArmor and FBAC-LSM. *International Journal of Information Security and Privacy*, 6(1):57–76, 2012.

[261] Michael I. Schwartzbach and Jens Palsberg. *Object-oriented type systems*. Wiley., 1994.

[262] Roger S. Scowen. Extended BNF-a generic base standard. Technical report, Technical report, ISO/IEC 14977., 1998.

[263] Konstantin Serebryany, Derek Bruening, Alexander Potapenko, and Dmitry Vyukov. Addresssanitizer: A fast address sanity checker. In *Proceedings of the 2012 USENIX Conference on Annual Technical Conference*, USENIX ATC'12, pages 28–28, Berkeley, CA, USA, 2012. USENIX Association. URL http://dl.acm.org/citation.cfm?id=2342821.2342849.

[264] Jérôme Siméon and Philip Wadler. The essence of xml. pages 1–13, 2003. doi: 10.1145/604131.604132. URL http://dx.doi.org/10.1145/604131.604132.

[265] Timo Soininen, Juha Tiihonen, Tomi Männistö, and Reijo Sulonen. Towards a general ontology of configuration. *AI EDAM*, 12(04):357–372, 1998.

[266] Ian Sommerville and Ronnie Thomson. Configuration specification using a system structure language. In *Configurable Distributed Systems, 1992., International Workshop on*, pages 80–89. IET, 1992. URL http://ieeexplore.ieee.org/xpls/abs_all.jsp?arnumber=152130.

[267] Matthias Springer, Hidehiko Masuhara, and Robert Hirschfeld. Classes as layers: Rewriting design patterns with COP: Alternative implementations of decorator, observer, and visitor. In *Proceedings of the 8th International Workshop on Context-Oriented Programming*, COP'16, pages 21–26, New York, NY, USA, 2016. ACM. ISBN 978-1-4503-4440-1. doi: 10.1145/2951965.2951968. URL http://dx.doi.org/10.1145/2951965.2951968.

[268] Richard M. Stallman. What is free software. *Free Society: Selected Essays of*, page 23, 2002.

[269] EBNF Syntaxt Specification Standard. EBNF: ISO/IEC 14977: 1996 (e). *http://www.cl.cam.ac.uk/~mgk25/iso-14977.pdf*, 70, 1996.

[270] Cristiano Storni. A personal perspective on research through design. *interactions*, 22(4):74–76, June 2015. ISSN 1072-5520. doi: 10.1145/2786974. URL http://dx.doi.org/10.1145/2786974.

[271] Thomas Strang and Claudia Linnhoff-Popien. A context modeling survey. In *First International Workshop on Advanced Context Modelling, Reasoning And Management at UbiComp 2004*, September 2004. URL http://elib.dlr.de/7444/.

[272] Ya-Yunn Su, Mona Attariyan, and Jason Flinn. Autobash: Improving configuration management with operating system causality analysis. pages 237–250, 2007. doi: 10.1145/1294261.1294284. URL http://dx.doi.org/10.1145/1294261. 1294284.

[273] Tommi Syrjänen. Including diagnostic information in configuration models. In John Lloyd, Veronica Dahl, Ulrich Furbach, Manfred Kerber, Kung-Kiu Lau, Catuscia Palamidessi, LuísMoniz Pereira, Yehoshua Sagiv, and PeterJ. Stuckey, editors, *Computational Logic — CL 2000*, volume 1861 of *Lecture Notes in Computer Science*, pages 837–851. Springer Berlin Heidelberg, 2000. ISBN 978-3-540-67797-0. doi: 10.1007/3-540-44957-4_56. URL http://dx.doi.org/10.1007/3-540-44957-4_56.

[274] Nguonly Taing, Markus Wutzler, Thomas Springer, Nicolás Cardozo, and Alexander Schill. Consistent unanticipated adaptation for context-dependent applications. In *Proceedings of the 8th International Workshop on Context-Oriented Programming*, COP'16, pages 33–38, New York, NY, USA, 2016. ACM. ISBN 978-1-4503-4440-1. doi: 10.1145/2951965.2951966. URL http://dx.doi.org/10.1145/2951965. 2951966.

[275] Éric Tanter. Contextual values. In *Proceedings of the 2008 Symposium on Dynamic Languages*, DLS '08, pages 3:1–3:10, New York, NY, USA, 2008. ACM. ISBN 978-1-60558-270-2. doi: 10.1145/1408681.1408684. URL http://dx.doi.org/10. 1145/1408681.1408684.

[276] Éric Tanter, Kris Gybels, Marcus Denker, and Alexandre Bergel. *Context-Aware Aspects*, pages 227–242. Springer, Berlin, Heidelberg, 2006. ISBN 978-3-540-37659-0. doi: 10.1007/11821946_15. URL http://dx.doi.org/10.1007/11821946_ 15.

[277] Zend Technologies. https://docs.zendframework.com/zend-config/. Accessed February 2017.

[278] Dave Thomas. The API field of dreams-too much stuff! It's time to reduce and simplify APIs! *Journal of Object Technology*, 5(6):23–27, 2006.

[279] Thomas Thüm, Christian Kästner, Fabian Benduhn, Jens Meinicke, Gunter Saake, and Thomas Leich. Featureide: An extensible framework for feature-oriented software development. *Science of Computer Programming*, 79:70–85, 2014. ISSN

0167-6423. doi: http://dx.doi.org/10.1016/j.scico.2012.06.002. URL //www. sciencedirect.com/science/article/pii/S0167642312001128. Experimental Software and Toolkits (EST 4): A special issue of the Workshop on Academic Software Development Tools and Techniques (WASDeTT-3 2010).

[280] Walter F. Tichy. Should computer scientists experiment more? *Computer*, (5): 32–40, 1997.

[281] Lucas Torri, Guilherme Fachini, Leonardo Steinfeld, Vesmar Camara, Luigi Carro, and Érika Cota. An evaluation of free/open source static analysis tools applied to embedded software. In *2010 11th Latin American Test Workshop*, pages 1–6, March 2010. doi: 10.1109/LATW.2010.5550368.

[282] Eirik Tryggeseth, Bjørn Gulla, and Reidar Conradi. Modelling systems with variability using the proteus configuration language. In *Software Configuration Management*, pages 216–240. Springer, 1995. URL http://link.springer.com/chapter/10.1007/3-540-60578-9_20.

[283] Dennis Tsichritzis and Oscar Nierstrasz. *Fitting Round Objects Into Square Databases*, pages 283–299. Springer Berlin Heidelberg, Berlin, Heidelberg, 1988. ISBN 978-3-540-45910-1. doi: 10.1007/3-540-45910-3_17. URL http://dx.doi.org/10.1007/3-540-45910-3_17.

[284] Eric Umuhoza, Hamza Ed-douibi, Marco Brambilla, Jordi Cabot, and Aldo Bongio. Automatic code generation for cross-platform, multi-device mobile apps: Some reflections from an industrial experience. In *Proceedings of the 3rd International Workshop on Mobile Development Lifecycle*, MobileDeLi 2015, pages 37–44, New York, NY, USA, 2015. ACM. ISBN 978-1-4503-3906-3. doi: 10.1145/2846661.2846666. URL http://dx.doi.org/10.1145/2846661.2846666.

[285] Sander van der Burg and Eelco Dolstra. Automating system tests using declarative virtual machines. In *Software Reliability Engineering (ISSRE), 2010 IEEE 21st International Symposium on*, pages 181–190. IEEE, 2010.

[286] Jilles Van Gurp, Jan Bosch, and Mikael Svahnberg. On the notion of variability in software product lines. In *Software Architecture, 2001. Proceedings. Working IEEE/IFIP Conference on*, pages 45–54. IEEE, 2001.

[287] Nicole F. Velasquez, Suzanne Weisband, and Alexandra Durcikova. Designing tools for system administrators: An empirical test of the integrated user satisfaction

model. In *Proceedings of the 22nd Conference on Large Installation System Administration Conference*, LISA'08, pages 1–8, Berkeley, CA, USA, 2008. USENIX Association. URL `http://dl.acm.org/citation.cfm?id=1496684.1496685`.

[288] Karina Villela, Adeline Silva, Tassio Vale, and Eduardo Santana de Almeida. A survey on software variability management approaches. In *Proceedings of the 18th International Software Product Line Conference - Volume 1*, SPLC '14, pages 147–156, New York, NY, USA, 2014. ACM. ISBN 978-1-4503-2740-4. doi: 10.1145/2648511.2648527. URL `http://dx.doi.org/10.1145/2648511.2648527`.

[289] Jan Vitek and Tomas Kalibera. Repeatability, reproducibility, and rigor in systems research. In *Proceedings of the Ninth ACM International Conference on Embedded Software*, EMSOFT '11, pages 33–38, New York, NY, USA, 2011. ACM. ISBN 978-1-4503-0714-7. doi: 10.1145/2038642.2038650. URL `http://dx.doi.org/10.1145/2038642.2038650`.

[290] Martin von Löwis, Marcus Denker, and Oscar Nierstrasz. Context-oriented programming: Beyond layers. In *Proceedings of the 2007 International Conference on Dynamic Languages*, ICDL '07, pages 143–156, New York, NY, USA, 2007. ACM. ISBN 978-1-60558-084-5. URL `http://dx.doi.org/10.1145/1352678.1352688`.

[291] Alexander von Rhein, Thomas Thüm, Ina Schaefer, Jörg Liebig, and Sven Apel. Variability encoding: From compile-time to load-time variability. *Journal of Logical and Algebraic Methods in Programming*, 85(1, Part 2):125–145, 2016. ISSN 2352-2208. doi: http://dx.doi.org/10.1016/j.jlamp.2015.06.007. URL `http://www.sciencedirect.com/science/article/pii/S2352220815000577`. Formal Methods for Software Product Line Engineering.

[292] Huai Wang and Wing Kwong Chan. Weaving context sensitivity into test suite construction. In *Automated Software Engineering, 2009. ASE '09. 24th IEEE/ACM International Conference on*, pages 610–614, November 2009. doi: 10.1109/ASE.2009.79.

[293] Yanlin Wang and Bruno C. d. S. Oliveira. The expression problem, trivially! In *Proceedings of the 15th International Conference on Modularity*, MODULARITY 2016, pages 37–41, New York, NY, USA, 2016. ACM. ISBN 978-1-4503-3995-7. doi: 10.1145/2889443.2889448. URL `http://dx.doi.org/10.1145/2889443.2889448`.

[294] Benjamin Hosain Wasty, Amir Semmo, Malte Appeltauer, Bastian Steinert, and Robert Hirschfeld. ContextLua: Dynamic behavioral variations in computer games. In *Proceedings of the 2nd International Workshop on Context-Oriented Programming*, COP '10, pages 5:1–5:6, New York, NY, USA, 2010. ACM. ISBN 978-1-4503-0531-0. doi: 10.1145/1930021.1930026. URL http://dx.doi.org/10.1145/1930021.1930026.

[295] Takuo Watanabe and Souhei Takeno. A reflective approach to actor-based concurrent context-oriented systems. In *Proceedings of 6th International Workshop on Context-Oriented Programming*, COP'14, pages 3:1–3:6, New York, NY, USA, 2014. ACM. ISBN 978-1-4503-2861-6. doi: 10.1145/2637066.2637069. URL http://dx.doi.org/10.1145/2637066.2637069.

[296] Peter Wegner. Concepts and paradigms of object-oriented programming. *SIGPLAN OOPS Mess.*, 1(1):7–87, August 1990. ISSN 1055-6400. doi: 10.1145/382192.383004. URL http://dx.doi.org/10.1145/382192.383004.

[297] B. Wielinga and G. Schreiber. Configuration-design problem solving. *IEEE Expert*, 12(2):49–56, Mar 1997. ISSN 0885-9000. doi: 10.1109/64.585104.

[298] Roel Wieringa. Design science as nested problem solving. In *Proceedings of the 4th international conference on design science research in information systems and technology*, page 8. ACM, 2009.

[299] Elizabeth Williams and Jeff Gray. Contextion: A framework for developing context-aware mobile applications. In *Proceedings of the 2nd International Workshop on Mobile Development Lifecycle*, MobileDeLi '14, pages 27–31, New York, NY, USA, 2014. ACM. ISBN 978-1-4503-2190-7. doi: 10.1145/2688412.2688416. URL http://dx.doi.org/10.1145/2688412.2688416.

[300] Niklaus Wirth. What can we do about the unnecessary diversity of notation for syntactic definitions? *Commun. ACM*, 20(11):822–823, November 1977. ISSN 0001-0782. doi: 10.1145/359863.359883. URL http://dx.doi.org/10.1145/359863.359883.

[301] Avishai Wool. A quantitative study of firewall configuration errors. *Computer*, 37 (6):62–67, 2004.

[302] Yingfei Xiong, Arnaud Hubaux, Steven She, and Krzysztof Czarnecki. Generating range fixes for software configuration. In *Proceedings of the 34th International Con-*

ference on Software Engineering, ICSE '12, pages 58–68, Piscataway, NJ, USA, 2012. IEEE Press. ISBN 978-1-4673-1067-3. URL http://dl.acm.org/citation.cfm?id=2337223.2337231.

[303] Tianyin Xu and Yuanyuan Zhou. Systems approaches to tackling configuration errors: A survey. *ACM Comput. Surv.*, 47(4):70:1–70:41, July 2015. ISSN 0360-0300. doi: 10.1145/2791577. URL http://dx.doi.org/10.1145/2791577.

[304] Tianyin Xu, Jiaqi Zhang, Peng Huang, Jing Zheng, Tianwei Sheng, Ding Yuan, Yuanyuan Zhou, and Shankar Pasupathy. Do not blame users for misconfigurations. In *Proceedings of the Twenty-Fourth ACM Symposium on Operating Systems Principles*, pages 244–259. ACM, 2013.

[305] Tianyin Xu, Long Jin, Xuepeng Fan, Yuanyuan Zhou, Shankar Pasupathy, and Rukma Talwadker. Hey, you have given me too many knobs! Understanding and dealing with over-designed configuration in system software. In *Proceedings of the 2015 10th Joint Meeting on Foundations of Software Engineering*, ESEC/FSE 2015, pages 307–319, New York, NY, USA, 2015. ACM. ISBN 978-1-4503-3675-8. doi: 10.1145/2786805.2786852. URL http://dx.doi.org/10.1145/2786805.2786852.

[306] Tianyin Xu, Xinxin Jin, Peng Huang, Yuanyuan Zhou, Shan Lu, Long Jin, and Shankar Pasupathy. Early Detection of Configuration Errors to Reduce Failure Damage. In *Proceedings of the 12th USENIX Symposium on Operating Systems Design and Implementation (OSDI'16)*, Savannah, GA, USA, November 2016.

[307] Zuoning Yin, Xiao Ma, Jing Zheng, Yuanyuan Zhou, Lakshmi N. Bairavasundaram, and Shankar Pasupathy. An empirical study on configuration errors in commercial and open source systems. In *Proceedings of the Twenty-Third ACM Symposium on Operating Systems Principles*, SOSP '11, pages 159–172, New York, NY, USA, 2011. ACM. ISBN 978-1-4503-0977-6. doi: 10.1145/2043556.2043572.

[308] Uwe Zdun. Tailorable language for behavioral composition and configuration of software components. *Computer Languages, Systems & Structures*, 32 (1):56–82, 2006. ISSN 1477-8424. doi: http://dx.doi.org/10.1016/j.cl.2005.04.001. URL http://www.sciencedirect.com/science/article/pii/S1477842405000205.

[309] Sai Zhang and Michael D. Ernst. Automated diagnosis of software configuration errors. In *Proceedings of the 2013 International Conference on Software Engineering*, ICSE '13, pages 312–321, Piscataway, NJ, USA, 2013. IEEE Press. ISBN 978-1-4673-3076-3.

[310] Sai Zhang and Michael D. Ernst. Which configuration option should I change? In *Proceedings of the 36th International Conference on Software Engineering*, ICSE 2014, pages 152–163, New York, NY, USA, 2014. ACM. ISBN 978-1-4503-2756-5. doi: 10.1145/2568225.2568251. URL http://dx.doi.org/10.1145/2568225. 2568251.

[311] Sai Zhang and Michael D. Ernst. Proactive detection of inadequate diagnostic messages for software configuration errors. In *Proceedings of the 2015 International Symposium on Software Testing and Analysis*, ISSTA 2015, pages 12–23, New York, NY, USA, 2015. ACM. ISBN 978-1-4503-3620-8. doi: 10.1145/2771783.2771817. URL http://dx.doi.org/10.1145/2771783.2771817.

www.ingramcontent.com/pod-product-compliance
Lightning Source LLC
LaVergne TN
LVHW060134070326

832902LV00018B/2792